Architectural
Illustration

Architectural Illustration

LEAVITT DUDLEY

The pencil is a rapid, flexible, and useful tool for the concept and visualization of any type of architecture. This sketch for Daniel, Mann, Johnson, and Mendenhall *is a design study of the firm's office building in Los Angeles.*

PRENTICE-HALL, INC.
Englewood Cliffs, New Jersey

Library of Congress Cataloging in Publication Data

Dudley, Leavitt.
    Architectural illustration.

    Bibliography: p.
    Includes index.
    SUMMARY: Describes different types of architectural
illustrations, their uses, the techniques used in their
execution, and how to master those techniques.
    1. Architectural rendering.   [1. Architectural
drawing]   I. Title.
NA2780.D82   720´.28   75-45472
ISBN: 0-13-044610-6

© 1977 by Prentice-Hall, Inc.
    Englewood Cliffs, New Jersey

10   9   8   7   6   5   4

Printed in the United States of America

PRENTICE-HALL INTERNATIONAL, INC., *London*
PRENTICE-HALL OF AUSTRALIA PTY. LIMITED, *Sydney*
PRENTICE-HALL OF CANADA, LTD., *Toronto*
PRENTICE-HALL OF INDIA PRIVATE LIMITED, *New Delhi*
PRENTICE-HALL OF JAPAN, INC., *Tokyo*
PRENTICE-HALL OF SOUTHEAST ASIA PTE. LTD., *Singapore*

Dedicated to my wife

Ruth

Contents

6

Useful Techniques   97

PART II

Application of Techniques   109

7

Exercises in Delineation   111

12

Cityscapes 179

13

Interiors 193

14

Sectional Drawings, Engineering Projects, and Land Use Studies 207

15

Freehand Sketches and Vignettes 221

16
Design Studies 233

PART **III**
Special Processes 249

17
Presentation Tips 251

18
Reproduction Techniques 261

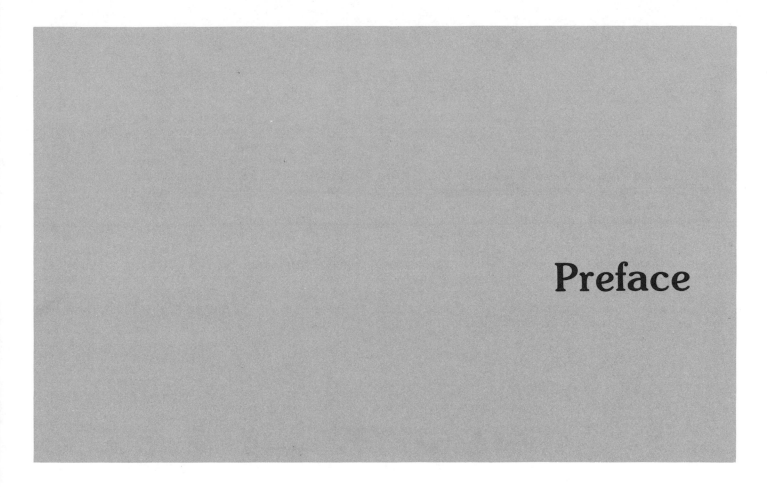

Preface

All of us are born with a certain degree of drawing ability. In some cases, that talent is pronounced enough to surface and be recognized at an early age. Its possessors, with proper training, progress naturally and easily into architectural illustration or some other form of art.

Other prospective illustrators may not realize their potential. They have to be shown how to visualize objects as simplified three-dimensional forms. They must discipline themselves to observe certain rules of composition, perspective, and technique. With practice, persistence, and constructive criticism, they can soon learn how to produce creditable architectural drawings.

Training can take an artist only to the limit of his talents. Very few may attain the skill and proficiency to lay out and render the complex, intricately detailed, highly finished artwork so important to the presentation of huge building projects.

Architecture and its related fields can offer many other avenues to illustrators. Many assignments do not require such elaborate presentations. Small projects may not warrant the expense of top-flight delineators.

Rendering services specializing in large volumes of relatively simple drawings may pool the talents of several artists for a single piece of work, assigning to each the part of the operation for which he or she is best qualified.

Studies for working out design problems may call for only rough, quick sketches to convey an idea. A draftsman, whose main job may be the preparation of working drawings, will benefit by the ability to visualize concepts in three-dimensional forms.

Architectural Illustration will help you, as a student, to find your niche by leading you through a series of achievement levels. From projects whose execution is based on following relatively simple formulas, you are introduced progressively to those more complex in concept and presentation. Some levels require more natural artistic talent than other levels; some are more technical; in some, a degree of design ability is as important as drawing.

As an illustrator, you will soon discover the level at which you work most effectively. As a professional, you will probably specialize in areas and techniques in which you are best qualified.

However, you will benefit from a working knowledge of other opportunities in architectural illustration and should develop the versatility for adapting to the needs of an industry constantly on the lookout for new ideas and techniques.

Contemporary requirements of the building industry call for many types of drawings. A final presentation drawing may have been preceded by dozens of quick sketches that are never seen by the public.

Therefore, this book is not planned as a showcase for outstanding examples of major architectural concepts and highly polished delineation techniques. Several handsomely finished illustrations are included, but only in proportion to their degree of usage in the industry.

Architectural Illustration presents a cross section of the kinds of assignments an artist can expect to encounter. They range from simple, formula-like depictions of mass-produced houses to vast projects where environmental and land use solutions are as important as the architecture itself.

Many drawings are for communication use only rather than for display or publication. Others are concerned with telling stories directly and simply by suggestion, through quick sketches rather than by painstaking detailing.

An author tends to lean most heavily on his own experiences in his preparation of a book. However, in an age of specialization, it is unlikely that any single artist could be proficient in all the wide variety of subjects and techniques included in the field of architectural illustration.

To be a practical and versatile teaching tool, a book also must draw upon the knowledge of others. I wish to extend thanks to those architects, publications, and business organizations who have been so necessary to my own experience, and to the other artists whose contributions have been so helpful to the production of this volume.

—LEAVITT DUDLEY

Acknowledgments

Most books of instruction reflect primarily the work and thoughts of their authors. But they are also heavily dependent, in one way or another, upon the efforts of others.

I am appreciative of the contributions of others, within or outside of the architectural field, which are included in this book. I thank valued clients and good friends, whose assignments have given me the background needed for the preparation of such a publication.

Many of its drawings were first reproduced in the Real Estate or Home magazine sections of the *Los Angeles Times.* Special Sections director Jim Toland (retired), Home editor Carolyn Murray, Dan McMasters, Real Estate editor Dick Turpin, and his predecessor, Tom Cameron, have been my contacts with the newspaper.

Most of the work on design studies and concepts has been provided by Daniel, Mann, Johnson, and Mendenhall, Architects and Engineers, whose operations are world-wide. For many years, I have worked with Anthony Lumsden, Principal for Design, and other members of the organization.

Gruen Associates, another office with an international reputation, is well represented in the book. Its Partner in Charge of Design, Cesar Pelli, and his staff are also long-time friends.

QA Architectural Arts is a nationally known delineating service whose owner, Ragnar Qvale, and his right-hand man, Walt Cole, provided excellent examples of tempera rendering.

Many of the pen and ink drawings of housing and commercial developments were originally done by me for advertising or public relations agencies. Some are not credited in the captions, but I thank such firms and individuals as Hubbert and Associates, Martin Advertising, Bergen and Lee, Lewis and Associates, Jean Lehnert Associates, Pat Penney, Ellis Flint, and many others for their help.

Motion picture illustrations are through the courtesy of Universal Studios, their supervising director William DeCinces, and unit art director Henry Bumstead.

Special thanks go to John La Monica, professor at California State University at Los Angeles and public relations director Bill Lloyd. An offer to teach an independent study course at that school led indirectly to the production of this book.

The manuscript was typed by my sister, Joanna Overby, who could decipher my handwriting as well as edit out split infinitives, dangling participles, and other grammatical errors.

I would also like to recognize the following Prentice-Hall co-workers for their diligent involvement in the production of this book: Howard Petlack, cover designer; Ros Herion, production editor, designer, and page layout supervisor; Jenny Markus, principal page layout artist.

The most important and personal thanks are reserved for my wife, Ruth, for patience and understanding during the long period of preparation of this book. Demands upon an artist's time in his normal routine are enough to try his family, without the additional complications of authorship.

—LEAVITT DUDLEY

Architectural Illustration

PART I

Opportunities and Approaches

Free-lancing specialists, commercial illustrators seeking new outlets for their talents, draftsmen adding another dimension to their work, recent graduates of art schools and universities—all will find architectural illustration a means of opening the doors to a broad and challenging field.

1

Purposes and Uses of Architectural Illustration

In the comparatively relaxed period of building prior to World War II, a few of the larger architectural firms were the major users of "architectural renderings." Drawings were usually executed elaborately in pencil, pen and ink, or were softly tinted with watercolor washes. But projects requiring such presentations were far and few between and assigned to a handful of top delineators.

Small offices designing residences or small commercial buildings could most often get by with a quick sketch by the head of the firm, or with a flat elevation touched up with colored pencil or chalk by a draftsman.

Home building contractors didn't need much more than sets of stock plans in order to sell their products to clients.

The housing shortage, the population explosion, and the migration from rural areas resulting from the war abruptly ended these comfortable procedures. The building booms of the late forties, fifties, and sixties demanded radical revisions in selling as well as in construction techniques, as suburban farmlands converted rapidly from row crops to row houses, and the skylines of major cities soared.

Land developers and contractors, jumping by droves into the mass housing market, quickly learned the necessity of efficient and effective merchandising for survival in a fiercely competitive business. Architects and designers found that hard-nosed businessmen, school boards, and similar committees needed a strong visual sales pitch before investing millions of dollars in giant new building complexes.

Circulation figures of home service magazines zoomed upwards as thousands of families took possession of the new housing units and became involved in beautification, improvement, and maintenance projects. And the trend extended to all other architecturally-related businesses.

Artists, particularly those who had architectural backgrounds, soon found more need for their services with the increasing emphasis on visual presentation. New organizations, formed to streamline and modernize the merchandising operations of land developers, opened a promising new market to them.

*On the wall of an architectural office, a display of watercolor
illustrations shows types of projects undertaken by the firm.*

Advertising agencies specializing in building accounts required the talents of figure, landscape, graphics, and layout artists in addition to those of the delineators.

Public relations firms, whose clients included publicity-minded architects and developers, created another outlet for illustrations.

Compared to handsome artwork displayed in the sales offices of contemporary building projects, early postwar sketches were often crude, and so were many of the tacky houses hurriedly thrown together during that initial building period as both contractors and artists felt their way into a business that was undergoing sudden expansion.

Illustrations and home designing have gained rapidly in sophistication as competition has stiffened. Today success in the field is difficult for any amateur—or professional—who does not develop his skills quickly enough to keep abreast of trends.

The categories of artwork dividing this chapter are extremely general and loosely defined. Many architectural illustrations tend to be multipurpose and may suit an office wall or a newspaper page as well as their limited original functions.

Techniques mentioned are recommendations only, not restrictions on what mediums may be used for effective presentations. The success of an illustration depends on how well it tells a particular story or suits a purpose, rather than on how it was produced. A practicing artist soon feels more at home with certain techniques than with others and should be innovative enough to develop their variations.

QUICK SKETCHES

These fast, flexible drawings are among the architect's most valuable tools in the concept and selling of large projects.

Relatively inexpensive, quick sketches may be revised or redone repeatedly to convey an idea properly before its final presentation as a highly finished rendering. During preliminary design phases, they help the draftsmens' visualization by the addition of another dimension to their flat planes and elevations.

As the design reaches more advanced stages, a more carefully prepared quick sketch may be sent to the delineator as the layout and reference for his presentation artwork.

Because of the spontaneity and casual appearance of its direct method of drawing, the sketch itself also can be an effective presentation. In that case, it is usually photographed and printed, with or without enlargement, and mounted on heavyweight illustration board.

Many architects find a series of sketches, prepared in this manner to show several facets of a subject, a very useful aid in selling their projects.

Quick sketch materials are simple. They usually include tracing paper tough enough to withstand repeated erasures, soft lead pencils, charcoal, felt markers, or other flexible drawing materials. According to their subject and content, sketches may be done freehand or with the aid of T-squares, triangles, or other instruments. Their rapid execution requires also that rules of composition, perspective, and scale be observed and may call for more natural artistic ability than some of the more formal techniques.

Architects are the major clients for this type of material; the artist works closely with the designers during the planning phases.

Away from the office, quick sketch notebooks are useful for architectural reference. The ability for quick sketches can do much to sharpen the observation and perception of a traveling artist.

Quick sketches must be bold and direct; details are suggestive. As this shopping area is only a preliminary proposal, atmosphere is most important, and much of the architecture is left to the discretion of the artist.

A quick sketch for reproduction in a newspaper. Technique is equally free and loose but must be clean and sharp for clear printing.

PRESENTATION DRAWINGS

These striking illustrations are the results of weeks or months of architectural planning. It is hoped that these final products will lead to contracts initiating construction of large projects or to the sale of completed structures.

They may depict a wide range of subjects, from small single residences to shopping centers, high-rise offices, or land developments many square miles in extent.

The delineator of a presentation drawing will usually, though not always, receive a complete set of plans and adequate background reference before starting work. Sometimes he is given an accurate quick sketch or a careful pencil perspective of the subject, which will save him hours of layout time.

Illustrations of single model homes for a typical housing project are generally routine enough that the artist can proceed directly with his rendering. Misunderstandings are avoided more easily in complex assignments, however, if rough preliminary sketches are submitted to clients for correction or approval before the final rendering.

Although watercolor washes and tempera are seen most often, other techniques are equally suitable. Meticulous airbrush drawings are less common and command high prices. While many clients specify color, pen and ink illustrations have gained in popularity in recent years, particularly when the artwork is to be reproduced. Pencil treatments are excellent for certain subjects. Many drawings combine different mediums.

An attractive tempera rendering of a large New Mexico residence, by QA Architectural Arts.

Careful penwork holds the detail, and tone is overlaid in this drawing of Pacific Center, Vancouver, British Columbia. Designer is Gruen Associates. Artist is Ben Althen.

Though less flexible than quick sketches, completed presentation drawings still must be adaptable to last-minute revisions prompted by clients.

Most commissions are given by architectural or engineering firms, land developers, or their advertising agencies. Display in sales or rental offices, submission to boards and committees, and reproduction for brochures and sales kits are major uses for this artwork.

Because of the necessity for high visual appeal in his product, an artist must be skilled and professional in the handling of his medium. An established delineator may employ others for the layout or initial stages of a drawing, so that he may concentrate his effort on the application of his own distinctive techniques to the finishing.

An illustration by a high-volume rendering service gains in consistency, versatility, and overall quality what may be lost in individual style. This may be done by several artists, each a specialist in layout, architecture, landscaping, figures, vehicles, or other details of production.

Some large architectural firms may employ one or more delineators full-time, but most are free-lancers who work on call with their clients. Some share the same office space to reduce expenses, help each other, and offer a wider range of services.

ADVERTISING AND PROMOTION

As a specialized form of commercial art, an advertising illustration must often sell a way of life as well as a product. Whether the presentation offered features a single-family residence, a condominium, an apartment, recreational activity, a sweeping view, or an environment, it should be presented in the most irresistible manner to prospective buyers.

Advertising agencies, the most promising clients for this field of artwork, reproduce the illustrations in brochures—or other related sales pieces—in newspaper and magazine ads. They tend to buy from established artists with reputations for meeting the all-important deadlines.

An ad by Wenger-Michael Advertising *relies upon a suggestion of gracious living in attractive surroundings to strengthen the sales appeal of the product.*

Landscaping and activity areas are featured with the architecture of a San Diego development, in an ad prepared by Marstellar, Inc.

A typical brochure requires drawings of each model unit of a development, vignettes of attractive architectural details, or atmospheric sketches of environmental qualities.

The models are usually reproduced from the presentation drawings also displayed in the sales office; the other art is ordered specially. Unless an expensive booklet calls for full color, illustrations are printed as one-color halftones or linecuts. Overlays for additional color or toning may be added.

Ads placed in periodicals may fill only a column or two, a full- or double-page spread, or any amount of space in between. Smaller ones often adapt existing presentation drawings to an agency artist's layouts. A larger size may require an elaborate and intricate illustration combining architecture with recreational activity, environment, or any other features an art director feels will best sell the product. The latter assignment calls for a versatile delineator.

For his concept, he may have to sift through bulky rolls of construction plans and elevations, landscaping and plot layouts, photographs, and other references to extract the essence of the project. He may have to visit the site to help capture its atmosphere. Figures, vehicles, activities, and other details must be filled in from his imagination or from other resources.

The drawing may be planned to fit an existing advertising layout, or the art director may prefer to compose the ad around the delineator's visualization.

In addition, the artist should be familiar with reproduction requirements and procedures. The size of the finished drawing is related to the amount of reduction or enlargement it can take; the use of benday or color overlays may be a consideration.

Because of its superior reproduction qualities, a pen and ink technique is best suited for use on coarse newspaper stock. Wash, tempera, and pencil drawings also print well if they are executed in a crisp and contrasty style. The slicker papers and finer screens used for brochures retain the qualities of the original artwork better than newsprint in halftone reproductions.

EDITORIAL ILLUSTRATION

The multitude of new living units constructed during the postwar building booms needed publicity as well as advertising in order to attract and interest potential buyers. Many young families were seeking their first homes; older ones were shifting to different types of accommodations or life styles. Migrating populations sought neighborhoods and environments compatible to their needs and desires.

Newspapers were able to tell prospective purchasers where to look, what they would find, and when they could move in. Once buyers were installed, publications could advise them how best to live in, improve, and maintain their new houses and apartments.

Real estate and building sections of newspapers now devote much of their space to editorial descriptions of new housing projects and commercial developments, including many architectural illustrations. Artwork may be reproduced from existing presentation drawings or commissioned specifically by editors, public relations firms, or representatives of the organizations for the purpose of publicity. Requirements and techniques for this type of drawing are similar to those for advertisements.

Home service magazines have expanded and proliferated to show their readers attractive examples of residential architecture and landscaping. They may explain the planning and building of a glamorous new patio, show how to line a wall with bookshelves, or discuss any number of enticing new projects. They even tell the customer how to cope with the thousand and one different problems of repair and maintenance in the modern household. The same subjects are often compiled and elaborated on in books.

Although photographs are used extensively, all these publications are heavily dependent on artwork to properly tell their stories. Artists are less concerned with the presentation of a structure in its entirety than with concentration on its specific details. Many illustrations use schematic or diagrammatic methods to explain procedures most clearly.

Clarity and good reproducibility are primary requisites of these drawings. Pen and ink—or pen and watercolor—are techniques that best meet the standards for one-color printing and, to the artist, have the advantages of quick execution. Wash or tempera illustrations are excellent for full-color reproduction.

A knowledge of construction and better-than-average design ability are frequently required for editorial art. As often as not, the artist finds himself working more with ideas and sketchy reference material than with the detailed plans provided for other forms of architectural illustration. He must be prepared to invent and improvise when necessary without straining the credibility of the subject.

These pen and ink illustrations, left and above, view their subjects from an angle at the level of the structures for a more intimate appreciation of the architecture and atmosphere.

Some publications may have staff artists capable of this type of work, but most editors assign these projects to free-lancers. Ability to meet a deadline is essential.

DESIGN STUDIES

As a starting point and necessary function in planning huge architectural and engineering projects, design studies can be a challenging, exciting, and demanding form of illustration.

Major commercial and residential complexes, highway and airport projects, resort areas, transit systems, and municipal improvements developed with the aid of these sketches can affect the living and working habits of an entire city or state. An artist must use his head as well as his hands in their concept and visualization.

He must be able to work closely with others, grasp ideas quickly, and proceed much of the time by his own judgment.

During the earlier stages of a project, reference material can be as minimal as a short conference with a busy architect or a few lines scribbled on a scrap of paper to suggest the composition and nature of the subject. Later, as tentative plans and elevations begin to shape up on the drafting tables, and rough study models define the volumes, the directions in which a design is heading will be more clearly designated.

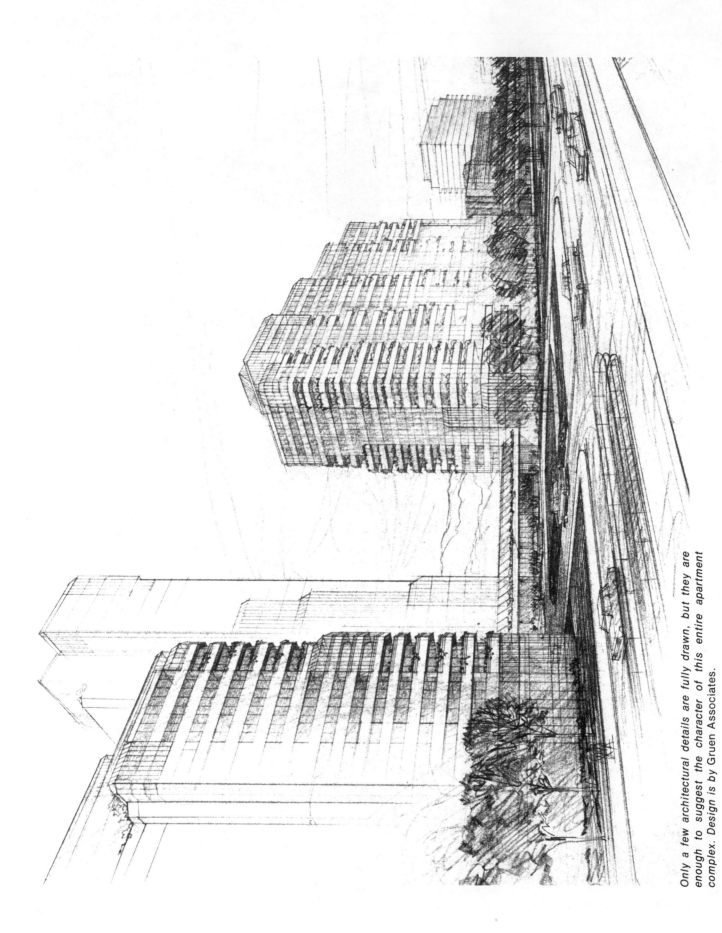

Only a few architectural details are fully drawn, but they are enough to suggest the character of this entire apartment complex. Design is by Gruen Associates.

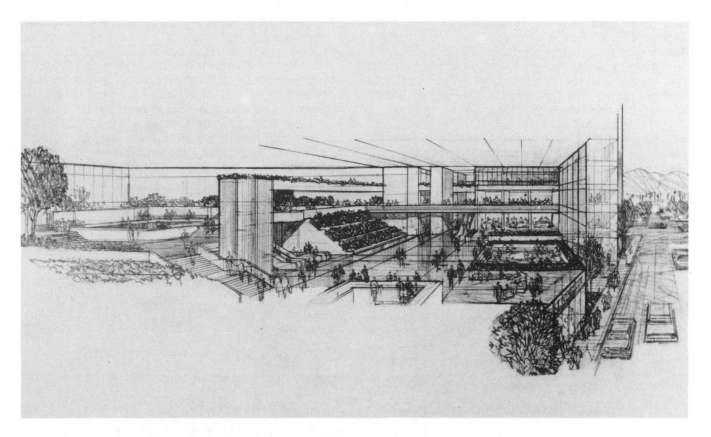

Design studies concentrate most of the drawing on centers of interest and treat the rest of the sketch loosely and suggestively. To better show the interior/exterior relationships of a Beverly Hills hotel, by Daniel, Mann, Johnson, and Mendenhall, *many walls were omitted from this panoramic view.*

Success of these sketches depends more on quantity and quickness than on quality. As they are subject to revision and change constantly, time cannot be wasted on minor design points or unessential detail. Soft pencils, charcoal, felt markers, or other flexible mediums on tough tracing paper convey ideas well enough for the architect's critique or initial conferences with his clients, or help designers determine where their concepts need further consideration.

In later design stages, the more usable of these drawings may be refined for showings to a client or sent to the delineator for use in preparation of more formal presentations.

In addition to quick sketch ability and an architectural background, an artist will benefit from a working knowledge of landscape design, plant materials, engineering projects, recreational facilities, and as much other related information as his background can provide. Travel in the United States and abroad is particularly valuable. Large architectural and engineering firms operate today on a global basis; their projects may be located in any part of the world. An illustrator may or may not be sent to such a job on

assignment, but his familiarity with building and living conditions in other regions will help him in any case.

Due to the necessity of close and continuous contact with other personnel, design studies most likely will be done by employees of organizations requiring them. Free-lance assignments are possible for qualified artists who are familiar enough with the staff and operations of a firm to be dependable sources of work.

INTERIORS

Illustration of the interiors of homes or commercial buildings is made more difficult by furniture and accessories than by architecture. Their irregular shapes and random relationships to the flat walls and perpendicular angles of the rest of the room can pose frustrating problems to artists who handle exterior elevations with ease and competence.

A specialist in this field must be an excellent draftsman. He must work with a direct, deft touch and a better-than-average sense of scale and proportion. Chairs, tables, sofas, and other pieces usually figure so prominently that perfection in the rest of the rendering is negated if the furniture is not up to standard. Unless the artist has originals for models, or an exceptional design ability, he will need a diversified file of clippings and photos to refer to for style.

Transparent water color, tempera, ink and wash, pencil, or pen and ink with overlays for benday or color are recommended mediums for delineation.

Illustrations may depict complete rooms, or they may be vignettes of home furnishings or products set against suggested backgrounds.

Interior decorators, designers, and architects use these illustrations as quick sketches or presentation drawings and for submission to their clients. Some are reproduced in brochures.

Department and furniture stores, or their advertising agencies, include interior illustrations in ads that merchandize household necessities.

A

B

*Interiors may represent many architectural styles and may be drawn in many different techniques. **A**, opposite, in pen and ink, is an ancient Mexico City palace remodeled into a sophisticated office building. **B**, above, is a comfortable sitting and recreation room, rendered in wash and ink. Both are editorial sketches for the Los Angeles Times.*

MOTION PICTURES AND TELEVISION

During the heyday of motion pictures, in the thirties and forties, architectural and art school graduates, as well as licensed architects, found employment in Hollywood studios as sketch artists, draftsmen, and art directors.

Illustrations, quick in execution and striking in technique, explained set design and construction to producers, directors, and back-lot technicians. Other sketches by the score were turned out to plot the action of the characters through the sets.

Although the advent of television soon made serious inroads into the heavy production schedules of major studios, the industry still uses architecturally trained artists.

Strong, dramatic compositions are distinctive qualities of this type of work. An artist should have a versatile knowledge of period and regional styles as well as contemporary design. An uninhibited imagination is helpful. Human figures and animals are often important elements in a sketch. Boats, cars, landscapes, and other nonarchitectural backgrounds are frequently featured.

Watercolor, tempera, charcoal, pencil, or any other medium best expressing the mood of the sketch may be used, either separately or as a mixed technique. As this field of illustration sells atmosphere and action rather than a product, the desired effect may be bright and gay, dark and somber, or drab and forlorn, the mood being the more important expression.

An atmosphere interior by Tom Wright *for art director Henry Bumstead for* The Sting, *a Universal Studios release.*

Moscow street scene, painted in tempera by Gary Meyer, *for the Universal Studios motion picture,* Girl from Petrovka.

2

Academic and Practical Background

A degree from an accredited school of architecture is helpful, but it is not essential to an illustrator.

Some highly successful delineators have completed their preliminary training in a college or university—and have even obtained licenses as practicing architects—before illustrating professionally. Many others have studied in good art schools, concentrating on learning to draw and picking up the mechanics of architecture in other ways.

The choice of school is a matter of individual preference and consideration of the directions a practice will take. A young person planning to include rendering ability in a career as an architect probably will find the more formal and better rounded background of a university education advantageous. One who intends to continue primarily as an illustrator can develop his talents more directly and rapidly through the emphasis on drawing at a specialized art school.

Some students compromise by combining outside art classes with academic studies or by carrying on postgraduate work. Some select an art school that includes architectural courses in its curriculum; others gain the necessary basics of design and construction by individual study or practical experience as draftsmen in architectural offices.

It is not impossible to parlay a natural talent, individual research, and a strong dash of persistence into successful architectural illustration without the benefit of either type of education. But, unless he is unusually gifted, an artist may lose out in the competition to those who have been given a head start with formal training.

Whatever methods have prepared you to enter this field of illustration, the ability to read plans quickly and accurately is an essential acquisition. Average laymen, including many actively engaged in construction and development, find it extremely difficult to visualize a project from the bulky roll of plans, elevations, details, diagrams, and other specifications included in a set of working drawings. Your knack for translating them into recognizable and attractive three-dimensional forms will be a major reason for others to employ your services.

All the facets of your educational background will be called upon sooner or later in your practice, particularly if you operate as a self-employed delineator. Your studio will be subject to the same demands as any other business or professional organization.

Well-composed letters must be written, account books kept in order, reports filed, sales talks given, taxes figured, and a multitude of other tasks and chores must be attended to in addition to artwork production. You will be exposed more to the business world than the artistic community; a good sense of its workings and an ability to satisfy client needs rank in importance with drawing ability.

Whether you are employed by an architectural office or agency or on your own, you soon discover how subject you are to deadlines. As opposed to the less rigid schedules of those painting or drawing for gallery sales, you are turning out custom products for which there is a specific, definite need.

Ideally, an assignment is given enough in advance to allow ample time for its proper thought and execution. But as often as not it may be a rush job due within a limited time—sometimes measured by hours or even minutes. Your calendar may list several commissions, all due within the same general period.

Under these circumstances, drawing must be direct and confident. Time does not allow for trial and error methods. Regular work hours must be ignored.

Like it or not, the tyranny of the deadline is one of the harsher facts of an illustrator's life. The sooner you learn to live with it the better. It is also an excellent, if stern, teacher; having to meet deadlines is a sure and rapid way to develop the skills and temperament demanded for quick, competent drawing.

Deadlines also curb the all-too-natural tendency toward procrastination, which can afflict an artist who is confronted with the blank emptiness of a fresh sheet of paper on his board. No matter how self-disciplined he may think he is, a circled date on the calendar is one of the surest ways to prod him into action. Many artists do better work when their schedules are full than when slack periods leave too much time for thinking about a project. The surest mark of the professional is the ability to produce under pressure.

In addition to academic background, talent, proper mental attitude, inventiveness, stamina, and other intangible attributes, an architectural illustrator needs a wealth of reference material.

An abstract painter can get by on imagination alone for the depiction of his subject, but the illustrator must be concerned with a creation whose value depends on its authenticity and believability. From the top of his head, he may do an occasional semiabstract visualization setting a mood or general theme for a project, but more of his work will reflect the function of a building, its construction and textures, its relationship to the environment, or a new architectural idea.

Books, magazines, clippings, and other references are helpful, essential supplements to your own creative abilities. Architects' offices are well supplied with these, but as a free-lancer you will have to build up your own library.

Architectural Graphic Standards, a thick volume by Charles G. Ramsey and Harold R. Sleeper, is the construction industry's bible. Highly detailed specifications, construction data, dimensions, and requirements for almost any type of architectural project are included. Although much of the technical information on building detail is more useful to draftsmen than illustrators, sections on recreational facilities, furniture, vehicles and equipment, site preparation, room layout, landscaping, perspective, and other miscellaneous subjects make it an invaluable reference.

Delineation books, prepared for both academic and professional use, are helpful aids to the study and development of techniques. A good illustrated volume on gardening indicates tree and plant conformations, sizes, and regional locations. The paper-back books on landscaping, patio design, and related subjects published by Sunset, House Beautiful, Better Homes and Gardens, and other home service magazines are rich source material for environmental ideas; decorating books by the same periodicals are excellent references for interior illustrations.

Articles from House and Homes, Architectural Forum, Architectural Record, Progressive Architecture, and other trade magazines cover a wide range of subjects, from housing to commercial to urban development. Subscriptions to these help an artist keep abreast of his field.

American Artist and other art magazines do not specifically treat the architect, but they introduce him to new ideas and techniques which may be incorporated into his own work.

These are only a few of the helpful publications available. As you gain experience, you will discover which others can best supplement your own library.

Start extensive clipping files as soon as possible, then add to and edit them to keep them up to date. As any variety of objects may be required by an architectural subject, useful scrap may turn up as a photo or illustration in any kind of magazine or newspaper. For easy reference, catalog them under general headings and subheadings, with each group of clippings in a separate folder or envelope. A useful list includes the following:

Activities: suburban; sports and recreation; vocations and professions; hobbies; armed services.

Commercial and Industrial: cityscapes; buildings; developments; schools; churches; interiors and furniture; agriculture and farm equipment.

Fauna: animals and zoos; fish and aquaria; birds; insects; reptiles.

Flora: trees; shrubs; ground covers; gardens; garden equipment; house plants.

Homes: contemporary; traditional; period; kitchens; bathrooms; utility rooms and shops; pools; patios; landscaping; greenhouses; remodeling ideas; decorating and interiors; furniture; accessories; table settings; residential developments; tools and equipment.

Miscellaneous: western; Victorian; foreign; other unusual or regional buildings or subjects.

Science: space programs; atomic development; hospitals and medicine; other.

Technique and Design: rendering techniques; painting and art; lettering and layout; graphics, maps; landscapes and seascapes.

Transportation: autos, trucks, highways; aircraft and airports; boats, ships, harbors; recreational vehicles; mobile homes and parks; trains and railroads; carriages and wagons.

Some of these subjects may seem far removed from conventional architectural reference, but you will find yourself using most of them at some time or other. Specialization in certain fields of illustration will indicate areas to emphasize, delete, or supplement with additional categories.

Catalogs from nurseries and mail order houses are also excellent sources of material.

Many illustrations require an authentic geographic or environmental background, or at least a good general representation, as a setting for the architectural center of interest. A grove of pines, for instance, is as unconvincing in a desert as a palm on a midwest prairie.

Although photographic or other references may be provided by a client, an artist must often draw upon his own resources for this information. Another division of your files can include books, magazines, or clippings on particular cities, suburban areas, mountains, deserts, shorelines, lakes, or other urban or rural areas in the process of development or where building pressures are likely to occur.

Chamber of commerce brochures and catalogs or promotional material by other developers are inexpensive and valuable additions. Builders' expositions, home shows, or sports and recreation centers also provide a wealth of material.

New single-family homes in Chartres are French-designed, have a European look, and have the modern conveniences of a similar American dwelling.

Model homes areas of project near Paris by American builders, Kaufman and Broad, closely resemble similar U.S. developments, even to swimming pools and recreation centers.

Don't limit your reference to your own local area, state, or country. Foreign lands are subject to the same pressures for housing, industry, and recreation as the United States, and much of their development parallels our own in concept, function, and form. American architects now work in all parts of the world; your drawings may depict an office building in the South Pacific or a resort in Switzerland, as well as projects a few miles from your home or office.

One of your most valuable assets may be familiarity with other areas and their regional characteristics and ways of life, gathered through your experience. A visit to a site or its general vicinity is the best way to capture its atmosphere. Travel as much as possible—either in direct connection with your work or on vacation—to broaden your field of knowledge.

Because of its far-ranging scope, architecture can present an artist with better-than-average travel possibilities. A trip may be only a short

visit to a nearby site, or it may involve a cross-country journey and several weeks' time. Longer travels are more likely if you are an employee of a large architectural firm, but they also are possible for free-lancers who can work them into their schedules.

If you do have such an opportunity, you may be able to familiarize yourself with the requirements of the project with quick sketches and a few days' stay, returning home to complete the balance of the assignment.

Vacation traveling can be a productive experience, made instructive and enjoyable by having more purpose than routine sightseeing. With specific objectives, you will have a better chance to meet and talk with others in your field, and you will understand their attitudes and problems better.

Through newspaper or magazine contacts, you may be able to arrange for the publication of articles and sketches pertaining to foreign

When traveling, a felt pen and sketch pad is handy for catching quick impressions of traditional and contemporary architecture.

building, landscaping, or decorating ideas. These may be written and illustrated to inform interested readers or to present ideas applicable to American usage.

Architects and developers may have branches of their own offices, or representatives, abroad. Correspondence with them—and arrangements made before leaving on your trip—can open up possibilities of acquaintance and inspection rarely available to the casual visitor.

Another tangible dividend of travel with a purpose may be realized at tax-paying time: all or part of your costs may be deductible as legitimate business expenses.

No matter how impressive your educational and practical background, or how handsome your portfolio of samples, you as a beginning illustrator still face the problem of proving yourself before you can be considered for the more exotic assignments. You must show yourself to be a dependable producer under the dictates and conditions of professional illustration.

To establish yourself, you may find employ-ment in an architect's office or with a rendering service. During the learning period your duties will consist largely of routine chores. With an architect, drafting ability will be a great help in obtaining a job, as only the larger offices have the volume of work to keep an artist busy full-time. You may spend more time preparing working drawings or in rendering plans and elevations than you will in delineating perspectives.

Even when your work is of professional quality, you may prefer the security and advantages of regular employment to the uncertainties and irregularities of free-lance operation. Hours, as well as paychecks, generally are more regular. You will qualify for the paid vacations, retirement programs, and other fringe benefits enjoyed by members of an organization. Work and duties are fairly well prescribed and are not complicated with salesmanship, bookkeeping, and other nonartistic business demands of self-employment.

Despite the advantages of organization employment, more delineators prefer the challenge and independence of free-lancing to the routine of a job. The ends justify the means—you can do your work when, where, and how you please. With a wider variety of clients and more types of opportunities, you will become more versatile, resourceful, and self-sufficient. The loss of one customer is not as catastrophic as the loss of a regular job. You can set your own fees, according to your valuation of your work and the demand for it.

Some artists work from studios in their own homes, saving the expense of office rental and separate utility charges as well as enjoying pleasant and convenient working conditions.

The home has a few problems also. Isolated in a suburban or rural area, you are less apt to keep in touch with developments in your field. Maintaining the necessary separation between business and household activities is often difficult. Tendencies toward procrastination are intensified. A successful home studio requires the utmost cooperation and self-discipline on the part of both you and your family. Other illustrators choose the more businesslike surroundings of a separate office and the stimulation of working more closely with clients and other artists. If this is your preference, sharing quarters with other compatible delineators has both economic and inspirational advantages.

Charges for secretarial, phone answering, janitorial, and other services can be reduced substantially and improved; office furniture and equipment can be acquired. You and your fellow-tenants can benefit from the exchange of ideas and information and assist each other during busy or slack periods.

A staff illustrator in a large firm soon becomes familiar with all phases of project planning and design.

Employment in a rendering service exposes an illustrator to the ideas and techniques of other artists, and proficiency develops rapidly in the high work output.

Each type of studio location has its own particular advantages and disadvantages. Whether you work at home, in a private office, or with a group is more a matter of personal preference than business necessity. Your own work specialties, types of clients, and reputation will also influence your choice.

As a beginning free-lancer, you cannot be too selective about the kind of work you wish to do. Until you gain experience and create a demand for your work, stick to jobs you can handle easily, rather than wasting your clients' and your own time on complex projects beyond your early capabililties.

Model home illustrations are good starters. A typical housing development offers buyers several different floor plans, each featuring a variety of differing front elevations. Their depiction requires a great number of separate drawings, each a simple eye-level perspective with minimum landscaping and decoration. This work can be routine and repetitious, but it will develop your skill and confidence rapidly.

As you become more proficient, you can branch out into the more difficult bird's-eye views, commercial buildings, interiors, or other subjects involving more study and rendering ability.

Some prefer to concentrate permanently on model home delineations; their large market can provide a steadier income than dependence on some of the more complicated assignments. If volume warrants it, you may hire assistants and streamline production into an assembly line type of operation.

Most delineators eventually tend toward specialization in certain techniques or types of illustration, depending on their own aptitudes and client needs. When and if you do reach this point, you will be able to command higher prices for your work than when you were less selective. However, do not become so stereotyped that you are unable to move in another direction if your market changes. Don't limit your goals; don't be overcautious about tackling an unfamiliar new opportunity.

Artistic ability and business acumen are not always found in the same person, but you will have to develop each in order to survive as a free-lancer. These are a few of the requirements the observations of which will help you to stay solvent:

Sell yourself by the quality of your work. Your best recommendation is a satisfied customer.

Keep a work or progress sheet on the status of jobs, prices quoted, and due dates.

Settle a mutual financial agreement with the client before starting a job.

Be realistic in your charges; value your work for what it is worth but don't price it out of the market.

Invoice jobs promptly; follow up on sluggish collections.

Keep accurate records of expenses, billings, and collections.

Refer work you cannot handle to another delineator. It is better to miss an occasional client because you are too busy rather than to lose him through sloppy workmanship or inability to meet a deadline.

3

Tools and Materials

A very modest financial outlay will equip a studio adequately enough to begin free-lance architectural illustration.

For a minimal start, you can improvise most of your working surfaces and storage facilities from sheets of plywood, sawhorses, boxes, and other expedients. Supplement them with an old chair or two. You can invest in more presentable and permanent fixtures as your business develops.

Although you can get by for a while with makeshift furnishings, drawing materials and tools used for production of illustrations should be of first-class quality right from the start. Much of this equipment should last for many years, or even a lifetime. Buy the best you can afford and the most suitable for your purpose.

Don't try to economize on paper, brushes, pens, and other expendable materials. The higher costs you pay for them over cut-rate or low-grade items will be more than offset by their easy use and more satisfactory results.

Professional quality artwork is virtually impossible using sleazy-surfaced illustration board, limp lifeless brushes continually shedding bristles, scratchy pen points which refuse to flow properly, or gritty pencils.

Exact specification of all equipment and materials is a personal matter, dependent on the techniques preferred and the directions taken by the individual artist. Certain articles are basic necessities in any studio. Specialized items may be added as required by particular types of work.

The more versatile tools and materials listed in the photographs, charts, and copy in this chapter are those whose satisfactory qualities have been proven in the most popular and conventional illustration techniques.

Brand names, when mentioned, are not necessarily a recommendation for one product only. Rather, they are suggested as a guide for locating similar items of comparable excellence.

The basic drafting equipment and miscellaneous tools shown here are those most useful for the layout and rendering of the average range of architectural illustrations. Rulers included show relative size of objects.

1. T-squares, transparent edges, 24″ and 42″ lengths.
2. Triangle, transparent, 30/60 degrees.
3. Triangle, transparent, 45/90 degrees.
4. French curve.

5. Scale rule, architects' (graduated in fractions of an inch to the foot).

6. Scale, civil engineers' (graduated in decimal parts to the inch: 10, 20, 30, etc.)

7. Dividers.

8. Compass (interchangeable pencil and ruling pen tips).

9. Ruling pen.

10. Metal-edged rulers, 15″ and 24″ lengths.

11. Erasing shield.

12. Straightedge (old T-square with head removed).

13. Straight edges (metal-edged rulers).

14. Bridge ruler.

15. Pencil sharpener.

16. Pencil pointer.

17. Magnifying glass.

18. Mat knife (with replaceable blade).

19. Frisket knife (with replaceable blade).

20. Scissors.

21. Paper cutter (not shown in folder).

22. Soft-bristle cleanup brush.

Expendable essentials that supplement equipment and tools are:

1. Push pins.

2. Drafting tape.

3. Workable fixative (spray can).

4. Rubber cement, thinner, and dispenser.

5. Scotch tape (translucent).

6. Drafting tape.

Basic drafting equipment and miscellaneous tools.

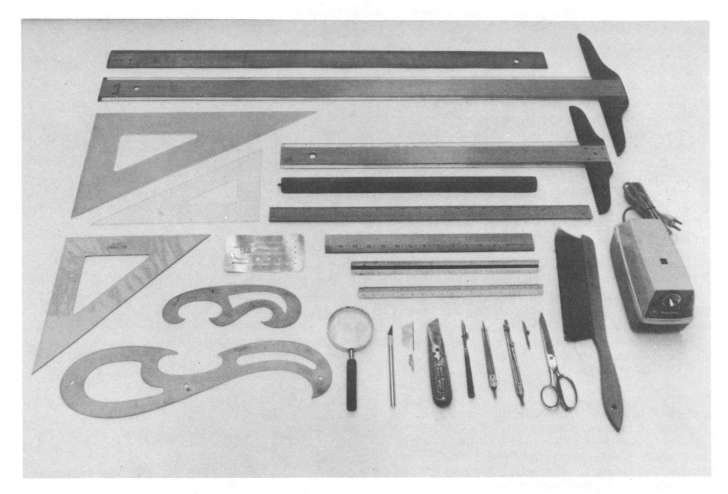

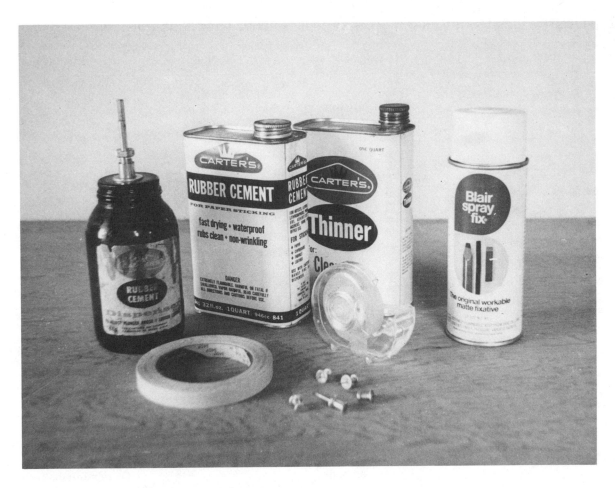

Expendable essentials that supplement basic equipment.

SOME SUGGESTED DRAWING SURFACES

No one type of paper or illustration board will satisfactorily handle all the popular rendering mediums, applied by conventional methods. Several different grades and surfaces, with completely different characteristics, are necessary for the expression of a variety of techniques.

A suitable range can be grouped roughly in these categories:

1. *Lightweight translucent papers:* May be white or buff in color; surface generally is smooth, but may have a slight tooth in the heavier grades. Used mostly for sketches and studies.

2. *Drawing papers:* White in color and opaque, although the lighter grades are translucent enough for tracing over a light table. Available in thicknesses one to several plies; both sides may be used for drawing. Texture may be a smooth glossy "plate finish" or a slightly rough "medium surface." Used mostly for pencil or pen illustrations.

3. *Illustration boards:* White in color, with durable high quality rag surface affixed to a backing of heavy cardboard. Surfaces available are "cold pressed" (CP) with a visible and tangible grain; "hot pressed" (HP) with a smaller shallow grain; "rough" (R) with large uneven grain; or a smooth plate finish. Used for presentation and reproduction work in watercolor, tempera, airbrush, or pen and ink, according to the surface.

4. *Mat board:* Lighter weight and of lesser quality than illustration board; available in white, buff, gray, and an assortment of muted colors. Used mostly for framing presentation drawings, but also suitable for tempera illustration.

From the general classifications of papers and boards, these brands, or their equivalents, can be recommended for the following techniques:

Pencil: For layout or sketching, Clearprint #160 tracing and sketch paper. Available in rolls up to 42″ wide; can be sawed into shorter lengths for economy and ease of handling. Is too fragile for other uses.

Technique	Drawing Surface	Medium	Equipment
Pencil	Tracing paper Technical paper Strathmore paper Bristol board	Graphite pencils Prismacolor pencils Carbon pencils Graphite sticks	Erasing shield Fixative Kneaded eraser Pink Pearl eraser
Pen and Ink	Illustration board Technical paper Vellum	India ink Opaque white watercolor (tempera)	Croquil pen Speedball pens Old sable brush Artgum eraser
Pen and Wash	Illustration board	India ink Transparent watercolor Opaque white watercolor	Croquil pen Speedball pen Sable brushes (round) Ox-hair brushes (flat)
Watercolor	Illustration board	Transparent watercolor Opaque watercolor (white and grays)	Sable brushes (round) Ox-hair brushes (flat) Wash brushes Bridge rule Masking tape
Tempera	Illustration board	Opaque watercolor or Acrylic paints	Sable brushes (round) Sable brushes (chisel point) Ox-hair brushes (flat) Bridge rule Masking tape
Flow Pen	Technical paper Illustration board Matte-surface photo paper Bond paper	Porous point flow pens Felt-tip markers	Bridge rule
Airbrush	Illustration board	India ink Opaque watercolor Transparent watercolor	Frisket paper Frisket knife Airbrush Sable brushes (round)

For more finished illustrations, Clearprint #1000H technical paper. Has the toughness and texture to withstand erasures and handling. Available in rolls to 42″ in width, or pads to 18″ x 24″ in size.

For finished illustrations, Strathmore medium surface paper, one ply. Has texture enough for linecut reproduction and is thin enough to use over a light table. Strathmore medium surface #65, five ply, when a heavier weight is required. Available in 23″ x 29″ sheets.

Pen and Ink: For quick sketching, 1000H technical paper. However, its thinness has a tendency to buckle during more protracted detail work.

For finished art, Crescent illustration board (CP) #79 or #100. Heavy enough to lay flat during a long job; takes an ink line without the "fuzzing" of softer surfaces. Slightly rough texture may bother some artists at first, but gives excellent control for line weights from very fine to broad.

Some prefer to work on a smoother surfaced

board such as Crescent #201 (HP) because it offers less resistance to pen strokes and ink flow.

These boards are available in sizes to 30″ × 40″, in medium or heavy weight. Because of its stiffness, the latter is preferable for larger illustrations, but both grades lie flat during rendering.

For small drawings, where a slight tendency to buckle is not a disadvantage, lighter weight materials are as satisfactory as the heavy boards. Strathmore #75, high surface, is a plate surface. Strathmore #65, medium surface, is a lightly grained surface. Five ply is recommended thickness for each; available size is 23″ × 29″.

For tracing in ink over a layout, Vidalon #90 heavyweight vellum is tough enough to withstand inevitable erasures.

Pen and Wash: This technique calls for a surface hard enough to hold a pen line without fuzzing, yet absorbent enough to take watercolor washes without "puddling" or uneven drying. Crescent watercolor board #112 (R), Strathmore surface, meets both these standards. Pen work is a little more difficult because of the roughness, but this can be overcome with care and practice. Available in 30″ × 40″ sheets.

Crescent #100 board will absorb watercolor, but to a lesser degree, and may be used if application is limited to lighter coats over small areas.

Watercolors: Crescent #112 has the qualities for this technique also, as have other comparable rough watercolor boards.

Watercolor papers have the required absorptive capabilities, but are less convenient to use for architectural illustration because of stretching and mounting considerations. Their buckling tendencies are not a drawback for large, loose paintings, but are a hindrance to fine detailing.

Tempera and Acrylic: Medium rough surfaces are best for these mediums. Absorptive properties are not a factor, as layers of paint do not penetrate the paper. Illustration board should be stiff enough to resist buckling under heavy paint applications. Crescent #100 has the backbone to stand up under this work.

Despite its lighter weight and lower quality, a good medium surface mat board also is suitable. When used, tones or colors of the background often are left unpainted and are incorporated into the composition.

Flow Pen and Felt Marker: These flexible devices work well on several surfaces, particularly those with a slight tooth or texture. Clearprint 1000H, Strathmore #65, Crescent #100, and medium surface mat board all are suitable.

Matte finish photographic paper, upon which pencil or pen drawings often are reproduced, will take tone or color added with a marker.

For quick sketching or travel notations, an artist's pad of #60 white paper or ordinary bond paper on a clipboard are good, inexpensive surfaces.

EXPENDABLE MATERIALS

Materials which are frequently replenished or replaced need not always be of the highest available quality. For instance, I have found a good grade of common office pencils produce results as satisfactory as those from more expensive, specialized drafting varieties. But beware of the cheapest grades on the market!

Experience, by trial and error, is the only way that an artist can standardize his supplies to those most useful to his own needs and preferences. Usually by that time, he has accumulated an excess of items that will seldom, if ever, be used. But, like an ardent fisherman, and his surplus tackle, he will keep it on hand just in case.

It's a good idea to check your inventory occasionally just to keep track of what you do have in storage and help avoid duplication.

This list of materials includes more than any one artist actually will need. It is broad enough to cover most of the normal requirements of the popular techniques.

Pencils:

For layout and illustration: Dixon Ticonderoga 2⁵⁄₁₀ (medium), 2 (soft), 1 (extra soft) in office type; or Eagle Turquoise HB, B, 2B in drafting type. Eagle Drafting #314 for extra soft large lead.

For applying broad flat tone: L. C. Hardmouth Graphite Drawing Stick.

For transferring layout to drawing surface: Eagle Turquoise 4H or 6H (very hard).

For color: Eagle "Prismacolor"; black, white, and wide range of intense color in soft lead. Eagle "Verithin"; same color range with harder leads.

For charcoal or smudge-type work: Eberhard-Faber Black Chalk Pencil; Wolff's Carbon Drawing Pencils, grades H to BBB.

Erasers:

For general use: Eberhard-Faber Pink Pearl.

For smudgy soft pencil: Eberhard-Faber Kneaded Rubber.

For clean-up of pencil from ink drawings: artgum.

Fixative:

Blair or Krylon workable fixative.

Ink:

Higgins or Pelikan Black Drawing Ink.

Pens:

For variable line, fine to heavy: Esterbrook #62 Lithographic Croquil, with Grifhold #47 holder.

For heavy linework and fill-in: Hunt "Speed-

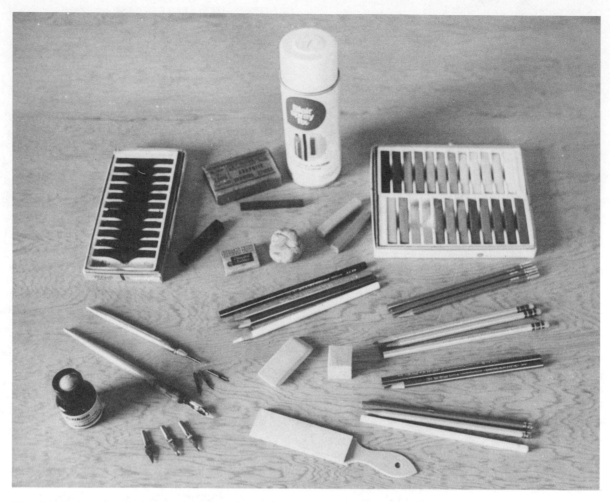

Materials and equipment for drawing: Charcoal sticks; graphite sticks; pastel chalks; kneaded erasers; fixative; colored, graphite, and carbon pencils; pink rubber and art-gum erasers; sandpaper pad; India ink; croquil and speedball pens with holders.

ball," #5 to #2, series "C" (flat chisel point). Old watercolor brushes are good for fill-in of large areas.

For continuous, uniform line: Rapidograph technical fountain pen with changeable points.

Brushes (for transparent watercolor or tempera):

For small wash areas and detailing: Red sable watercolor, round, #1, #3, #6, and #10 (must be of high quality with springy bristles, and come to a sharp point when dipped in water and shaken out).

For corners and small regular areas: Red sable lettering, chisel point, #3 and #6 (also must be of high quality).

For medium to large wash areas: Sable or ox-hair, flat, sizes ½", 1", and 1½" (do not need to be of same quality as above; less expensive ox-hair is suitable for most work).

For skies or other large free primary washes: Fitch bristle easel brush or house painter's sash tool, 1½" and 2" (should be of sufficient quality

that bristles stay in ferrule while in use).

For special effects: old toothbrushes for spattering; stiff bristle brushes for stippling, foliage effects, and textures.

Watercolor:

Professional quality transparent, in ½" or ¾" diameter tubes. Some colors remain moist for years in the containers; others may dry up. Larger tubes are practical for specialists in the technique, but occasional users are advised to buy the smaller sizes and learn to paint from a limited palette. Lamp black is used for noncolor washes.

Tempera:

Professional quality opaque watercolor, in jars from ½-oz to ½-lb or more in capacity. The 2-oz size is most practical for average occasional use, as paint will dry out or deteriorate in time. Check them frequently and add water if moisture is needed.

Unlike transparent colors, opaque colors do not

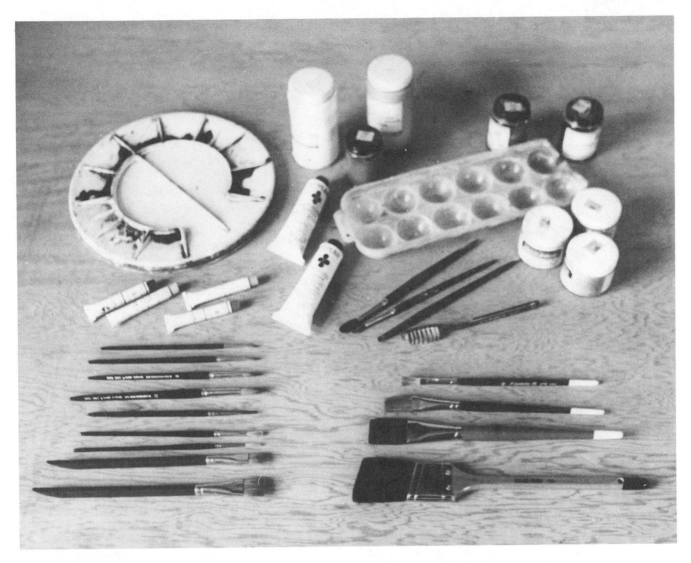

Materials and equipment for painting: Transparent watercolors in tubes with palette; tempera colors in jars; acrylic colors in tubes and jars; plastic cups for opaque colors; round and chisel-point sable brushes; flat ox-hair brushes; broad wash brushes; old brushes and toothbrush for stippling, inking, and splatter effects. (Larger quantities of color may be mixed in shallow individual pans, and some artists prefer a flat slab of porcelain or glass as a palette.)

mix well and often result in muddy hues. Buy a variety of colors and shades, combine them cautiously. Lighten them with white, or darken them with black.

Middle tones for black and white illustrations can be mixed, or purchased ready-mixed in six different shades of neutral gray.

Acrylic:

Similar to tempera in application and final appearance, but dries to a harder, more durable surface. It will not "bleed" or show through when overpainted, and will not peel off when drafting tape masks are removed. On the other hand, acrylic is hard on brushes and they must be given extra care. Never let the paint dry in them; wash frequently with soap and water, and sus-

pend in alcohol between uses to help cut any remaining paint.

Flow Pens and Markers:

A variety of lines from fine to heavy are possible with the range of porous point pens now on the market, in black, brown, all primary and secondary colors, plus a few miscellaneous hues.

Felt-tip markers also offer a wide spectrum, including earth colors, delicate tints, and muted shades particularly suited to architectural work. Grays, in both warm and cool tones, cover a span of values from very light to black.

Test each marker on a piece of white paper before buying from the huge selection available; true colors and tones are impossible to tell by looking at the tips.

Flow pens with different-sized tips are used for linework. Felt-tipped markers apply broad flat tones.

SETTING UP A STUDIO

An adequately large drawing surface, a comfortable chair, and a good light source are the three essentials in furnishing a studio properly. Your need for them will be constant and relatively unchanging, so they should be of a sturdy and substantial enough quality to provide years of service.

An adjustable tilt top drawing table can be stationed at a height for comfortable sitting or raised when standing is a more convenient working station.

A 31″ x 42″ top is not at all too large. It must accommodate the illustration plus the miscellaneous array of reference material, papers, and small tools that inevitably accumulate on the board during work procedure.

To protect and provide a smooth, even backing for drawing on thinner papers, cover the top's surface with vinyl. Pale green or ivory shades are more restful to the eyes than white. As a vinyl substitute, plastic-coated paper may be used. Both materials are available in rolls, and can be cleaned with soapy water.

As you will spend a good many hours in it, a good swivel chair with a well-upholstered seat and back will be appreciated. Rollers on the legs add to its convenience.

Fluorescent lamps, which produce a more even light and hold color tones more truly, are more satisfactory than incandescent bulbs. Ceiling fixtures, built in or suspended, give good general illumination but should be supplemented with a table-mounted lamp for spot lighting.

Sooner or later, a studio needs additional drawing surface. A drafting table, accompanied by a stool, is useful for handling larger pieces of work. Good commercial models, with adjustable tops, foot rests, and storage space are excellent but expensive. If your need is only occasional, improvise an acceptable substitute from a flush door or other one-piece smooth surface.

Next to the drawing board, a small service table or taboret helps to keep the work surface clear of excessive crowding.

A light table or light board, with a translucent glass surface illuminated from below, is a necessity if you do many tracings. It is an in-

This type of drawing table, with a top adjustable for height and slope, is convenient for smaller illustrations or studios with limited floor space. Parallel rule can be moved out of the way when not in use.

Large, durable steel drafting tables with built-in drawers for storage are the most useful all-around drawing surfaces.

Work space is always at a premium in a busy studio. Tack boards on wall and on drawing board help relieve the pressure. Plastic squeeze-bottles are handy dispensers for acrylic paint.

valuable aid to any artist. The board type is more convenient in small studios, as it can be placed on an existing table and stored when not in use.

Provide as much additional counter, shelf, and storage area as studio space permits. Tools, materials, references, drawings, and other paraphernalia accumulate rapidly.

Upright filing cabinets handle reference and business papers; sliding-drawer flat files are best for the storage of large sheets of paper. Heavyweight boards may be stacked on edge in

vertical racks. Commercial facilities for these purposes are expensive, but an innovative artist can find adaptable pieces of furniture in second-hand stores or improvise his own solutions.

SUPPLEMENTARY EQUIPMENT

To supplement basic tools and equipment, you can go as far as you want (or can afford) in the acquisition of "luxury" items. Indulgences

A light board simplifies tracing of layouts or drawings over its frosted glass surface.

such as these make your work easier, faster, more efficient, or more varied and versatile.

Parallel Straightedge: Attached to drawing board, maintains constant horizontal position as it moves. Can be more accurate than the T-square, but can't replace it entirely.

Magnifier: Large adjustable lens with built-in light. Attaches to drawing board, leaving hands free for drawing. Invaluable for very small-scale detailing in pen and ink and other techniques.

Electric Pencil Sharpener: Well worth its cost in convenience and time saved in soft pencil techniques. Heavier duty models, plugged into a socket, recommended over battery powered models.

Airbrush: A delicate spray gun used primarily for smoothly rendered illustrations or special effects. Operated by electric-powered air compressor or compressed air tank.

Electric Eraser: For neatness, accuracy, and saving time in correcting or highlighting areas in pencil drawings. Variety of interchangeable rubber tips available, including ink erasers.

Camera Lucida: A precision instrument with prism and interchangeable lenses. Reflects a subject in reduced or enlarged image on a drawing surface. Good for scaling layouts, preliminary sketches, or reference materials to a desired size.

Reproduction Machines: Compact, relatively inexpensive copiers now available operate from an electrical socket, need no additives, produce single photographic copies within minutes. Handy for reproducing reference material, business papers, layouts, or other small volume occasional jobs. Overall size is limited; print quality too low for other than file copy or reference use.

For reproductions that can be brought to presentation quality with pencil or color touch up, a table top model "whiteprinter" turns out prints in sepia, blue, or black line on white sensitized paper. Handles work up to 42″ wide but is limited to originals drawn on translucent materials.

An airbrush operated by a compressed air tank. Higher pressures are used for spraying large areas, lower pressures for fine detail.

HOMEMADE DRAWING AIDS AND STORAGE IDEAS

TRANSFER PAPER

Cover one side of lightweight tracing paper with soft pencil or graphite stick. Dampen a cotton swab with rubber cement thinner; rub to dissolve and "fix" graphite.

When dry, insert between layout paper and illustration board. Use like carbon paper to transfer drawing by pressure from 4H or harder grade pencil.

This paper results in a strong clean line, does not smudge the board, and can be used repeatedly.

VANISHING POINT

Drill a hole in a 2″ or 3″ concave metal disc, push a sixpenny nail through, and solder in place. Drafting tape holds the device to the drawing board. This is a strong pivot for a straightedge to a faraway vanishing point.

(Warning: file the end off the nail; a kibitzer might lean on it accidentally!)

Pushpins are compact pivots for vanishing points located within the drawing itself. They also are useful for points off the drawing. To reduce marring of the work table surface, protect it with a small scrap of heavy illustration board taped in place.

BRIDGE RULE

This rule is essential for drawing a straight clean line with a brush, raising a straight edge high enough to guide the ferrule and clear the bristles. Rules may be shaped to convenient lengths or forms from ¾″ hardwood, or from plexiglass strips cemented together. Small rollers cemented to plexiglass allow for quick alignment of a series of parallel lines.

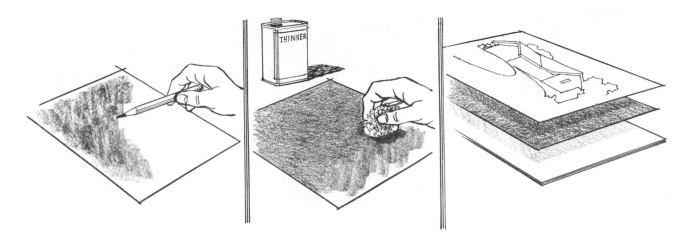

Making transfer paper.

A useful type of vanishing point.

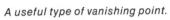

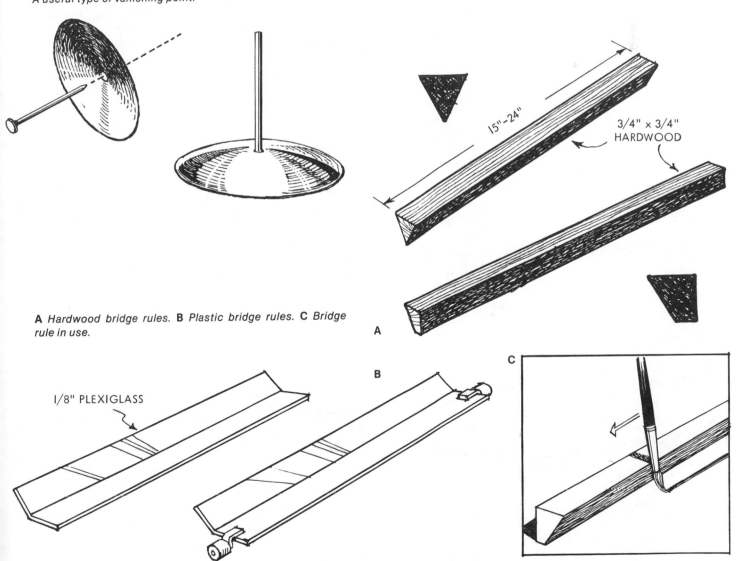

A *Hardwood bridge rules.* **B** *Plastic bridge rules.* **C** *Bridge rule in use.*

15"–24"

3/4" × 3/4"
HARDWOOD

A

B

C

1/8" PLEXIGLASS

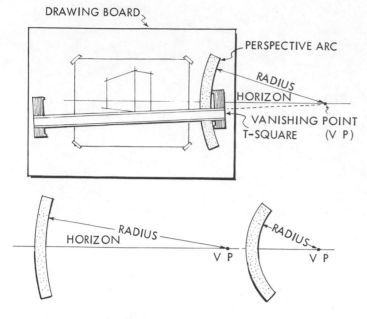

Perspective arcs and their use. Note shape of T-square head for proper alignment of upper edge of blade. Head on other end permits use from either side of board.

PERSPECTIVE ARCS

These establish remote vanishing points without the necessity of working beyond the edge of the drawing board. Cut them from ⅛" masonite, or have them made up in plastic. The small-headed T-square used with them can be cut down from an existing T, or made up from hard wood.

The radius of the arc determines the distance to the assumed vanishing point. For instance, the point would be 18" from the inside curve of an arc drawn with an 18" radius, or 36" from the inside curve of an arc drawn with a 36" radius.

DRAFTING TABLE TOP

¾" plywood, chipboard, or other one-piece material is cut to a convenient and practical size. Trim with hardwood to provide even, easy-sliding edges for T-squares. Cover surface with vinyl top. For ease in changing a worn-out surface, the vinyl can be affixed to the table top with strips of drafting tape around its edges.

Adjustable sawhorses, a low set of filing cabinets, or improvised storage units provide a portable base.

LIGHT BOARD

For occasional use, a homemade version can be an adequate alternative to a commercial board with built-in lighting.

Cut an opening as shown in a piece of

An easily-made drafting table.

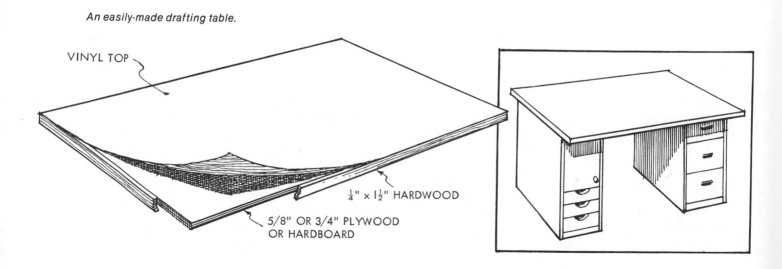

¾" plywood or chipboard. Trim with hardwood, leaving a ⅛" projection above the top.

⅛" masonite fits within the trim for the working surface, with opening cut to expose a ½" margin of the board below. ⅛" frosted glass, fitted snugly into the masonite, completes the top. A 100-watt incandescent bulb, in an ordinary light fixture, is placed about 10" below the board for illumination. This can be removed between usages.

To improve the diffusion of light from an incandescent bulb, a plastic lens from a household lighting fixture can be attached to the under surface of the board. The lens must be large enough, however, to cover the glassed area.

Dimensions given can be adjusted to suit your own needs.

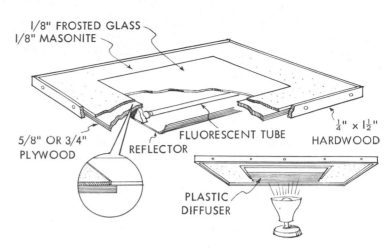

This simple type of portable light board can be stored against a wall or under a table top when not in use.

TABORET

Take a small secondhand chest of drawers, add a larger top (with a rim to keep items in place) and a set of casters. You have a convenient service table and storage unit.

STORAGE IDEAS

Scrap lumber and an afternoon's carpentry transform a closet into an efficient storage area.

Tracing paper, mailing tubes, and rolls of drawings are easily accessible in a wine bottle rack or stack of aggregate blocks.

Keep shelves for books and magazines high; save floor and wall space for production purposes.

Built-in storage unit for small space.

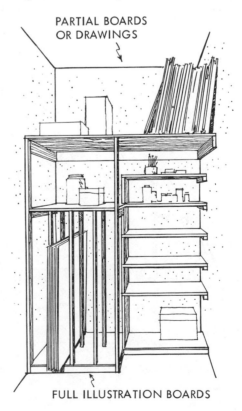

A homemade top converts a storage chest to a taboret.

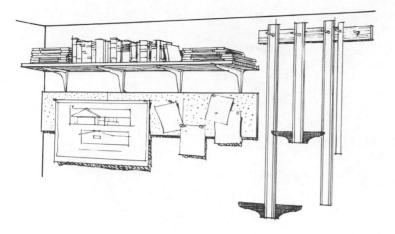

High shelves, tack boards, and racks keep reference material and equipment off table and counter tops and keep them visible for easy accessibility.

A setup for copying artwork.

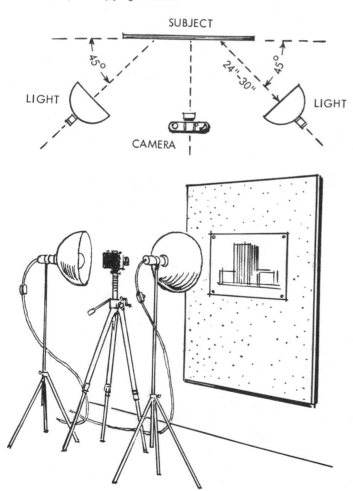

TACK BOARD

Cork panels, cemented to the wall in front of the drawing board, keep schedules and reference material visible and handy to the work area.

PHOTOGRAPHIC EQUIPMENT

No illustrator should overlook the value of cameras, projectors, and photographic processes as drawing aids. You will need only a few articles of equipment to realize impressive savings of time and effort.

CAMERAS

Two cameras, a Polaroid and a 35-mm single-lens reflex, are sufficient to cover most of the needs of the average studio.

You can use the Polaroid at a building site as a substitute for reference sketches. Or, if atmospheric conditions are unfavorable for outdoor photography, it can supplement general sketches by close-ups of details.

Plans, elevations, or models are frequently in preliminary stages and cannot leave the drafting room. Polaroid shots catch enough of their detail to be used as general reference.

Layout of a perspective from a complex plan can be a tedious process. Enlarge a photo of the plan, shot from the proper angle, and trace it to save hours of work.

Polaroid copies record finished artwork for your files.

Unbeatable as it is for instantaneous results, the Polaroid has limitations imposed by its print quality. Lack of a negative also restricts further usage of an exposure.

The versatile reflex camera covers areas the other cannot. A good model of a reliable make, with interchangeable lenses, produces high quality photographs of everything from outdoor shots to close-up copy work in the studio.

A 35-mm wide angle lens has the scope for outdoor and much of the general studio work. It can be supplemented by a telescopic lens for long-distance shooting.

For copying artwork, the standard 50-mm lens has a proportion best suited for most drawings. It should be capable of focusing to a distance of 18″ from the subject. Inexpensive supplementary close-up lenses, snapped over the normal lens, can enlarge the image enough to photograph a small portion in great detail.

Using fast film, color transparencies of artwork can usually be shot with a handheld camera in natural light.

Black and white copies, of reproduction quality, are better taken with a tripod mounted camera. Two blue photoflood bulbs, 150 watts each and positioned as shown, illuminate the subject.

With Kodak Plus-X Panchromatic film, a shutter speed of 1/60th second, and an aperture setting of F/11 or F/8, your camera makes satisfactory copies of pen and ink and most other techniques, unless your light meter indicates otherwise. Play safe by shooting at a couple of f-numbers.

PROJECTORS AND VIEWERS

In a projector, your color slides can serve several useful and time-saving purposes. A site or building, photographed from the proper viewpoint, can be focused to the right size on an illustration board and its outlines traced in pencil. An image projected on the wall in front of your drawing board is also better reference for details than trying to discern them from a small transparency.

Projected slides of artwork are effective aids for selling your work and are far easier to carry than a bulky portfolio of original drawings.

Quick editing, or study of several slides simultaneously, is possible with an inexpensive viewer holding up to 36 transparencies on its sloping plastic front. Illuminated from the rear, and leaving your hands free for drawing, it has obvious advantages over the small, handheld, single-exposure viewers.

An opaque projector reflects an image printed on nontransparent material. Although it is flashed to another surface by mirrors rather than by light through a slide, the size of the image can be controlled for tracing or study.

PHOTO PROCESSING

Your own darkroom can be a useful addition to your studio for developing, printing, or enlarging your camera work. But, unless processing is an active sideline or a particular hobby, a reliable photo service is the more convenient route to follow.

In addition to routine processing of slides and prints, it can offer enlargements of reproduction quality up to 30″ x 40″ or more, inexpensive enlargements (from prints or negatives) on lightweight paper for tracing or transferring, line drawings on transparent acetate, matte-surface prints which will take color addition, photostatic copies and enlargements, and whiteprints in several colors of line.

This can all be done in any quantity. Per unit costs drop drastically as the number ordered increases.

4

Construction Principles

An illustrator's work is more concerned with a building's skin than with its bones. Usually, the spacing of the studding behind stucco wall, the steel framework of a skyscraper, or the depth of a foundation are important only in their relationship to the size and spacing of window openings or other visible features. It is possible to render an aesthetically pleasing representation of an exterior without an intimate knowledge of interior details.

Although you may have little reason to structurally dissect a building, you need more than a casual acquaintance with its superficial characteristics in order to depict it in a convincing and authentic manner. You must understand enough of its construction to fit a doorway properly into position, correctly relate a roofline to the rest of the house, or draw a practical flight of steps.

The ability to read the plans, elevations, and sections of the working drawings of a building is absolutely essential. These items tell you what to draw and how to do it. Larger projects involve you with plot plans, landscape layouts, traffic patterns, and other details of an entire site. They, too, must be interpreted. From contour maps, you must be able to figure slopes, grading, and terrain features.

A better-than-average sense of proportion, scale, and design is as important to architectural illustration as a working knowledge of construction. Without it, an artist will have problems translating a set of plans into a three-dimensional form.

The projection of a complicated structure into a perspective by completely mechanical means is possible, but it is a tedious and time-consuming task. Professional illustrators speed the process by filling in details from their own educated judgment, after a preliminary blockout of volumes and major features. Maintaining proper relationship among all the elements demands a trained eye and thoughtful application.

Correct indication of the scale and texture of the materials of roof and wall surfaces cannot be overemphasized. Courses of shingles or masonry, shown too large or too small, can destroy the credibility of an otherwise well-drawn structure. Stone, wood, brick, tile, and other types of material should be detailed in a self-explanatory manner.

Charts and diagrams included in this chapter introduce a few basic construction types, differing building materials, ranges of style and function, and tips helpful to an artist's understanding of a very broad subject.

Regional requirements and preferences vary too widely for us to be able to describe the subject in more than a general, simplified way. Different projects, as well, may have their own particular specifications.

Architects and contractors must follow changing economic and social trends. High costs of materials, labor, and land virtually have forced custom-designed homes off the market. Semistandardized, more efficiently constructed units of the sprawling suburban developments are replacing them.

Condominiums, apartments, and other forms of compact cluster housing are gaining popularity. Landscaped parks of mobile homes are other attempts to counter the expenses of older, more traditional building methods.

Leisure time is increasing, and many Americans are investing in small second homes in vacation and recreational areas.

Commercial building is changing as well. Stores, markets, and services are concentrated in well-planned suburban shopping centers whose proliferation no longer is confined to the United States. The size and scope of high-rise buildings in major cities call for innovative building methods.

As an artist whose responsibility is the visualization rather than the design of a subject, your thorough knowledge of its mechanics is neither expected nor necessary. However, the more familiar you are with construction basics, the quicker you will grasp the essentials of a new assignment from a set of plans.

HOW TO READ PLANS, ELEVATIONS, AND MAPS

A. *Floor plan of a residence.* Shows location of walls, rooms, divisions, doors, windows, and built-in features. Additional floors have separate plans. A roof plan is a useful reference for aerial views.

B. *Elevation of the residence.* Shows proportions of building; shapes and sizes of windows, doors, and other exterior features; shape and type of roof; and materials used for finish surfaces. Elevations of all sides are provided.

C. *Section of the residence.* Shows type of ceiling and floors, and treatment of walls and built-in features. Interior wall elevations may also indicate section details.

D. *Floor plan of a commercial building.* Shows location of walls, entries, and windows; and support members of framework, elevators,

and other interior features. Plans provided for ground floor and all upper floors.

E. *Elevation of a commercial building.* Shows shape and proportion of building, door, and window arrangements; and finish details and materials. Elevations of all walls are provided.

F. *Section of a commercial building.* Shows general type of framework, spacing, and thickness of floors; and major interior features.

G. *Plot plan.* Shows compass orientation, location and orientation of buildings, change of grade, landscaping features, walkways, drives, parking areas, relationship to streets, or other exterior planning details. Often includes contour lines.

H. *Contour map.* Shows slopes, valleys, ridges, peaks, and other terrain features. Lines indicate height at that particular spot above sea level or any other given elevation. The more closely spaced the lines, the steeper the slope.

I. *Dimensions.* On elevations, plans, and sections of all working drawings, measurements are indicated in feet and inches by architectural scales. These are based upon fractions of an inch to the foot (i.e., $\frac{1}{8}''$ = $1'0''$ means $\frac{1}{8}''$ on the drawing equals one foot on the actual building).

Civil engineers' scales are used for land measurement and often for preliminary building plans, based on the number of feet to the inch ($1''$ = $40'$, $1''$ = $100'$, etc.).

Measurements on many foreign projects are figured by the metric system (1:50, 1:100, 1:500, etc.).

Roof plan for small residence.

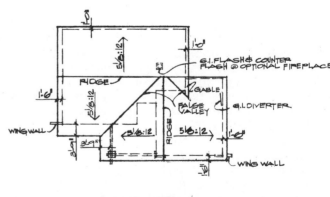

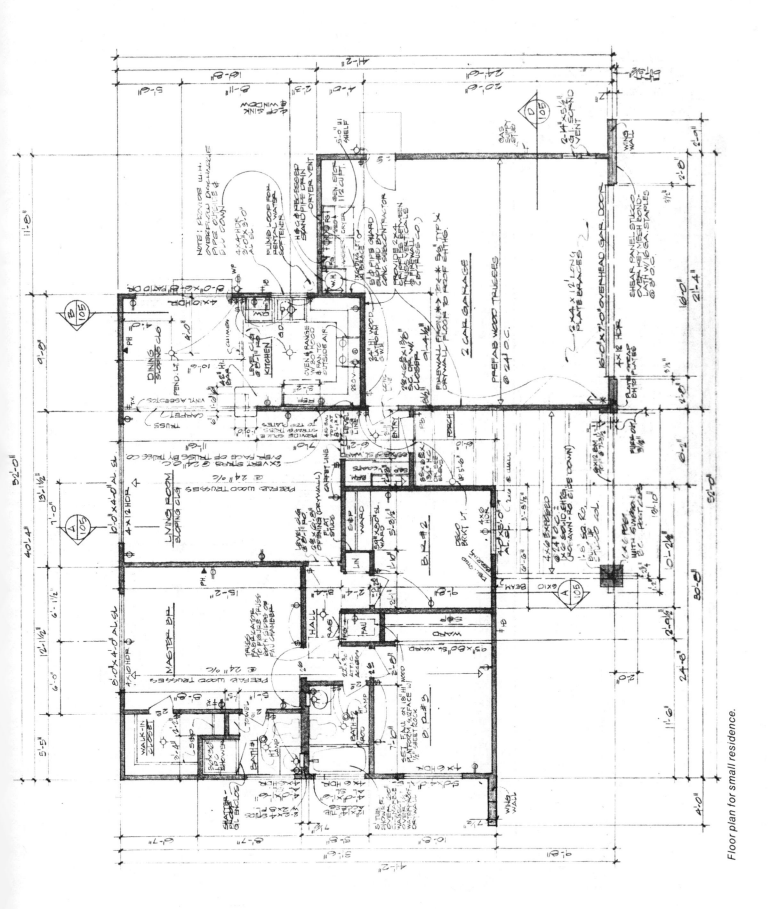

Floor plan for small residence.

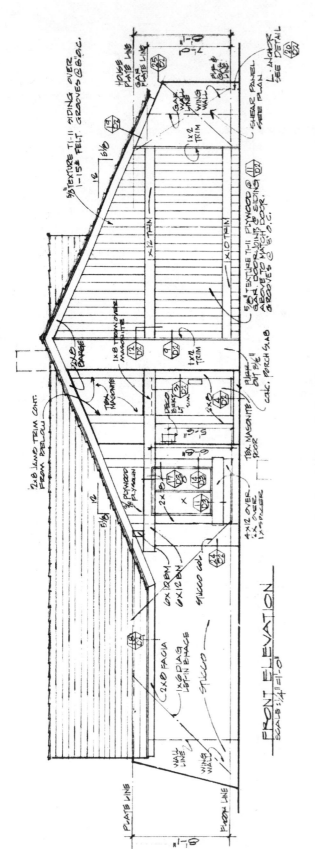

An elevation for a small residence.

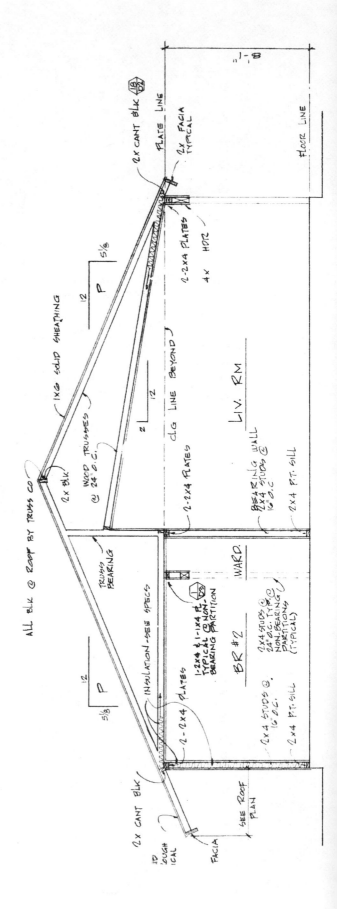

A section for a small residence.

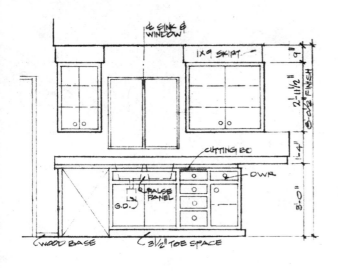

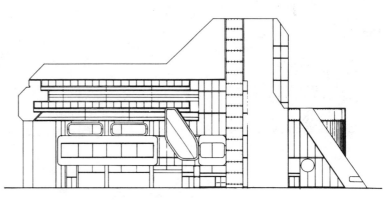

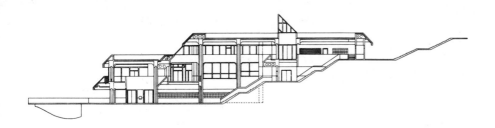

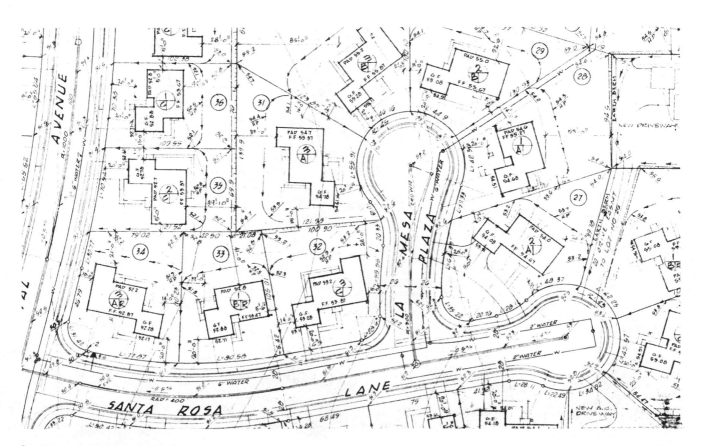

Section and elevation of a kitchen.
Elevation of a commercial building.
Portion of a plot plan for a residential development.

BUILDINGS

65

65

60

55

50

45

32

27

STEEP SLOPE

ROADWAY

RIVER

GENTLE SLOPE

50

55

55

55

58
HIGH POINT
(ELEVATION
IN METERS)

59
HIGH POINT
ON KNOLL

FOUNDATIONS

The foundation is one of the most important elements of a building. Unless seen in a section or cutaway, however, it seldom shows as a separate part in the average perspective illustration. Whether visible or not, its form and function must be considered for an accurate depiction of the subject.

A slab foundation is laid directly on the ground, raising the floor only a few inches above grade level. The crawl space, or built-up type, raises the floor level and increases the distance between the ground and the eave line. In a rendering of a cantilevered building or a sectionalized illustration, the details and shape of the foundation may be visible features and must be included in the drawing.

Several varieties of foundations are used to support residential structures; some are a combination of more than one type. Character of terrain can dictate which is used, although sloping ground in most developments is usually graded into flat pads for slabs.

Footings and slabs are of concrete; piers may be of concrete, wood, or masonry. Other foundation parts may be of wood, steel, or masonry.

LEVEL GROUND FOUNDATIONS

In milder climates of the country, the slab is the most used and least expensive type. The footing for a two-story building is widened to support the additional load. Larger footings may be T-shaped to save concrete.

A crawl-space type of foundation is used most in areas where winters are severe. Because of frost lines, its depth is enough that basements commonly are included in eastern and midwestern houses. The raised floor requires additional interior footings—or piers—at stress points.

Split-level on flat ground is a combination of slab and built-up foundations. The irregular floor heights provide for a sunken living room or other special architectural features.

SLOPING GROUND FOUNDATIONS

The combination slab-crawl-space type is economical on this terrain. The built-up portion is supported by footings and piers.

A split-level steps down the slopes, the ends of its two sections supported by a common footing.

On steeper grades, the cantilever is the most dramatic type of foundation. The reach of the cantilevered section must not exceed more than half the width of the section supported by footings. Longer cantilevers must rest on piers and beams and may need diagonal bracing or steel cantilever beams.

FOUNDATIONS FOR COMMERCIAL BUILDINGS

Foundations for large commercial buildings must be massive enough to support enormous loads. Some are similar to those used in residential construction but are scaled to the buildings they carry. Others are of more complicated design.

A heavy low-rise structure rests on a slab, its weight distributed over thick pads below the floor.

Surface soil conditions may not be suitable for the support of a high-rise building. In that case, huge pilings or caissons, driven deep into the earth to a more solid layer, may be needed. A lower section of the structure, such as a parking level, may incorporate the caissons into its design.

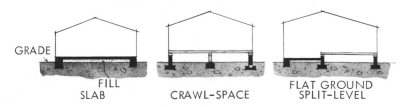

Types of residential foundations commonly used on flat building sites.

Types of residential foundations commonly used on sloping building sites.

Types of foundations used for commercial buildings. These are extremely variable due to soil structure, size of building, and other conditions.

COMMERCIAL WITH PADS

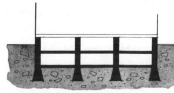

COMMERCIAL WITH CAISSONS

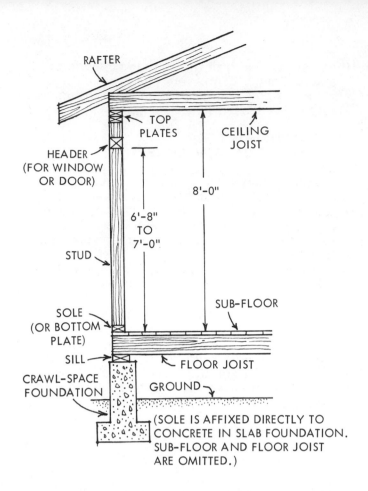

RAFTER

TOP PLATES

CEILING JOIST

HEADER (FOR WINDOW OR DOOR)

8'-0"

6'-8" TO 7'-0"

STUD

SUB-FLOOR

SOLE (OR BOTTOM PLATE)

SILL

CRAWL-SPACE FOUNDATION

FLOOR JOIST

GROUND

(SOLE IS AFFIXED DIRECTLY TO CONCRETE IN SLAB FOUNDATION. SUB-FLOOR AND FLOOR JOIST ARE OMITTED.)

FRAMING AND FINISHING DETAILS

The framework of the great majority of mass-produced light residential structures is basically the same. Whether exterior and interior surfaces are wood, stucco, brick, stone, or other material, most are applied over wood skeletons.

Floor-to-ceiling distances, and spacing of studs and rafters, are generally standardized. Dimensions may vary with split-level styles, vaulted ceilings, and custom designs. Check their specifications for correct measurements in such cases.

Little framing is visible in the average illustration, but consider it for building proportions, eave overhangs, placement and setbacks of doors and windows, and similar details. Rafters, beams, or trusses may be exposed in open-type ceilings, and their construction and spacing must be considered.

Framing can vary according to the style of the house and its regional location, but this type of construction and these dimensions are typical of most conventional usage.

Different types of buildings use their own terminology for the nomenclature of their parts. The labels used on the sketch of this small residence are typical terms used on the elevations in its working drawings. The wording is also subject to change by regional differences.

RIDGE

GRAVEL ROOF

OPEN EAVE

FASCIA

EAVE

STUCCO FINISH

PLANTER

BOARD AND BATT SIDING

MASONRY VENEER

Sections through one-story, two-story, and split-level houses show floor to ceiling heights the same in all stories. If a "cathedral ceiling" with exposed rafters is used on the second level, the floor to upper plate distance may be less than with a flat ceiling. Two types of roof framing are included: the one-story and split-level buildings use "conventional" framing; the two-story example has the "truss" type.

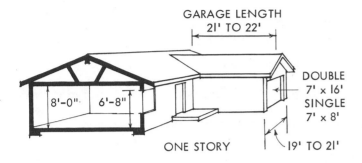

GARAGE LENGTH
21' TO 22'

8'-0" 6'-8"

DOUBLE
7' x 16'
SINGLE
7' x 8'

ONE STORY

19' TO 21'

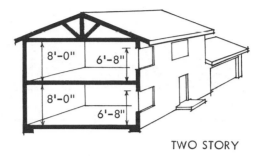

8'-0" 6'-8"

8'-0" 6'-8"

TWO STORY

8'-0"

8'-0"

SPLIT LEVEL

HIP RAFTER RIDGE BEAM RAFTER EAVE OVERHANG

SOLE PLATE
OR SILL PLATE

SUB-FLOOR
OVER SLAB

The slab foundation in the foreground of this photograph by William Aplin is ready for the framing of the building. Rough framing has been completed in the background structure.

51

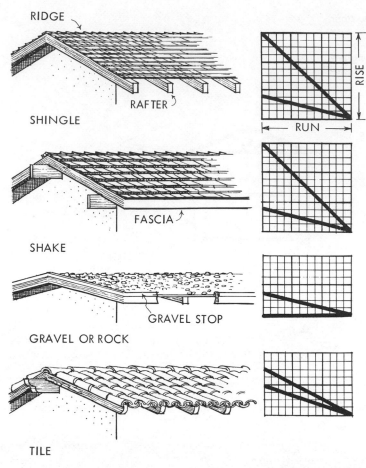

SHINGLE

RIDGE
RAFTER

SHAKE

FASCIA

GRAVEL OR ROCK

GRAVEL STOP

TILE

RISE

RUN

Frequently-used roof materials for residential construction. Diagrams at right indicate the typical ranges of slope for different materials.

ROOFS

A. The slope of the roof is determined by the desired appearance of the building and the type of material used for its surfacing. A shingled roof, for instance, may slope up to an extremely steep angle, while a built-up rock roof must be relatively flat. Slope is usually shown by the number of units in the "rise" (vertical) to those of the "run" (horizontal).

B. Roof construction obviously must be considered in an illustration. Many variations are possible with the types shown in this diagram. Rafters may be closed in by a fascia, left open, or extended beyond the shingles.

Scale is very important to the indication of the surface. Shingles and shakes of split wood resemble each other, but the latter are larger and heavier. The average range of slope for different roofing materials is shown.

Most roofs are distinctively directional in character. A shake roof, for instance, is strongly horizontal. Vertical lines of individual shingles are less obvious; their placement is random. A tile roof is primarily vertical in feeling with a fairly regular horizontal alignment of individual tiles. Before final rendering in an illustration, guidelines must be drawn in order to maintain accurate perspective.

C. Popular roof styles are distinctive, but many variations are possible with each. Several types are often combined in a single building.

SIDINGS

Materials for surfacing exteriors are areas that lend themselves to the development of character and interest in an illustration.

Most surfaces are applied over a conventional wood framing; brick or stone are usually veneers. In masonry construction, such as concrete block, adobe, or solid stone, the material itself is both support and surface.

Study the particular properties and textures of the many types of wall finish and render them just enough to suggest their characteristics. Subordinate their detail to the major features of the structure.

With the exception of such materials as random stone or stucco, most exterior wall surfaces indicate strong linear directions from their methods of construction. Brick courses are horizontal, for instance, while boards and batts are vertical. Preliminary guidelines will help keep their drawing in perspective, scale, and alignment.

Popular roof styles.

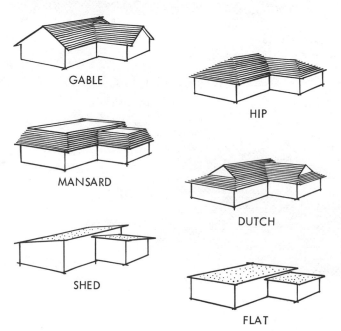

GABLE

HIP

MANSARD

DUTCH

SHED

FLAT

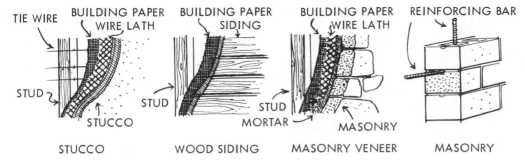

STUCCO — WOOD SIDING — MASONRY VENEER — MASONRY

Simplified diagrams of common types of exterior residential wall construction. First three are applied to conventional framing. Masonry construction is unframed.

A sampling of small residential structures on this and the following page shows a wide range of styles, building material usages, and architectural details. Examples are representative of many different parts of the United States. Several techniques suitable for residences are illustrated. B and D are by QA Architectural Arts. E is a project on the outskirts of Paris built by a European division of a large American building firm.

C

D

RUE
DU REVEILLON

LEAVITT
DUDLEY

E

WINDOWS

Windows used in residential housing change with the introduction of new materials and with economic considerations. In the 1940s, wood framed double-hung, casement, and sliding types were popular.

Casement and sliding steel windows took over in the 1950s. Double-hung versions are difficult for workmen to paint, and have been phased out.

Since that period, the convenient and maintenance-free sliding aluminum sash, in stock sizes, is the most commonly employed style. Jalousies are secondary ventilation units.

Stock sizes are measured mostly in multiples of two feet in width and varying depths at six-inch intervals. The first dimension specified is the width, and the second is the depth. In terminology used to describe them, 4050, for instance, means four feet wide by five feet deep.

A window in a home is set close to the exterior wall surface, but it shows a slight setback. Often a trim applied to the wall around the window emphasizes the recess more. A setback is also indicated on the interior wall.

The details show framing and placement of a window.

Fixed panes of glass are used for custom work but are expensive compared to conventional sash.

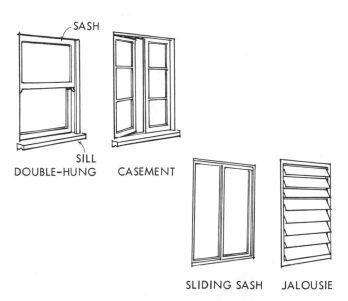

Types of windows for residential construction. Aluminum sliding sash, by far the most commonly used today, may be double thickness (Thermopane) for insulation in cold climates.

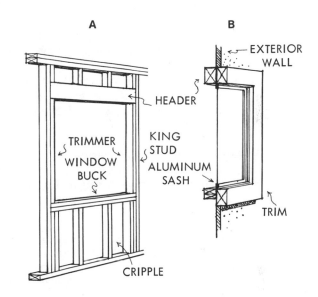

A Framing detail for a window. Aluminum sash is affixed to outside edge of the frame. If untrimmed, the only setback noticed is the thickness of the exterior wall surface. When trim is applied, however, much more recess will be seen (**B**).

Pen and wash vignette of a fixed glass window installation.

DOORS

Doors come in many types and styles but, like windows, are usually specified in stock sizes. Unless intended for custom installations, the usual height for doors is 6'8" or 7'0".

The average front entry is three feet wide. This is often doubled by an additional unit in larger homes, although one of the doors may be fixed in place. Wall surface of the same material sometimes extends its height visually. Exterior door thickness is 1¾."

Doorways may be simple slabs of wood or paneled in a variety of designs. Glass inserts for light may be used, but these have declined in popularity in recent years.

Exterior service doors, and most interiors, are 2'6" wide and 1⅜" thick. Bathroom and closet doors save space with a two-foot width.

French doors span 2'6" or 2'0" per section. Bifolds, usually room dividers, average 18" per leaf.

The aluminum-sash sliding glass door largely has replaced the French as a passage to private outdoor areas. Its width, ranging from six to eight feet, is divided into sliding and fixed panels.

Doors are framed in a manner similar to windows, and a setback is shown in a drawing. An exterior installation shows a sill at its base.

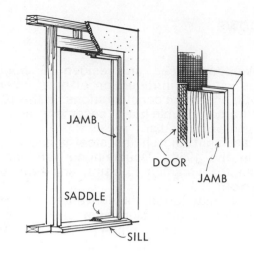

Framing of a door. When installed, one side will be recessed the width of the jamb; the opposite will be flush with the wall.

Pen and wash drawing of an entryway.

Typical home door styles. For effect, a front door may be doubled in width though one section is open. In loftier entryways, the material of the door also may extend vertically for additional effect. French doors, once popular for both exterior and interior wall usage, have largely been supplanted by sliding glass units in exterior surfaces.

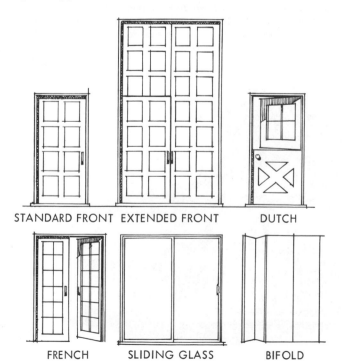

STANDARD FRONT   EXTENDED FRONT   DUTCH

FRENCH   SLIDING GLASS   BIFOLD

FIREPLACES AND CHIMNEYS

A fireplace is complex in construction. Unless it appears in a sectioned drawing, however, you will be concerned only with its location and its visible parts.

If it is installed on an interior wall, just a small portion of the chimney will be seen extending above the roof. From the plan and elevations, position it in proper relationship to the ridge.

The entire length of a chimney on an exterior wall is usually visible. Whether or not it is enclosed by the fascia or barge depends on the width of the eave. Its conformation is indicated on the elevations.

If you are not working from plans, remember that the chimney extends at least two feet above the ridge of a gable roof, and three feet above a flat roof.

Within a room, the opening of a medium-sized fireplace is approximately 30″ in height and 36″ – 40″ in width.

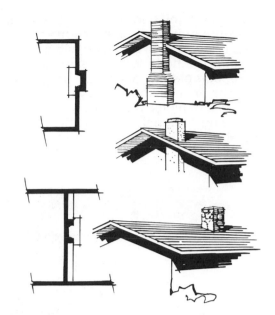

Appearance of chimneys installed on exterior and interior walls.

Minimum heights for chimney extension above flat and ridged roofs.

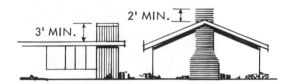

COMMERCIAL BUILDINGS

The construction methods of commercial structures are just as varied as the shapes they take and the purposes they serve.

As nearly all the structures are custom de-

Progress photos (this page and the following) of stages of construction of an office building in Oakland, California. Architects are Gruen Associates.

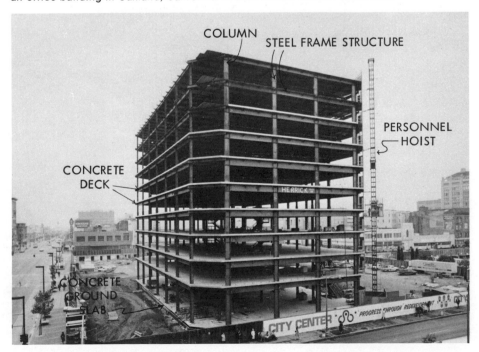

signed and built for particular sites and functions, the more standardized procedures of light residential construction are impossible to parallel. Building methods of massive apartment blocks are completely dissimilar to those of single houses or small multifamily units, and are closer to those of high-rise offices.

Styles and materials for commercial buildings vary all the way from rustic interpretations featuring heavy timbers and tile roofs, to soaring, ultrasleek creations of glass and steel.

A word to artists who propose to illustrate this type of building: working drawings for a single large building can run to many dozen sheets of plans, elevations, sections, and other specifications. To simplify their use, sort out only the sheets that will be applicable to the pictorial interpretation of the subject.

B

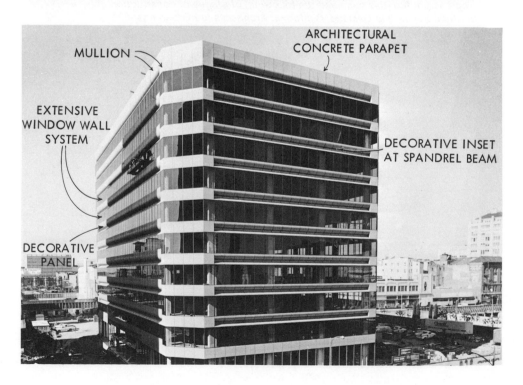

C

5

Drawing Principles

Simpler types of architectural illustrations, such as eye-level views of single houses, can be broken down into a series of formula-like operations. Though his artistic background and experience may be limited, a conscientious and industrious beginner can soon produce creditable results by rigid observation of a few rules of drawing and rendering. Through practice, many steps of execution can become almost automatic. Complex renderings call for more imaginative concepts and design abilities. Solutions are not always available from a neat routine of formulas.

Certain basic principles and theories apply to all forms of art, not just architectural illustration. Knowledge and use of those presented in this chapter forward the artist's progress toward more difficult and complicated delineations.

ANALYSIS OF FORM

Do you remember children's "learn-to-draw" books, with animals or human figures portrayed by a series of circles, cylinders, or other simplified shapes?

This same analysis of form through separation into geometric shapes is a sure, logical aid to drawing architecture as well. Regular contours of the average building make this visualization relatively simple.

Think of your subject in terms of its broadest geometrical configuration before involving yourself with its details. Only when you are satisfied with the correct relationship of major masses should secondary features be added to the layout. Doors, windows, trim, textures, and decoration cannot assume a proper scale unless the primary forms are visualized accurately.

COMPOSITION

Arrangement of the various elements of a drawing into a pleasing and well-related whole is a fundamental essential to successful artwork. The most skillful drawing and rendering is ineffective unless it is presented in a well-composed manner.

Good composition depends on a proper choice of viewpoint and a sense of scale as well as the harmonious arrangement of the elements of the picture. Observation of the principles covered in this section will help develop your facility in this all-important phase of illustration.

Study of the sketches shows that their subjects

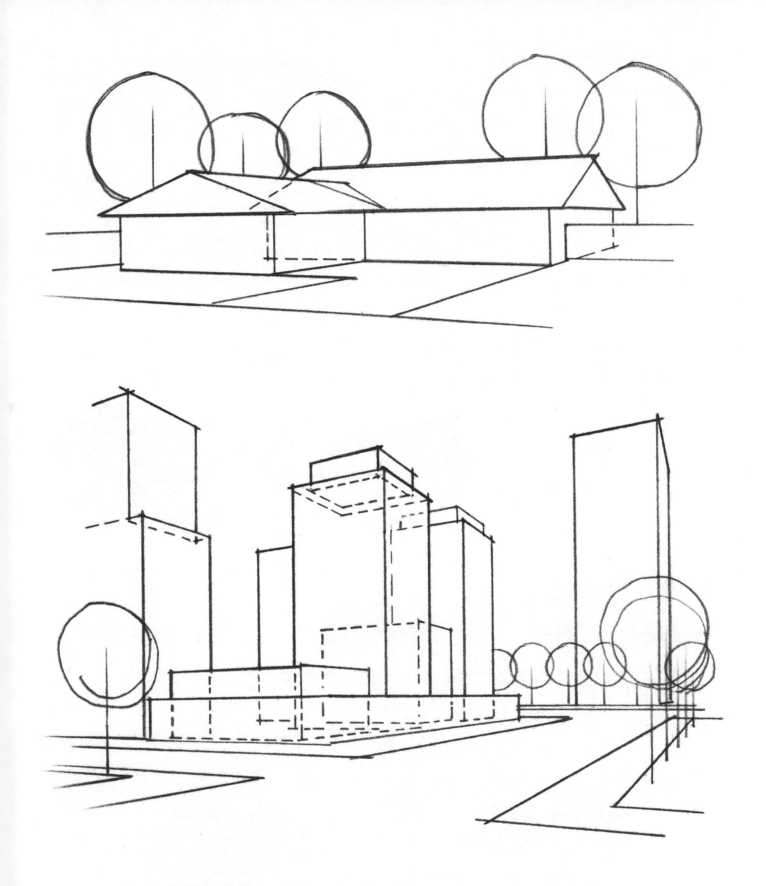

readily break down into simple geometric shapes.

PRELIMINARY SKETCHES

Before committing yourself to the layout of a final drawing, settle upon a suitable concept from a series of "thumbnails." Small rough sketches, executed in a few minutes with a minimum of drawing, visualize a subject from different viewpoints and are invaluable savers of time and effort.

FORMAT

The general layout of an illustration should complement the shape of its major element. A vertical format, for instance, is usually more suitable for a thirty-story high-rise. A rambling ranch-style residence fits more easily into a hori-zontal arrangement. Adjacent buildings or environment also can affect the layout, according to their importance in the composition.

Usually, a building is positioned to "look" into a picture. Its main facade or prominent features are located to direct the eye toward the center.

For advertising or editorial assignments, the space that is available sometimes dictates the format. Whatever the subject's contours are, they must be compressed into a layout of given size and shape.

In any format, preplan and roughly block out all elements to be included before starting the detailed layout. Unless boundaries are set, even an experienced illustrator can run out of drawing surface at a critical point.

A few minutes spent on thumbnail sketches help you decide composition questions in advance. Time is, then, less likely to be wasted on final layouts that may be unsatisfactory.

The style and type of building will determine the format of the illustration. Notice how both examples "look" into the composition, holding the viewer's eye at the center of interest rather than leading it off the page. Leave plenty of margin space to avoid cramping a composition. Surplus can be cropped later.

VIEWPOINT

Selection of the "station point," the assumed spot from which your subject is viewed, is important to attractive presentation.

Generally, the viewing angle should feature the main facade of a building. A major entrance should be visible, not masked by a garage or other protuberance. One should look into—rather than around—an angular conformation.

Distance from station point to subject varies the effect. A remote point flattens the perspective; a close one accents its angularity. Unless you are trying to achieve a dramatic impact, avoid the distorted appearance of a too-close viewpoint.

The average residential structure is best presented at the eye level of a person standing on the ground (approximately six feet high). Eye levels below that point tend to exaggerate foreground features—a factor that is often exploited in motion picture sketches or others requiring striking compositions. A "bird's-eye," or aerial perspective from a high eye level, can show an extensive subject in its entirety or relate it to its environment.

However, a choice of viewpoint is an extremely variable matter. Your own experience and your client's objectives best indicate your selection of viewpoint. For any such complex presentation, try several thumbnails before deciding.

A more distant view, top, is a more pleasing perspective. Too close a station point, below, results in a distorted appearance.

The more pleasing composition, **A**, looks into the angle of the building and the entry. In **B**, the center of interest is blocked by the flat wall and bulky garage.

A

B

All three of these compositions are good, and the height of the horizon may depend upon what features of the subject are to be emphasized. Avoid too high an angle, which might show a great, unrelieved roof expanse at the expense of more interesting architectural details.

CENTER OF INTEREST

The focal point will be some particular element. It may be an entry, a facade, a fireplace, pool, or landscaped area. It may be a group of buildings in a large complex, or a recreation center.

Whatever it is, emphasize it and subordinate other features. Directional lines of the composition should lead the eye toward—rather than away from—it. More detailed drawing, or stronger tonal contrasts than those used in the rest of the illustration, can accent its importance.

The strong directional lines leading to the center of interest are apparent when the illustration is diagrammed.

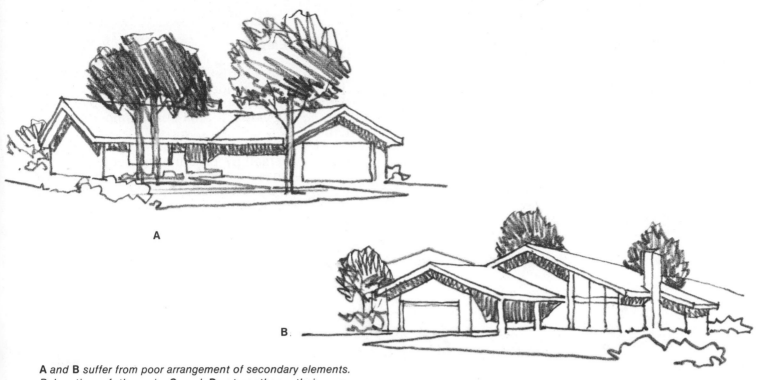

A

B

A and B *suffer from poor arrangement of secondary elements. Relocation of them, in* C *and* D, *strengthens their compositions.*

C

D

SECONDARY ELEMENTS

Landscaping, trees, hills, or other structures must not conflict with or detract from the center of interest.

Avoid backgrounds of plantings, hills, or other elements that coincide with or repeat rooflines of the building. Beware of tree trunks or other foreground elements lining up on a structure's corners or cutting across its major features. Use them instead to break the monotony of blank walls.

DEPTH

Trees, driveways, and landscaping in the immediate foreground add depth and spaciousness. Similar background elements, in proper perspective and tonal values, extend the feeling even farther.

Do not let them become isolated units, however, which are unrelated to the center of interest. Thoughtful placement of foreground pieces, and their connection to the main subject by line or tone, make them valuable assets to the interest and attractiveness of a drawing.

MOVEMENT

To a skilled artist, good composition is more than a static arrangement of forms. He creates definite movements in his illustration by subtly leading the viewer's attention to important features.

A less experienced illustrator can broaden his own versatility by studying such pictures. Place a sheet of tracing paper over a good example, plot its movement with a few sweeping curves or bold lines, and incorporate the observations into your own work.

Isolated elements result in a spotty composition. Connecting them with tone and line, right, organizes the drawing as a more cohesive whole.

In a more difficult subject, line quality, tone, scale, and movement all combine to suggest depth while holding the composition together. Background is strong and definite, but does not overpower the foreground center of interest.

Rhythmic movements throughout the drawing lead to and soften the firm line of architecture, while strong verticals in the foreground prevent the undulating lines from becoming too dominant.

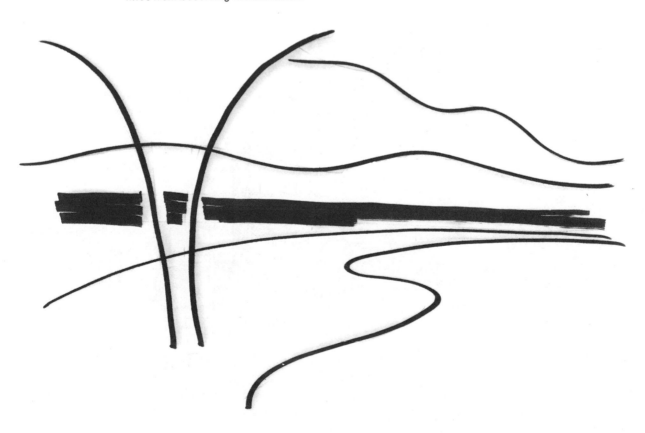

PERSPECTIVE

Composition allows an artist considerable latitude in its interpretation. Perspective, on the other hand, does not permit straying very far from its strict and confining rules.

The artist can stretch these regulations a bit (and does so as often as not); he can take shortcuts with them—which is necessary in order to complete a layout in a practical length of time—but he never can ignore them.

Anyone who is able to read and follow directions can project the plans and elevations of any building into a perspective drawing, provided he observes academic instructions. But if he goes entirely by the book, his patience must be as unlimited as his time.

A practicing illustrator must work within the framework of these regulations while expediting them for convenience and speed of execution. He must also recognize what liberties he can take to improve the presentation of his subject without affecting its credibility.

"Eyeballing" is the term given to the compromise between strict adherence to academic rules and the following of one's judgment and instincts. This ability enables the artist to project perspectives quickly and with relative accuracy.

More academic methods of perspective projection will be more fully described in the appendix of this book. Study and practice them until you are familiar enough with their mechanics to use the expedients discussed in this chapter.

If you are unsure of your ability to gauge proportions, you can project, in an orthodox manner, a module to be used as a reference for horizontal and vertical dimensions.

A convenient module for the plan and elevations shown would measure 8′ × 10′ × 10′, although size is secondary to proportion, and dimensions can be changed arbitrarily (the same module could be 4′ × 5′ × 5′ or 16′ × 20′ × 20′).

Assuming that a normal eye-level, two-point perspective is desired, project as shown in the diagram (opposite, bottom) for an average pleasing view of the subject. Establish the height of the horizon according to dimensions chosen for the module.

Before starting a perspective layout, very rough thumbnail sketches help you to plan the composition and to roughly approximate the location of horizon and vanishing points.

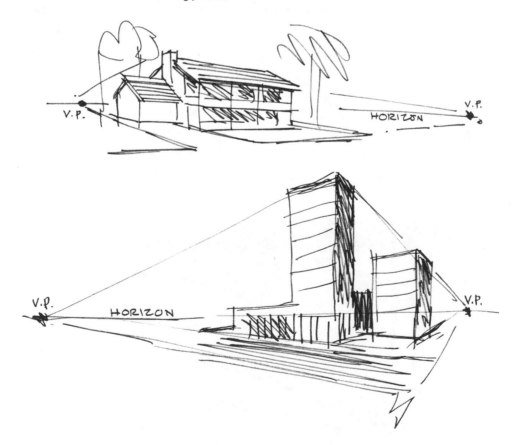

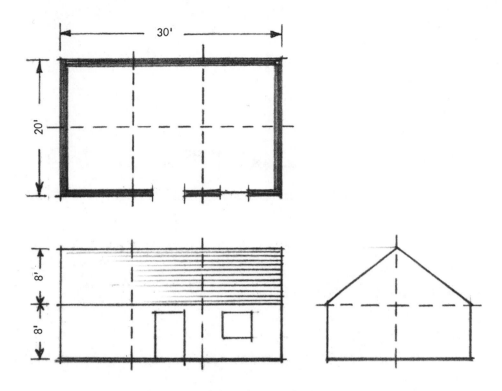

Dividing plan and elevation into modules prior to projection.

Projection of a module by the "office" method.

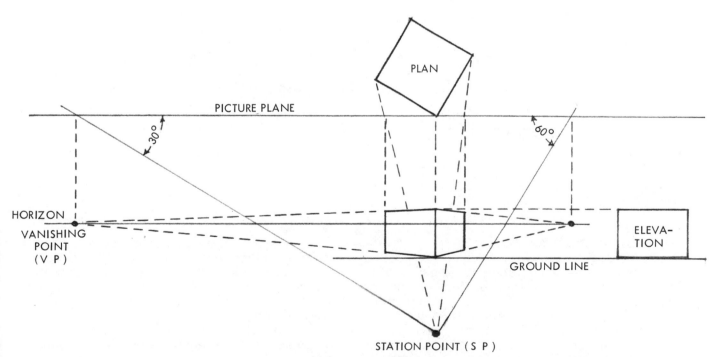

PICTURE PLANE

PLAN

30°

60°

HORIZON

VANISHING
POINT
(V P)

ELEVA-
TION

GROUND LINE

STATION POINT (S P)

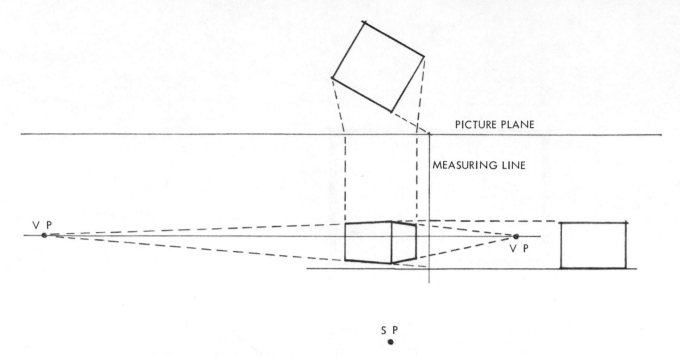

Move subject away from picture plane to reduce its size in perspective.

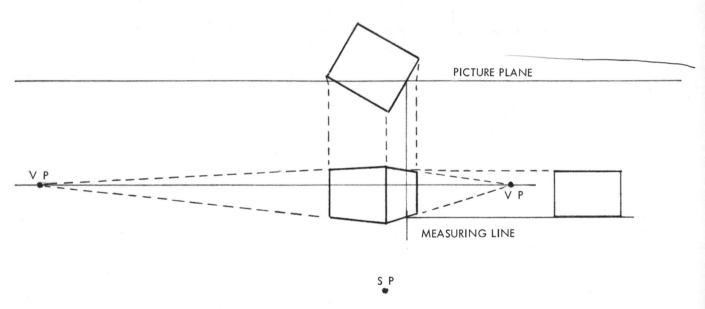

Overlap the picture plane with the subject to enlarge its size in perspective.

Moving the plan farther away from the picture plane results in a smaller perspective; overlapping the plane gives a larger one as shown in the diagrams above. If no line on the plan touches the picture plane, a measuring line must be added for true height measurements.

A vertical scale can be indicated for any desired elevation to project heights. Modular dimensions can be extended or divided as shown to add the balance of the structure and aid in the location of details.

An experienced eyeballer can establish a module, either visually or mentally, by more direct methods. But, however the proportions are determined, the same general procedure is used for developing a two-point perspective of any building.

Perhaps a given area must be divided into modules, as, for example, a wall where equally spaced windows are to be located. A simple, accurate projection does it almost as quickly as gauging it by eye.

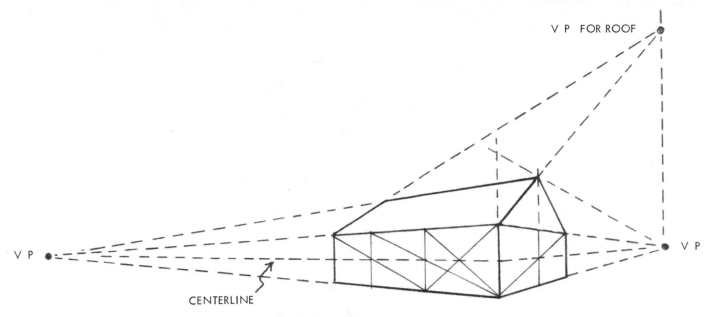

VP FOR ROOF

VP

VP

CENTERLINE

Method of extending modules in perspective, establishing roof height and vanishing point for roof plane.

Dividing a given shape into modules. Length of line B-E is arbitrary but must be divided into equal parts.

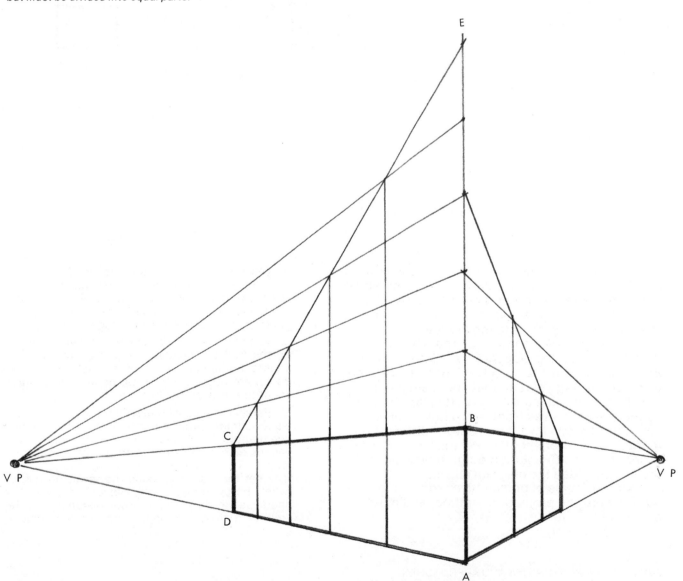

E

C

B

VP

VP

D

A

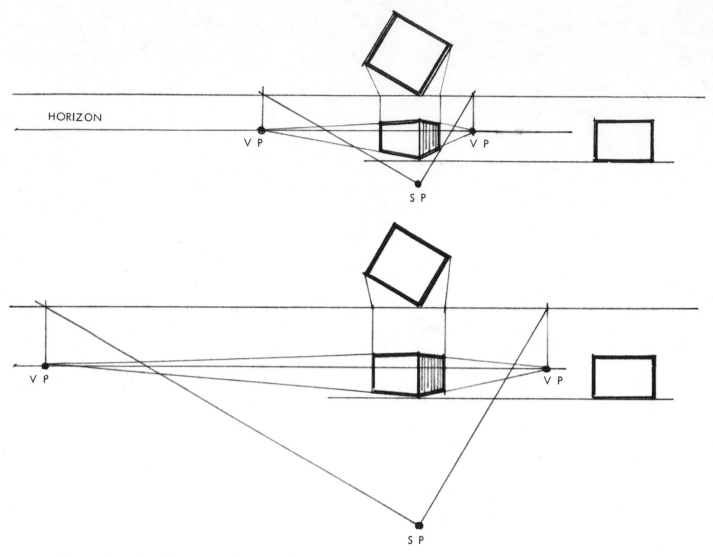

HORIZON

VP   VP

SP

VP   VP

SP

Effects of changing distance of station point from subject.

Extension *BE* is drawn to any length from given wall *ABCD.* Divide *BE* into as many equal parts as the required number of modules. Lines dropped from intersections of line *CE* and projections from *VP* indicate the modules.

Changing the location of the station point greatly affects the appearance of the subject. Experiment with the variety of possibilities before committing yourself to its final selection.

Different planes of a structure are featured as the station moves from left to right. Raising or lowering the eye level emphasizes different elements more prominently. Perspective is more pronounced as the station point moves closer to the subject. (See the diagram above.)

Certain rules of perspective remain fixed, no matter what the projection method, and must be observed.

1. The horizon is always established at the selected eye level, whether you assume a "worm's-eye view" from a prone position, a bird's-eye from 2,000 feet, or any altitude in between. Only one horizon may be used in a single drawing.

2. Vanishing points for all lines or planes parallel to the horizon must be located on the horizon. Points for nonparallel planes, such as pitched roofs, are not, but still must be in vertical alignment to those on the horizon.

3. Parallel planes of a given regular object, such as a building, project to the same set of vanishing points. The planes of a differently-aligned adjacent object will project to a different set of points. The distance between the two points of any set must be the same, however, no matter what the positions of the objects may be. Any increase or decrease of this distance will result in a distorted appearance of that object.

A group of buildings on a sloping site. All share the same set of vanishing points, but the angle of view changes as each structure drops further below the horizon.

LEAVITT DUDLEY

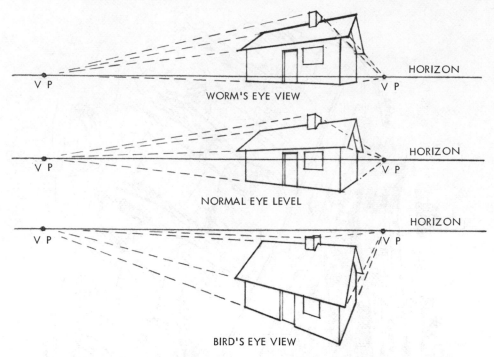

HORIZON
V P · · V P
WORM'S EYE VIEW

HORIZON
V P · V P
NORMAL EYE LEVEL

HORIZON
V P · V P
BIRD'S EYE VIEW

Only one horizon can be used in a perspective, at the height of the selected station point.

Distance above or below the horizon for vanishing points for rooflines is determined by the pitch of the roofs. Note method of locating center of gable.

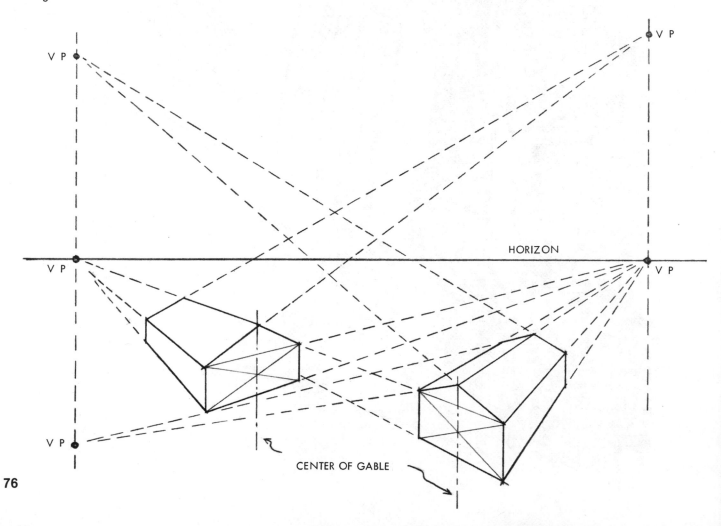

HORIZON

V P

V P

V P

V P

V P

CENTER OF GABLE

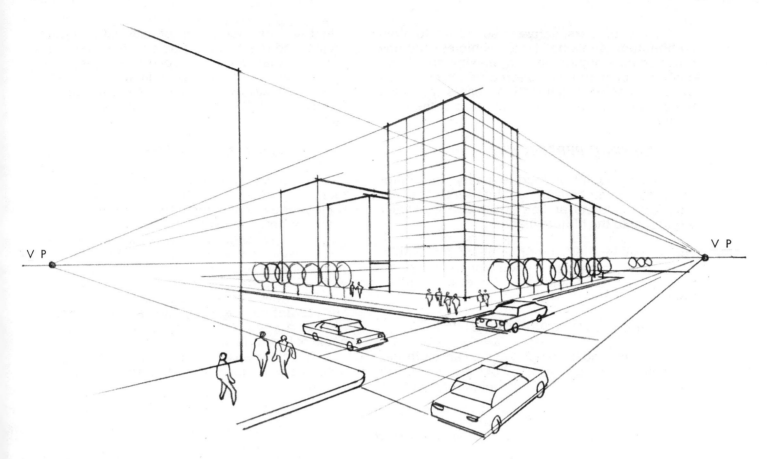

V P

V P

All planes parallel on the plan project to the same vanishing point.

Planes not parallel in plan project to different vanishing points. Distance between each set must be the same, however.

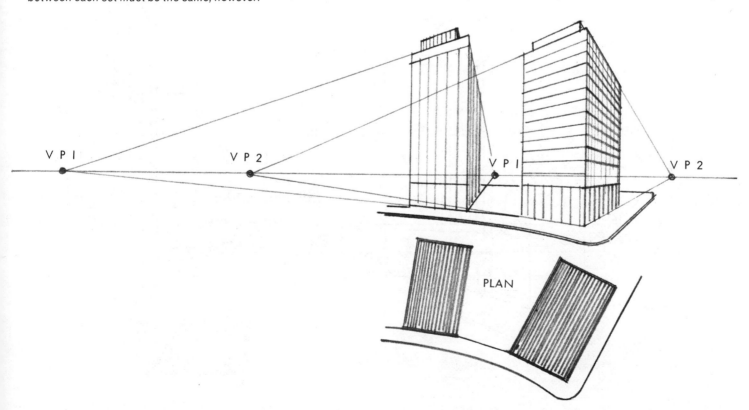

V P I

V P 2

V P I

V P 2

PLAN

Rules of perspective also apply to non-architectural subjects. Trees, vehicles, and any other objects appearing in a drawing should be analyzed for their basic geometric shapes; their three-dimensional delineation shares the same horizon and station point as the rest of the illustration.

ONE-POINT PERSPECTIVE

The one-point method is a very useful process for perspectives of interiors, head-on exteriors, sections, and other subjects in parallel alignment to the picture plane.

With only one vanishing point on the horizon to consider, projection is quick and simple. Lines of the planes perpendicular to the line of view are parallel and may be drawn with a T-square.

THREE-POINT PERSPECTIVE

This method is complicated by an additional vanishing point above or below the horizon to which all vertical lines of the subject project. Its effect is most obvious in oblique aerial photographs and must be considered when drawing a structure that will be included in such a photo.

It can also achieve a dramatic effect in a close high- or low-level view of a tall building. Otherwise, it is seldom used in the average delineation.

CIRCLES IN PERSPECTIVE

Circular shapes are often featured in architecture. In perspective, they appear as ellipses. If incorrectly drawn, they detract from an otherwise competent illustration.

Improper alignment of its axis is the most common cause of a faulty ellipse. Any circle on a plane parallel to the horizon will show an ellipse with its axis parallel to the horizon, from any point of view. The axis of an ellipse drawn on a surface not parallel to the horizon, as a pitched roof or a vertical wall, will correspond to the angle of the surface.

To help keep an ellipse properly aligned and proportioned, block in its tangent lines in perspective.

A group of buildings projected in one-point, or parallel, perspective.

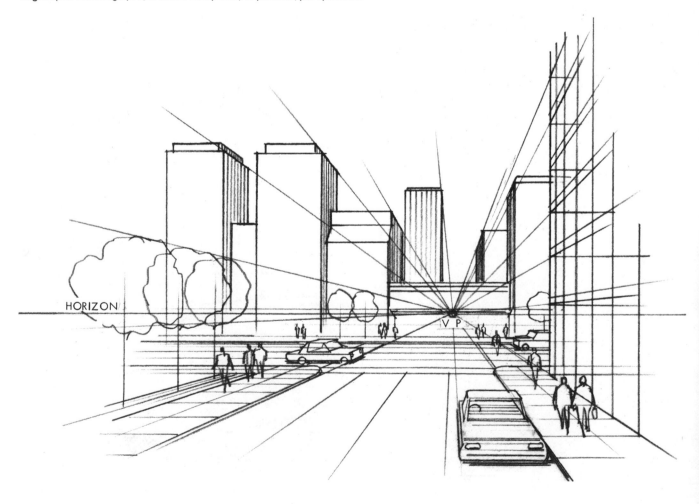

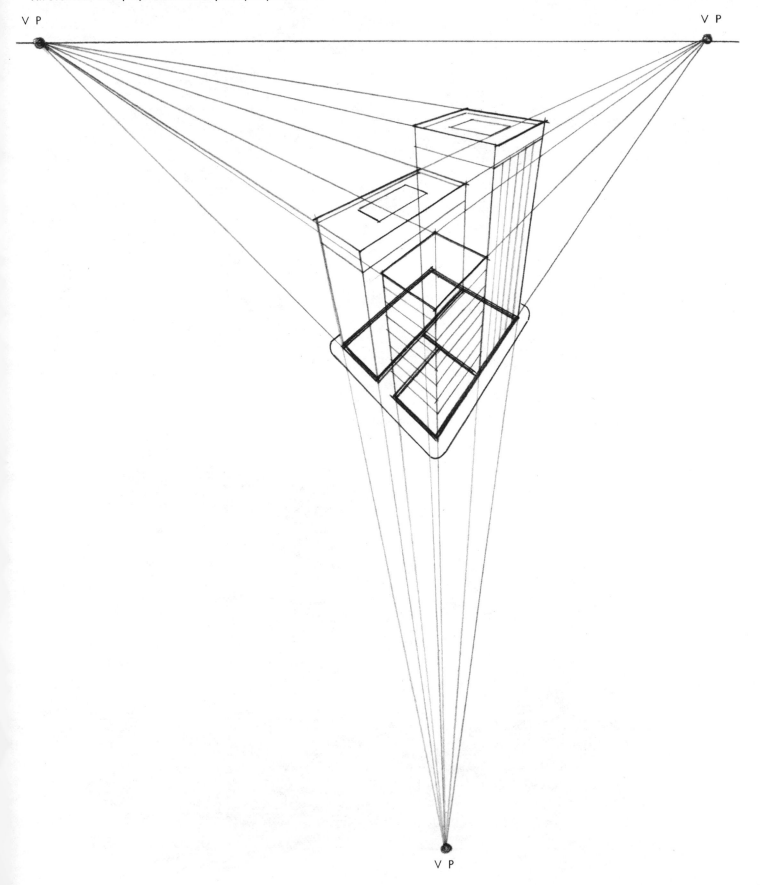

An overhead view projected in three-point perspective.

V P

V P

V P

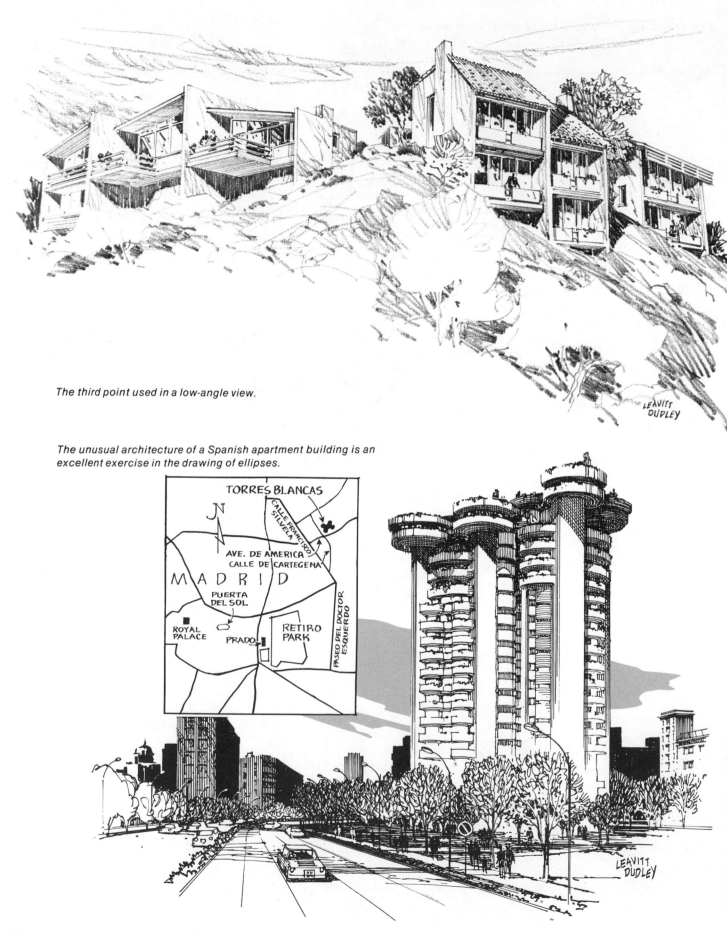

The third point used in a low-angle view.

The unusual architecture of a Spanish apartment building is an excellent exercise in the drawing of ellipses.

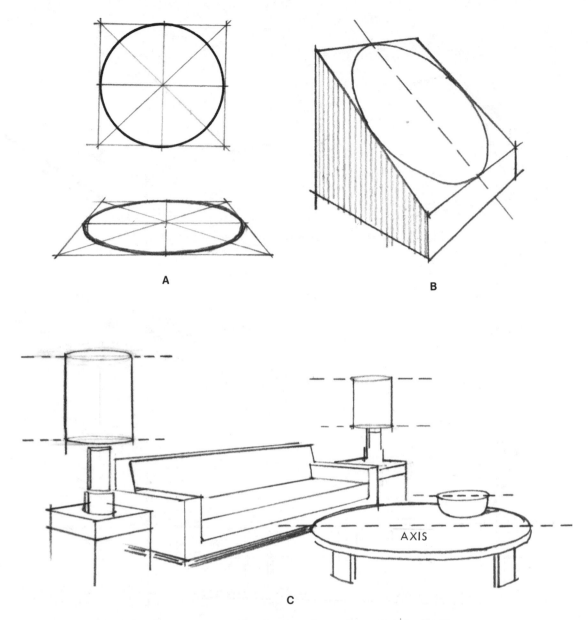

A *Tangent lines help the drawing of an ellipse.* B *Axis of ellipse on sloping surface.* C *Ellipse axis of planes parallel to the horizon.*

PERSPECTIVE CHARTS

Time-saving perspective charts are ready-made grids which can calculate much of your projection for you. Divided into modular units which may be given any convenient dimension, the grid shows through the tracing paper overlay on which the perspective is drawn. Dimensions from plans and elevations are figured quickly over the grid.

A typical series of charts include grids for subjects aligned at 45 degrees to the picture plane (to feature two facades equally), 30/60 de-grees to the picture plane (to feature one facade over the other), and parallel to the picture plane (for one-point head-on views). Normal eye-level and high-horizon grids are provided.

The charts are most useful for drawing buildings of a regular conformation and alignment, and for subjects, such as model homes, which tend to be repetitious.

The lack of setups for irregular alignment and the limited choice of horizon levels are limitations to the use of charts on more complex, exotic assignments. If much of your work tends toward similar layout, you can make charts to fit your needs with ink on vellum.

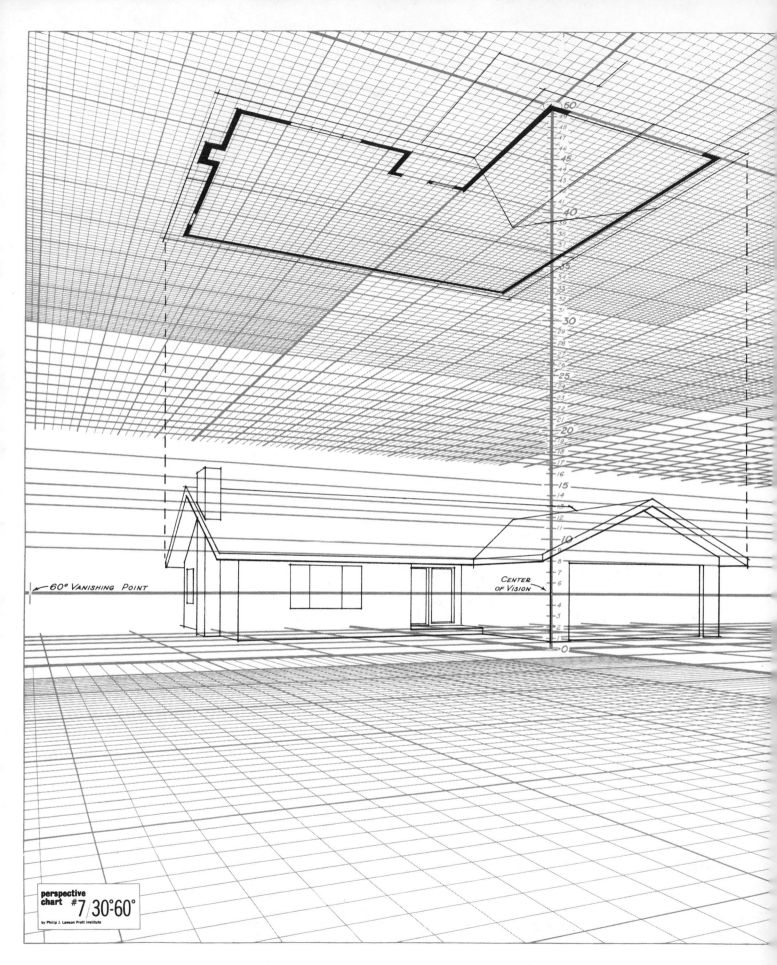

60° VANISHING POINT

CENTER OF VISION

perspective
chart #7 / 30°·60°
by Philip J. Lawson Pratt Institute

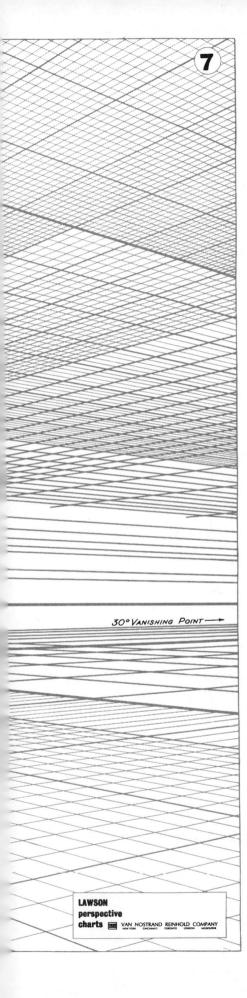

30° VANISHING POINT ⟶

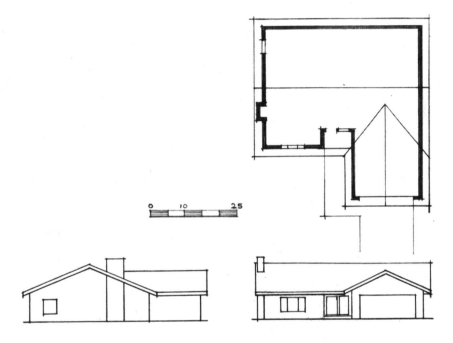

0   10   25

Plan and elevations of a small house projected by means of a commercial per-spective chart, using a 30/60 degree view pattern and a scale of one foot to each unit of measurement. From plan drawn in perspective on grid, reference points are projected downward to the construction of the three-dimensional view. Vertical measurements are projected from the scale on the center-of-vision line. A facade may be emphasized more or less by moving the plan right or left to change its relationship to the center of vision. The size of the drawing may be increased or decreased by using a different scale for a unit of measure-ment.

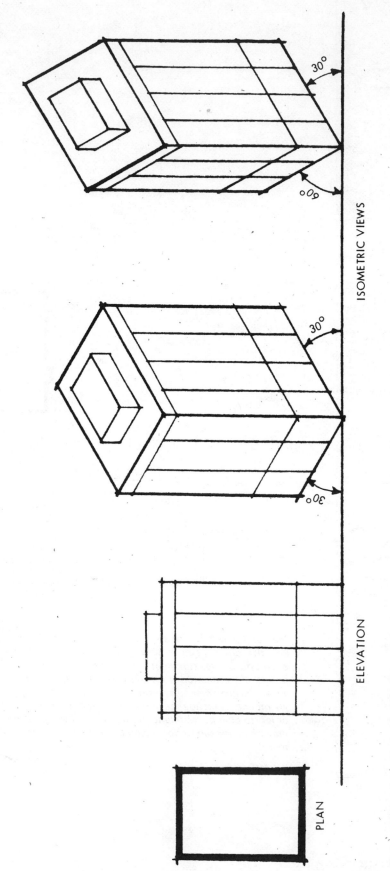

PLAN

ELEVATION

ISOMETRIC VIEWS

30°

60°

30°

30°

A structure projected in two types of isometric views.

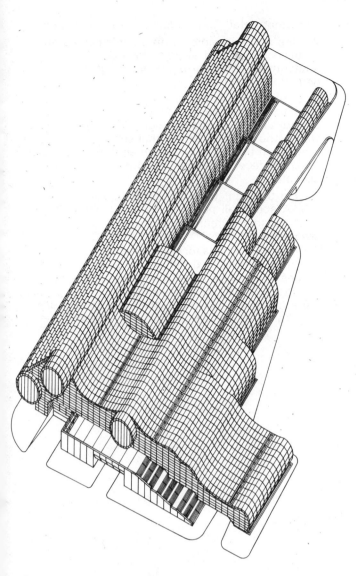

Mamoru Shimazu *drew the complicated structure in isometric for* Daniel, Mann, Johnson, and Mendenhall. *Curvilinear planes remain the same throughout its length, simplifying the delineation of the remainder once the initial lines were correctly established.*

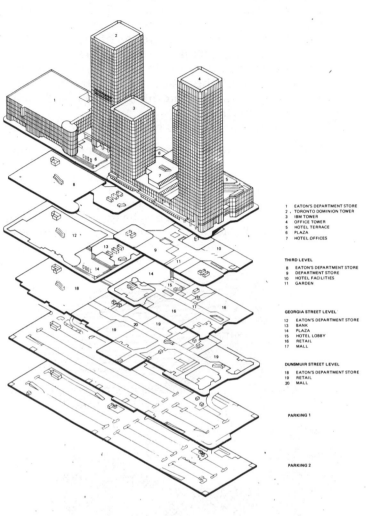

1   EATON'S DEPARTMENT STORE
2 . TORONTO DOMINION TOWER
3   IBM TOWER
4   OFFICE TOWER
5   HOTEL TERRACE
6   PLAZA
7   HOTEL OFFICES

THIRD LEVEL

8   EATON'S DEPARTMENT STORE
9   DEPARTMENT STORE
10   HOTEL FACILITIES
11   GARDEN

GEORGIA STREET LEVEL

12   EATON'S DEPARTMENT STORE
13   BANK
14   PLAZA
15   HOTEL LOBBY
16   RETAIL
17   MALL

DUNSMUIR STREET LEVEL

18   EATON'S DEPARTMENT STORE
19   RETAIL
20   MALL

PARKING 1

PARKING 2

A metropolitan complex of buildings, designed by Gruen Associates, *and schematic views of its different levels. All are isometric projections.*

ISOMETRICS

Although it is less visually pleasing, an isometric is easier than a perspective to draw and tells a clearer story. Its mechanical method of projection is virtually foolproof, providing that you read and follow plans accurately.

Usually associated with engineers' designing machine parts, the isometric is a useful type of three-dimensional illustration for architects as well. Its qualities are suited to the explanation of the complexities of larger projects.

Its drawing procedure results in a distorted appearance, making it more appropriate for inter-office communication than for presentation to clients.

Lines which would converge to vanishing points in a perspective are drawn on parallel planes isometrically, usually at thirty degrees from the horizontal or vertical. Dimensions are transferred directly from plans and elevations without the complication of diminishing proportions.

Explanation of form and detail is a primary purpose. Techniques for delineation usually are pencil or pen line. Further rendering, if necessary, should be limited to simple, flat tones or shadows.

LINE VALUES

Illustrations by brush and paint define their subjects with masses of pure tone. Pen and ink techniques, and many in pencil, must depend on line to achieve these results. The rich shades and textures of an intricate ink sketch are created by many individual strokes of the pen.

Confidence, skill, and variety are required to achieve these results with such a simple instrument. Lines of the same weight and character throughout usually produce a dull and uninspired illustration.

These suggestions help avoid such lifelessness:

1. Vary line weight by exertion of more or less pressure on the point of the instrument. Use heavier lines to define major shapes or foreground elements and emphasize shadow-casting edges; lighter lines for secondary areas and less important detail, tone values, and backgrounds.

2. Line patterns indicate different qualities and textures: clean and straight for rigid structure; squiggly for foliage; irregular for rough shingles; and stipple for stucco.

3. Control lines at all times, even in areas treated most freely and casually. Keep them on course by careful drawing, straightedges, or other aids. Don't stop short of corners that should intersect. Keep even the finest lines firm all the way; don't let them fade out vaguely at their terminals or skip areas.

4. Use the right tools for different parts of the job. A speedball pen fills in solid areas or outlines coarse foregrounds better than a fine croquil.

Use softer pencils for bold loose areas; medium for tight architectural detailings. Slightly harder grades of pencils are used on textured paper than on smooth stock, with similar results.

For transferring layout to illustration board, use the hard 4H or 6H pencils for clean lines.

A variety of line values and textures possible with a croquil pen.

Different line treatments give interest to this pen sketch of a simple vacation structure. Additional interest is gained by texturing the tones of the screened area with lines of white tempera, drawn with a No. 1 pointed sable brush and a bridge rule.

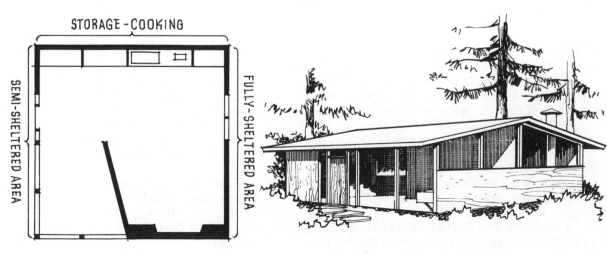

STORAGE - COOKING

SEMI-SHELTERED AREA

FULLY-SHELTERED AREA

A sketch using pencil tones with a minimum of hard lines for definition.

A sketch delineated by tones only, with no hard lines to define the planes.

TONAL VALUES

Unless planned for line only, an illustration in any medium requires a wide range of tonal values for its effective and attractive presentation. Pure white gives sparkle; black provides strength and contrast; middle grays add variety and interest. Color work also needs the same span of values.

Much of the detail is developed in the middle shades. It is often lost or obscured in the dark areas of shadow or the bright patches of light.

In pen or pencil sketching, a built-up tone can eliminate a hard line to define a change of plane, suggesting a more natural shaping of the subject by the play of light on its surfaces.

Pen and wash drawings depend upon tone to establish major forms, with line used primarily for delineation of detail within them.

Wash, tempera, airbrush, and related techniques apply their mediums broadly, and rely almost completely upon values to depict their subjects. Tonal patterns should be planned in advance, so that the mediums can be applied as directly as possible. Excessive working over can destroy crispness and result in a muddy appearance.

Try to achieve a proper balance. A rendering is weak if it is too light in tone, is heavy if too dark. Without proper middle values the unity is lost.

SHADES AND SHADOWS

Shades and shadows shape architectural forms and tonal contrasts. In an exterior view, their placement is governed by a single source of light, striking all surfaces from the same angle.

Once it has been assumed, the light direction must remain constant. Cast shadows are not seen on surfaces receiving no direct light, such as a wall on the opposite side of its source, or the underside of a roof area.

Such a surface is in shade, which is never as dark as a cast shadow. A wall struck by a glancing light may have a light tone to differentiate it from one in full sun and will show a cast shadow.

Shadows fall in only one direction—away from the light source. You are permitted some liberties with placement and sizing, but tread cautiously and without violation of basic principles.

Except for a rare night effect, the source is clear, bright sunshine. (Weather conditions in the typical rendering are invariably perfect!)

Interiors may be illuminated by artificial and reflected light as well as by that from outdoors. This need not be confusing if one source, such as a window, is kept dominant. The additional sources can usually justify the juggling of shades and shadows for a desired effect.

To visualize the various effects of light play on its surfaces, center the structure on an imaginary clock face and move the light source around its perimeter. Notice the deeper shadow cast on the wall least perpendicular to the light (see the diagram below).

To create the most pleasing shade and shadow pattern, light intensity should be greatest on the main facade (or facade at the least angle to the picture plane). Secondary or receding walls receive less intensity and are lightly shaded. Roof planes are treated in the same manner. Shadows are drawn with the same perspective as the structure (see the diagram to the right).

Cast shadows should be deep enough to strengthen and emphasize the eave line, but not so deep as to overpower the architectural design with a too-heavy effect (see the diagram opposite, bottom).

Windows or other glass areas are more subject to the action of reflected light and normally do not receive shadows. Draperies or other opaque materials behind the glass will, however, receive shadows.

Irregular surfaces can create tricky shadow problems. Lines projected at the angle of the light to the receiving surfaces can help determine their shapes. With practice, and a little applied logic, you should soon be able to eyeball them (see the diagram opposite, bottom).

Shades and cast shadows with light source from different directions.

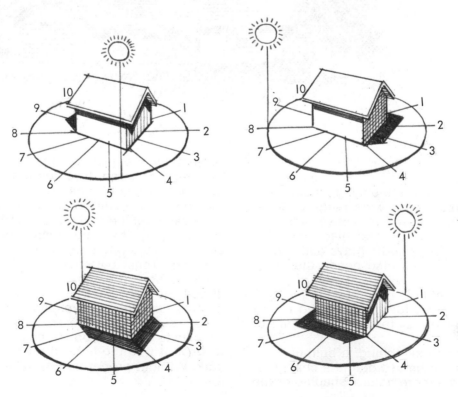

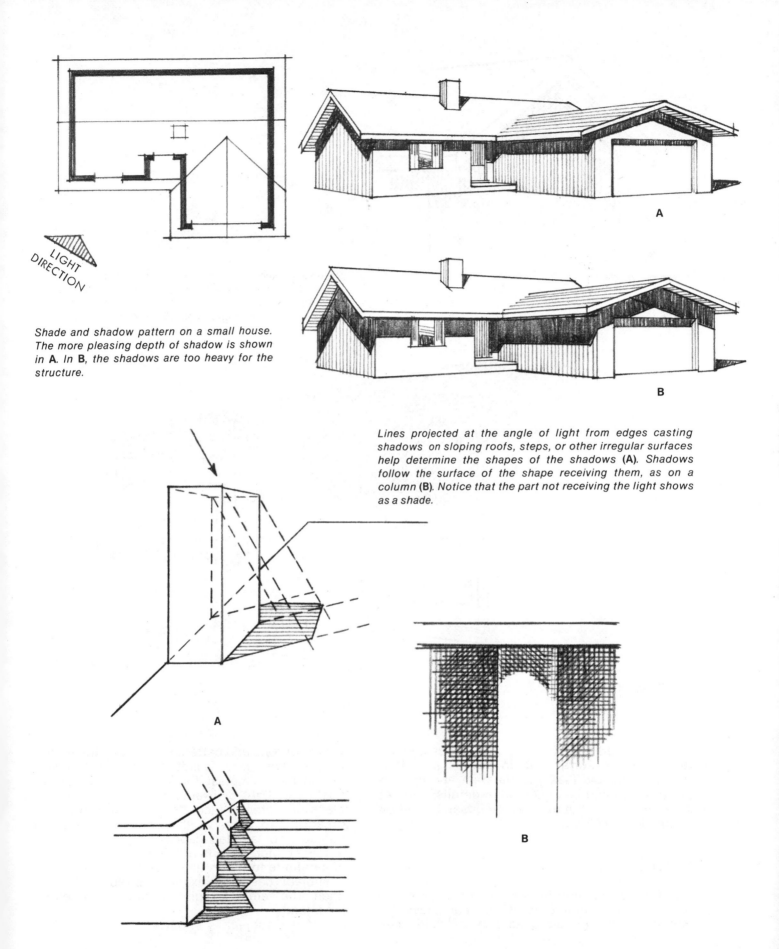

LIGHT DIRECTION

Shade and shadow pattern on a small house. The more pleasing depth of shadow is shown in **A**. In **B**, the shadows are too heavy for the structure.

Lines projected at the angle of light from edges casting shadows on sloping roofs, steps, or other irregular surfaces help determine the shapes of the shadows **(A)**. Shadows follow the surface of the shape receiving them, as on a column **(B)**. Notice that the part not receiving the light shows as a shade.

A

B

A

B

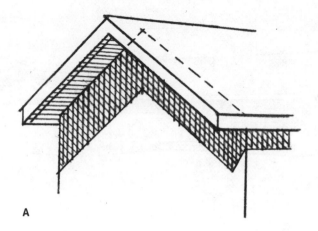

A

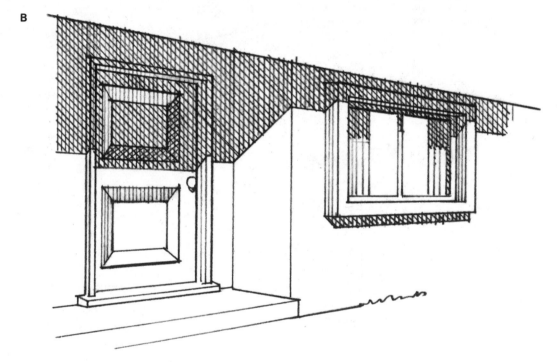

B

Shade and shadow patterns. In **A** *, note shade under eave and the portion of the shadow covered by the overhang of the roof. Shadows are irregular in shape from projections and recesses at windows and doors* **(B)**. *Part of the door panel in shadow shows as shade from reflected light from below.*

Reflected light from below causes a shade on the under surface of an eave, lighter than its cast shadow (see the diagram above). This principle should be observed in details rendered at larger scales, but may not be possible to show in smaller drawings.

REFLECTIONS

Reflections add interest to the surface of a lake or pool. Their careful use can prevent a window from appearing as a black hole; their variety of tone and pattern can relieve the monotony of the glass facade of an office tower.

In their simplest form, reflections may be flashes of light or irregular shadings across a glass or metal surface. Their patterns must be organized to preserve the unity of the whole subject, not applied haphazardly.

Even more care is required in the reflection of a definite form. On the calm surface of a lake, a subject casts an exact inverted replica of itself. The same vanishing points are shared by the image.

If the subject is situated at water's edge,

its entire image will be seen from any angle of view. When located away from the water, its distance and the viewing angle determine how much, if any, of the image will show (see the diagram on the next page, top).

Images are broken, but not destroyed, by ripples on the surface. Only casual suggestions of the subject can be used with increasing roughness of the water.

Image sizes of other buildings, trees, or vehicles reflected by the facade of a structure are governed by rules of perspective. Those of foreground elements will be reduced; those the same distance as their subject from the picture plane will remain the same (see the diagram on the next page, bottom).

Cloud reflections on the front facade come from conditions beyond the station point and out of the illustration. They may vary to suit the composition. However, clouds in the background are reflected in their true images on the side of a building.

A lake, a side of a building, or other reflective surface can be simulated with a large mirror for the study of these conditions. Blocks, cut paper clouds, and other props can be viewed in different positions at different eye levels to help verify your concepts.

Mirror image of a building in a pond is broken up by foreground elements.

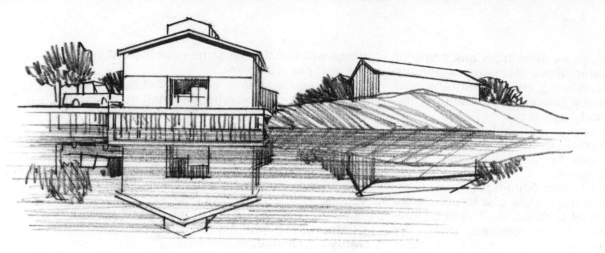

From a distance at a low angle, water reflects a mirror image of a subject. From a high angle, or from a near viewpoint, perspective reduces the visible amount of reflected background.

Perspective can reduce the size of an image reflected by a glass-walled building. Clouds in the background, however, will reflect as a mirror image on a plane perpendicular to them.

DETAIL

Detail is necessary to any well-finished illustration, whether it is a complicated watercolor or a quick pencil sketch. A drawing lacking scale, texture, and interest just does not tell its story.

If poorly drawn or overdone, however, detail can be a detraction. Too "busy" a picture is bewildering, and its main purpose is smothered in a welter of minutia.

A skilled artist recognizes this important fact: what is left out of a drawing can be as significant as what is put in. Rather than cover the entire surface with intricate patterns, he concentrates detail around centers of interest. Enough is included to describe fully essential elements and features. In secondary or unimportant areas, it is suggested, subordinated, or omitted.

Study of photographs with a wide range of tonal values will help you understand how and where detail should be played down or eliminated. Notice its tendency to disappear in strong sunlight or deep shadow, how apparent it becomes in middle value areas, how much foliage is massed together rather than separated in individual clumps. You will also learn much by examining the work of other illustrators.

Detail strongly indicated at one end of a surface can vanish almost totally at the other and yet leave no question of its continuity throughout. A few simple lines in the background can effectively suggest a cluster of other buildings without detracting attention from the main subjects. Equally simple outlines or silhouettes can unmistakably define foreground elements, and

Detail and contrast are worked into middle values of the center of interest in this pencil sketch but are lost or merely suggested in areas of strong light or shadow. Less important structures or elements are simplified tone patterns.

A pen illustration of villas in Sardinia suggests bright sunlight by strong patterns of light and dark values, elimination of hard definition lines, and only enough detail to identify textures.

yet they do nothing to hinder the movement of the eye to the center of interest.

Requirements of differing subjects govern the relationship of highly detailed to relatively open areas more than hard and fast rules. Some other points, however, may be stated more flatly:

1. Keep the size of any particular detail in scale with the rest of the structure. (Shingles and bricks are easy to draw too large.)

2. When the drawing area is too small to show detail to scale, treat it as texture or tone.

3. Don't let the drawing of single details dominate the whole illustration. Keep all tones or linework in harmony with one another.

4. Detail wood siding, bricks, shingles (and other materials of a regular construction pattern) to conform to the contours of a structure and the rules of perspective.

An effective sketch by Barry Zauss *for* Gruen Associates *tells its story with tones only and a bare minimum of detail.*

The croquil pen holds all the complicated detail with a delicacy that doesn't conflict with the overall scale of the structure, a building at the University of California at Irvine.

Only a few washes block in the tonal patterns of a block of town houses. After the pen work, a few highlights were picked out with tempera.

Useful Techniques

Certain delineation techniques may enjoy more popularity over a particular period than others. Prior to World War II, for instance, the most commonly used styles were careful pencil studies, built-up wash renderings, and pen sketches.

Much of the work of that time now looks rather academic, but a few of the artists worked with a power and competence equal to the best contemporary delineation.

Following the war, the field was led by bright watercolor techniques, often combined with tempera for additional flash and stronger definition. Their vivid colors and strong patterns could not help but draw attention to sales office display walls of the mushrooming housing developments. These techniques, along with tempera, are still favorites for presentation work.

In recent years, some of the older styles have been on an upswing. Pen and ink, and pencil, are commonly used, but with stronger, bolder treatments and more dramatic compositions than in the past.

Mixtures of different mediums are often featured. Pen and wash, pencil and acrylic, airbrush and tempera, color under acetate line overlays—these are only a few of the combinations. Anything portraying the subject well is acceptable, as long as it pleases both artist and client.

Some techniques lend themselves better to certain uses than others. Reproduction quality counts in one job, quickness of execution in another, and visual impact in a third. With the variety of usages now possible for illustrations, all effective rendering styles can find a market.

You will probably adopt one or more of the following techniques, or variations of them, as best suited for your particular specialties. Don't overlook the others; keeping up to date on them will increase your versatility.

PENCIL

No other medium matches the pencil for versatility, flexibility, and speed.

Design studies, constantly subject to change, can be erased and revised again and again. Durable tracing paper that can stand the

This sketch depends upon middle values to emphasize its woodsy subject.

LEAVITT DUDLEY

The pencil is ideal for catching the atmosphere of a reconstructed Western town.

strain of alteration, and medium, soft, and very soft grades of pencil are recommended materials.

A study or quick sketch can be drawn directly on the paper with graphite, or can be blocked in first with a nonphoto blue pencil. For a cleaner and more finished sketch, the latter process saves the step of retracing or transferring a layout to another surface. Graphite can be applied directly over the blue. The color is too recessive to detract from the finish medium, and drops out completely when photographed.

Smudgy drawings reproduce and print best in halftone, but well-prepared, high-contrast sketches can be processed as linecuts as well.

Handsome photographic enlargements are possible from pencil illustrations. They can be developed in a quality to hold the middle values or to intensify the blacks and whites boldly.

Copies from a whiteprinter may be printed in

sepia, blue, or black tones; color can be added to the background with pencils or felt tip markers.

Work by soft pencils smears easily, unless protected by a matte finish workable fixative. It may be sprayed after completion or during the drawing process. Although pencil can be added to the sprayed surface, application becomes more difficult as the fixative builds up. To reduce this problem, mask off untouched surface and spray only finished areas.

Paper overlays as hand rests and strips of cardboard to reduce the drag of the T-square also help protect the surface.

For the cleanest, sharpest results, tape a careful layout to a light table. Redraw it on an overlay thin enough to transmit the image from below.

Other mediums for this technique include graphite sticks, Prismacolor or sanguine pencils, charcoal and carbon pencils.

PEN AND INK

Crisp linework and high contrast make pen and ink a superior reproduction technique. Reduced or enlarged, its quality holds up on any type of paper.

Pen illustrations are widely used for presentations. The artist can work to a small and convenient size, saving hours that might be spent detailing the subject on a large surface. When complete, the art may be enlarged photographically to any desired dimension, and gains in power by the bold accentuation of its line quality.

Color may be added to an original on illustration board with watercolor wash, colored inks, or felt markers. Photographic prints can be tinted with markers or rubbed-on oils.

If color is to be included, reserve a copy of the artwork in the black and white stage to use for linecut reproduction or for variations.

Major corrections are difficult, so draw the illustration carefully in pencil before starting to ink. A preliminary tracing paper layout can be transferred, or the drawing may be made directly on the final surface.

Minor inking mistakes are salvaged easily, lines can be broken for texture or detail added to blacked-in areas with a fine sable brush and white tempera.

Don't make corrections or alterations, however, until the inking process is completed. Ink cannot be satisfactorily applied over tempera. If you do have to add detail on a painted surface, try lampblack watercolor and a fine-pointed brush.

When finished, remove the pencil marks with an artgum eraser. To prevent dulling the intensity of the ink, don't scrub more than necessary or use hard-textured erasers.

Some artists prefer a flexible croquil pen and a chisel point speedball for inking on a lightly-textured illustration board. Others would rather work on a smoother surface, such as plate-finish paper or board. Rapidograph technical fountain pens give good results on vellum.

Handled loosely and boldly, ink can be a good quick sketch medium.

With its bold shadow pattern and sparing use of line, this drawing will reduce to a small scale with little loss of detail.

WASH AND INK

Watercolor wash and ink line is another excellent reproduction technique, especially for advertising and editorial purposes.

The simplicity of its flat grays, the clarity of the pure whites, and the clean line detail combine nicely with the typography and other graphic material on a page layout.

If you are not sure of your drawing surface, test first for good absorbency of watercolor and ability to take a pen line without "fuzzing." These are essential.

First, transfer a tracing paper layout carefully to illustration board, and prepare a rough value study as a guide to tonal intensities. The charm of this is the directness of its washes laid down in the first application as close as

The lightness of an Oriental-style home is caught with soft washes textured with fine pen lines.

Bold splashes of wash are detailed with a few quick pen strokes in a rapid delineation of this building group.

possible to their final values. These are put in ahead of the inking, carefully confined to their proper areas. A bridge rule helps keep edges sharp. Add secondary washes as necessary for interest and further definition. Use the ink line for detail, texture, and emphasis. Wherever possible, let the edge of a wash shape a major area.

Finally, clean up rough edges or pick out detail from toned sections with a fine brush and tempera, white or mixed to the desired shade of gray. When thoroughly dry, erase pencil lines with artgum. Don't overdo this, as scrubbing lightens the tones of a wash area.

As a variation, the ink drawing may be completed first, with flat washes added for emphasis and unity of specific areas.

WATERCOLOR WASH

Watercolor wash is a traditional technique whose popularity has held through many generations of artists.

Though styles have changed from the more delicate renderings of the past to bolder, more direct contemporary delineations, the visual appeal and photographic reality of watercolor have kept it a favorite for presentation to clients.

Most wash drawings are in full color, but they can be done in black and white, as well. With competent craftmanship and good use of values, they reproduce well in brochures or on other slick-surfaced papers.

Unlike wash and ink, they are completely dependent on brushwork for definition and detail The choice of drawing surface is based on its ability to take washes. Most of its specialists prefer cold pressed rough surface illustration board.

The usual first step of delineation is the transfer of a pencil study to the board. Primary washes are applied as directly as possible to establish primary tonal values. Contrasts and textures are built up with succeeding layers.

Brushes are well-charged with color to keep the paint flowing freely onto the surface. Large flat brushes fill in the big areas; smaller round ones add the detail. A "dry brush" technique, with a minimum amount of water diluting the medium, often is used for particular textures.

Hold the overpainting to a minimum, however. Too much will muddy the color and destroy the spontaneity of the illustration.

After washes have been applied, tempera is used to add trim to a structure, even up rough edges, define windows or textures, highlight landscaping, and create other detail.

Thin tempera washes will suggest reflections on glass or subdue detail. A few spots of bright tempera also can add sparkle to relieve a muddy or too-dark area.

Transparent watercolors cannot be applied over tempera. Make sure that all preliminary washes are laid satisfactorily before using the opaque medium for detailing or correction.

Transparent watercolors are capable of a wide range of tonal values and light effect variations, as shown in the illustration of a hospital by Robert Jackson.

TEMPERA AND ACRYLIC

Although it is a completely different technique, tempera illustrations give the same visual effect as wash drawings and are used for the same purpose. They are equally popular in color or black and white.

Because its opacity and denser consistency make it a more tightly controlled medium than transparent watercolor, tempera is recommended as well for cutaway drawings, industrial installations, and subjects featuring intricate detail.

A suitable surface for tempera does not need the same absorptive qualities as watercolor board. Most of the material remains on the surface.

After transferring the pencil layout to the illustration board, major areas are painted broadly but in correct values. A rough preliminary value study is an essential guide.

Secondary areas and details are overpainted, but use caution to prevent undercoats from "bleeding" through or from lifting. Drafting tape can be used to mask areas already painted, to hold clean, sharp edges. Care must be taken in its removal to prevent lifting the color below it.

Landscaping and similar elements are usually added over the preliminary painting.

Acrylics are gaining popularity for this type of work. More durable than tempera, their fast-drying, hard, impervious surfaces will take unlimited overpainting. They do not flake off when masking tape is removed. Application techniques of this new medium are similar to those of tempera.

Both mediums are frequently and effectively used on colored mat board, which is usually of muted shades in the medium value range. Paint is applied in lighter or darker tones to contrast with the background. The unpainted surface often is exposed in a vignette effect.

Renderings in tempera or acrylic are solid and substantial in appearance and have strong value patterns. This is by QA Architectural Arts.

This illustration on colored illustration board uses the value of the surface for the sky and foreground. It was painted by Ross Barr for architect Marvin Johnson.

104

FLOW PENS AND FELT-TIPPED MARKERS

These verstile devices are ideal for quick sketches, in color or black and white. Travelers appreciate their self-containment.

Nearly any kind of drawing paper, from smooth to medium surface, is suitable for a background. Tracing paper, a sketch pad, or ordinary bond paper is most used, but you can get satisfactory results on an old grocery sack and many other convenient expedients. Bleeding of the medium can occur on some lighter-weight papers, and can sometimes be utilized for interesting textural effects.

Freehand sketching is the common technique. Drawing is very direct, with a few guidelines to indicate composition. If a straightedge is needed, use a bridge type to protect the felt tip from the edge.

A flow pen line drawing is similar to a pen and ink sketch, although the point is not capable of the croquil's flexible variation. Different sizes may be used for thicker or thinner lines. Tone, if desired, is added with a wide-tipped marker in gray or color.

To achieve the effect of a wash and ink drawing, apply tonal values first. Detail and definition as necessary are then delineated with the flow pen.

Markers lay down one uncompromising shade that allows little variation. Values may be built up, or colors modified, with careful overlays by the same or a different tip.

Because of the direct approach and the difficulty of changes, you need a good sense of proportion, scale, and detail to handle this technique.

Although mostly used for sketches or studies, these instruments can produce beautiful presentation drawings in the hands of a capable illustrator. More preliminary work is necessary for these. A clean pencil layout may be drawn on the working surface or placed under technical paper for tracing on a light table.

QA Architectural Arts *emphasized the highlighted office structure with bold strokes of flat tone.*

PASTEL CHALK

Although one of the more exotic techniques, pastel chalks produce colorful and dramatic quick sketches. The dash and flair of the medium allow considerable latitude for an artist's creative abilities.

Heavy tracing paper, medium surface illustration board, or colored mat board may be used. Black mat board—or paper—particularly sets off the medium for theatrical effects.

Rubbing and shading the chalk after application gives the rendered surface a smooth appearance. The strokes may be left as is for a rough-textured look.

The drawing is sprayed with workable matte fixative during its process to prevent smearing. Architectural detail or textures can be added with flow pens or tempera.

AIRBRUSH

This most mechanical of techniques produces some of the most striking presentation drawings. The artist using this tool must control it completely to achieve its smooth color applications, subtle shading, slick highlightings, and special effects.

Because of its complexity, the illustration must be thoroughly planned beforehand with a comprehensive sketch.

Before rendering, the drawing surface is first covered with frisket paper. With a frisket knife, the covering is cut and peeled away from areas to be exposed to the first color application by the airbrush. Successive sections are unmasked as the spraying operation progresses.

Because value comparisons are difficult when other sections are covered, be careful not to spray too light or too dark on the isolated area. Gauges, of white and tonal variations, held next to the sprayed area, help judge its intensity.

To build up different values within a given masked area, frisket paper may be removed in sections between spray coats. The last to be removed is the lightest in tone.

Fine architectural details, landscaping, figures, and other elements which are difficult to airbrush are added with tempera when spraying is completed.

An airbrushed area is extremely vulnerable to spots, drips, spatters, scratches, and other difficult-to-correct hazards. If a serious blemish occurs that won't be covered later by a tree or other brushworked object, remask and respray the area.

Medium surface illustration board is a good background material. The color medium may be India ink or tempera. The latter offers a wider range of colors but its consistency is more likely to clog the fine apertures of the brush.

For best results, flush the instrument frequently with pure water and clean thoroughly when the job is finished.

When ink is the medium sprayed, airbrushed drawings combine successfully with pen line. With other techniques, it may be used for smooth skies, highlighting, fogging, or other special treatments.

A pastel chalk rendering by Barry Zauss for Gruen Associates shows the broad treatment characteristic of this medium. Lettering and highlights are added with tempera.

An airbrush illustration by Ben Althen *for Gruen Associates shows the extremely smooth color application and delicate shading that identify this type of artwork.*

Oil color, applied with cotton swabs, combines with pen and ink line and tempera to produce this handsome illustration for Gruen Associates *by Ben Althen.*

MIXED MEDIA

While subject to certain controls not always present in less disciplined forms of art, architectural illustration is by no means closed to new techniques or methods of expression.

Traditional methods of presenting an architectural subject are open to new concepts. Illustrators more recognized in other fields have been commissioned for delineations that feature activities and figures as prominently as structure.

These imaginative artists often introduce ideas in technique and composition that are well worth studying.

Tried and true methods included in this chapter are responsive to experimentation. Frequently many of them are combined, often with more striking results than when used in a "pure" manner.

Observe their rules until your command of them is sure and confident—then explore their variations!

Figure 1 A layout for a pencil sketch with a nonphoto blue pencil on technical paper can be corrected and revised many times without affecting the surface of the paper or the application of the final medium. When the layout is redrawn with a graphite pencil, the blue recedes to an unobtrusive background undertone. The color drops out completely in photocopies. From Daniel, Mann, Johnson, and Mendenhall, Architects and Engineers.

Figure 2

Figure 3

For these renderings by Ben Althen for Gruen Associates, pen and ink line drawings were transferred photographically to matte finish print paper and mounted on heavyweight illustration board. Oil colors were added, as will be described in Chapter 17. Clouds were picked out of the color with a kneaded eraser.

Figure 4

Figure 5

Figure 6

These examples of well-handled transparent watercolor rendering are by John Hollingsworth *for* Daniel, Mann, Johnson, and Mendenhall, Architects and Engineers. *Tones are built up from light to dark, with trees added after the washes of the architecture are completed. Notice the change in value of the water in the canal, from the gradual addition of stronger pigmentation as a wet wash progresses. Fine detailing of the architecture and entourage are completed with tempera.*

Figure 7

Figure 8

Tempera is a medium for stronger, definite tonal patterns and the expression of architectural solidity. Structures and major areas of the background and foreground were finished first in these examples by QA Architectural Arts. Trees, shrubs, vehicles, and figures were added by overpainting.

Figure 9 Tempera application is carefully confined in the furnishings of this interior by QA Architectural Arts and is handled loosely in the rest of the vignette. It was thinned with water on the ceiling, and texture was added by stippling with a sponge.

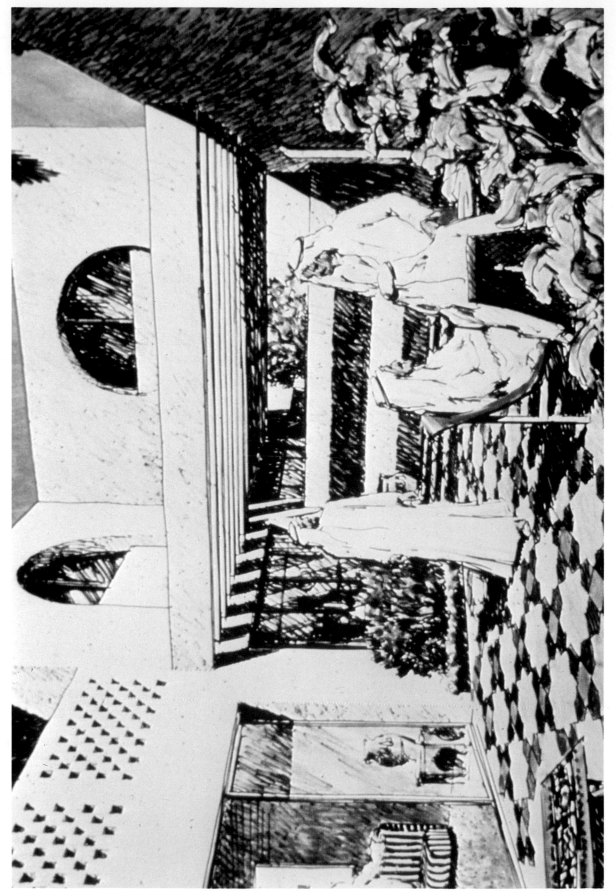

Figure 10

Figure 11

Original art for these felt-tipped pen illustrations of a Saudi Arabian project was by Tom Tomonaga. Dark and light tonal patterns were well established. Oil color was then added to photographic prints for the final results. Both figures are from Daniel, Mann, Johnson, and Mendenhall, Architects and Engineers.

Airbrush is an excellent medium for expressing the glittering sleekness and structural materials of many contemporary buildings. Artist Uri Hung *first drew the illustration carefully in pencil on illustration board, then airbrushed the main shapes and tones of the architecture and the environment. Final delineation of fine details, landscaping, vehicles, and figures is tempera painting. Clouds are in tempera in Figure 13 and are shaped with the airbrush in Figure 14. Figures 12, 13, and 14 are from* Daniel, Mann, Johnson, and Mendenhall, Architects and Engineers. *Figure 15 is from* Gruen Associates.

Figure 12

Figure 13

Figure 14

Figure 15

Figure 16 *Mediums are mixed for the crisp effect of this illustration by QA Architectural Arts. Painting was completed first in acrylic colors and allowed to dry to a hard, durable finish. Linework was then added with pen and ink. (This type of line addition is difficult over tempera, as the medium dries to a softer finish than acrylic and the ink tends to spread.)*

Figure 17 *Felt-tipped markers color the architecture and its surroundings, while trees and bright accents are brushed in with tempera. The base for the color addition is a white print of a pencil rendering by* Barry Zauss *for* Gruen Associates.

Figure 18 On a photographic print of a pen line drawing, tone is added to the railings and floor with an airbrush. Figures, trees, and wall decoration are painted with tempera. Leaving the rest of the architecture untouched to emphasize its linear quality, artist Barry Zauss achieves a strong, poster-like pattern with the mixture of mediums. From Gruen Associates.

Figure 19 *Brilliant ornamentation of the tile facade of the building in Figure 14 was planned with many design studies. Felt-tipped markers are used to color a white print of a quick pencil sketch in this example by Philo Jacobson for Daniel, Mann, Johnson, and Mendenhall, Architects and Engineers.*

Figure 20 In this example by QA Architectural Arts, a line drawing in felt-tipped pen was photographically reproduced on transparent acetate. Acrylic color was applied to the reverse side of the acetate. The illustration was mounted over craft paper, which provided the background color.

PART II

Application of Techniques

Few artists are proficient in all categories of architectural illustration. An expert at quick visualization may flounder in the concentrated detail of presentation drawings. Another works best from a thick roll of plans and elevations, preferring to leave more innovative subjects to others. Some excel at fluent expression of design ideas in rough sketch form.

The progression of an illustrator to different work levels is not in any fixed order. For the student, however, the ten chapters of Part II are arranged by increasing complexity of work levels and the degree of independent thought and action required for the development of each.

7
level one

Exercises in Delineation

Drawing and rendering a subject as simple as this small residence can be an almost unchanging formula. Turning out a creditable job by this approach is within the capabilities of anyone who is at all familiar with drawing materials and drafting tools, and can follow directions.

A subject may differ in composition, size, and viewpoint, but it can still be handled by the samp step-by-step procedure, as long as it conforms to the following factors:

1. Viewing angle is at eye level and uncomplicated;

2. Major forms are simple geometric shapes;

3. Perspective is mechanical;

4. Rendering steps are taken in proper sequence;

5. Recommended tonal values are used;

6. Landscape is stylized;

7. Variation is possible through resizing, rearranging, or adding more geometric shapes.

Within these limitations, you can delineate many types and styles of small homes. Despite their simplicity, the examples shown in this chapter include many elements and processes used in the illustration of more complex structures.

Skill in pencil, pen and ink, flow pen and marker, and wash and ink illustration should develop fairly rapidly. Control of wash or tempera usually takes longer.

Airbrush is the most difficult. It is shown here only as an introduction to an excellent technique. It is usually confined to more elaborate presentations.

THE LAYOUT

Study of the plan and elevations indicates the building basically is formed by two rectangular boxes topped by intersecting triangular shapes (see the top diagram on the next page).

Develop the pencil layout from these forms as follows:

1. Set up the station points, picture plane, horizon, and vanishing points; project the major

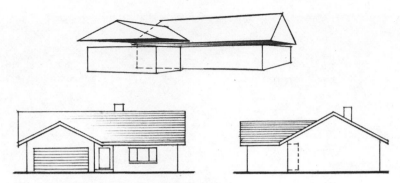

Plan, elevations, and basic geometric shapes.

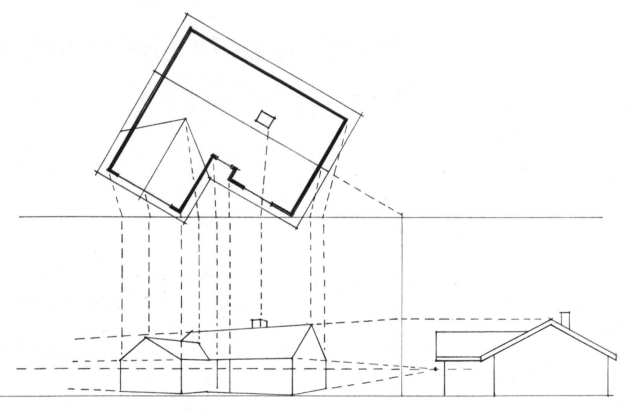

Layout step 1, perspective projection by "office" method.

shapes of the architecture. (For easier rendering on first attempts, keep your subject about 10″ – 12″ in width.)

2. Project roof overhang, chimney, door and window openings.

3. Draw doors, windows, trim, other detail, and guidelines for textures. Much of this can be carefully eyeballed for proportion. (A rough indication of a six-foot human figure is a good scale reference.)

Assume light source, draw shadow patterns.

4. Block in rough shapes of landscaping, drive-

way, walkways, and fences. (Keep all in perspective.)

The same layout is used for all the following techniques. A perspective chart can simplify the procedure, although with practice you will eyeball more and more, and you will often draw directly on the finish surface.

Before starting any rendering, practice with the medium and check the results against your value scale in order to familiarize yourself with its possibilities and limitations.

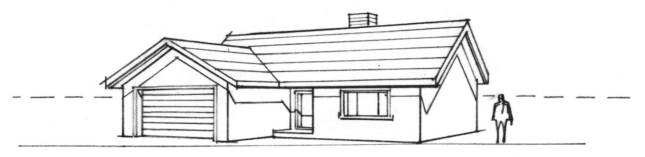

Layout steps 2 and 3.

Layout step 4.

Before rendering in any medium, plan values with a rough thumbnail sketch.

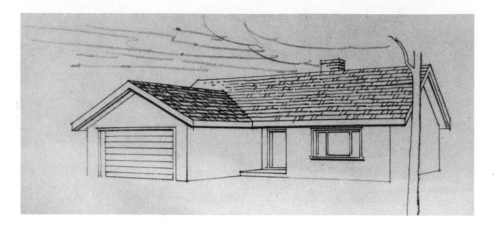

Steps 2, 3, 4, and 5.

Steps 6, 7, and 8.

PENCIL

When drawing on a translucent paper, place the layout underneath it. Trace the layout with a sky-blue pencil, a recessive color, and render over it.

On an opaque paper or illustration board, use transfer-paper to shift the layout to its surface. As cleanup of superfluous lines is difficult after rendering, the transfer must be neat and accurate.

Rendering surface: 1000H technical paper, medium surface Strathmore paper or Bristol board.

Medium: Medium, soft, and extra soft grade pencils (#2%10, #2, #1, or HB, B, 2B according to grading method of manufacturer).

Equipment: T-square, triangle, erasing shield, fixative.

Procedure:

1. Transfer layout to drawing surface.

2. Suggest sky with soft pencil strokes.

3. Outline tree trunks, branches, or other elements cutting across the architecture. Make lines away from light source heavier.

4. With sharp #2%10 pencil and straightedge, firmly draw in outlines of architecture. Strengthen the edges casting shadows, as the under surfaces of eaves or door and window trim, with #2 pencil.

5. Freehand, with #2 pencil, add courses of shingles and bricks. Follow guidelines to keep courses in perspective, notice areas where detail is lost in light, and use heavier pencil pressure on receding roof and chimney planes. Suggest a few individual shingles.

6. Add shingle pattern freehand at ridges and edges of roofs. Note reversal of direction of shingles at center of ridge. Add linear toning to underside of eaves, following guidelines.

7. With #2 pencil, bevel point, add middle tones to receding walls, highlighted surfaces, roof planes, and glass to suggest play of light and reflections. Use medium to light pressure, varying tones from darker, where a change of plane is defined, to lighter.

8. Render cast shadows with #2 pencil (notice that shadows are darker on receding walls.) Add dark areas to glass.

9. Add tree branches with sharp point of #2

pencil; foliage with point held flat. Darken under-surfaces of foliage area for perspective effect.

10. Complete landscaping, fence, and foreground. (Notice greater tone contrasts near subject; use of lighter values or outline only in other areas.)

11. Spray with fixative.

Throughout the sketch, drawing with a straightedge maintains control and alignment. Freehand rendering of foliage and texture and irregularity of secondary tonal values prevent a too-mechanical appearance.

Steps 9 and 10 and value scale.

For a clean, straight edge to shadows, draw them against a triangle placed on the illustration.

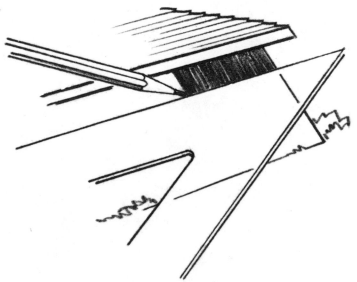

PEN AND INK

Procedures and strokes of pen delineation are similar in many ways to pencil work. Dependent on a finer instrument and a medium of one intensity only, pen rendering is more precise in appearance. Vary line weights by pressure on the point (croquil), or by drawing edgeways (chisel point speedball).

Rendering surface: Medium rough surface illustration board or paper, plate surface illustration board or paper, 1000H technical paper (experiment to find your favorite).

Medium: Waterproof India ink; white tempera.

Equipment: T-square, triangle, metal-edged ruler, croquil pen, #C4 chisel point speedball pen, #1 round sable brush.

Procedure:

1. Transfer layout to illustration board.

2. Suggest sky with a few light pen lines.

3. Outline tree trunks and elements cutting across architecture with croquil. Darken line on side away from light source.

4. Outline architecture with croquil, pressing more heavily on edges casting shadows. Use the metal edge of the upside-down ruler as a straight-edge and bridge to prevent ink smears.

5. With croquil, draw courses of shingles and bricks freehand. Use heavier pressure on receding planes. Lose some detail in sunlit area. Suggest individual shingles.

6. With medium pressure on croquil, draw freehand the shingle patterns at ridge and edge of roof. Add tone under eave with light but firm line.

7. With croquil, light to medium pressure, add middle tone values to receding walls. Suggest light play on highlighted surfaces.

8. With speedball, add cast shadows on receding walls (let a few white flecks show for sparkle); add darkest window areas. Use croquil for shadows on other surfaces, cross-hatching with medium to heavy pressure to vary intensity. Vertical parallel strokes indicate shadow on different material.

9. Add tree branches with croquil; foliage with speedball.

10. Finish other elements of sketch, using croquil for detail work and speedball for dark accent areas.

11. Correct any smears or mistakes with tempera and brush. Erase pencil lines with artgum.

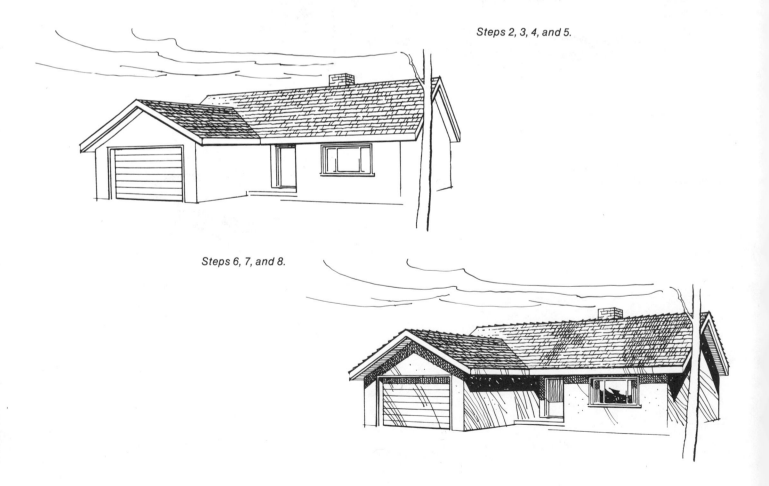

Steps 2, 3, 4, and 5.

Steps 6, 7, and 8.

Steps 9, 10, and 11 and value scale.

Held upside-down and used as a straightedge, a metal-edged ruler helps prevent smeared pen lines.

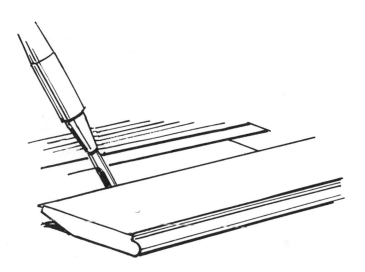

WASH AND INK

In this technique, tones are applied first by brush and watercolor. Pen and ink lines are added as needed for definition and detail.

Its charm and quick execution depend on its directness. The initial washes should be in their proper values, requiring a minimum of overlaying washes to build up their tones.

Transparent washes are deceptive. Their values when dry are much lighter than when wet. Because of this, timidity of application is a common fault and results in too pale a tone.

Experiment with middle values on another board before rendering; compare them with light and dark extremes.

As much as possible, hold washes to three applications. The first establishes primary values; the second defines planes or suggests light variations; the final adds shadow and accents.

To avoid spotty drying, mix plenty of material for larger wash areas, use the right brush for the job, and keep it well-charged. Flow the material freely, tilting the illustration board slightly during the process to keep the edges of the paint wet and moving evenly across the surface.

Finish a wash with clean crisp edges; pick up surplus material with an empty brush.

Don't let a freshly painted area touch another until the latter is thoroughly dry, to prevent "bleeding" of one into the other.

Rendering surface: Crescent #112 illustration board or similar.

Medium: Transparent watercolor, lamp black (or color), waterproof black India ink, white tempera.

Equipment: T-square, triangle, bridge rule, metal-edged ruler, ½″ flat brush, #6, #3, and #1 round sable brushes, croquil pen, #C4 chisel point speedball pen.

Procedure:

1. Transfer layout to illustration board.

2. Indicate sky with loose strokes of #1 value by ½″ brush. Indicate lawn with #4 value by #6 brush.

3. With #6 brush, apply #2 value to receding walls, chimney, fence, entry, and garage doors, draperies, undersides of roof; #3 value to upper roof planes.

4. With #3 brush, tone glass area with #3 value leaving a little white at top for sparkle. While still wet, tilt board and touch bottoms of windows with black, let dry for "accidental" varied effect.

5. With #6 brush, apply second wash coats to architecture. Give an even tone of #3 value to receding roof plane, a few irregular strokes to other roof planes. Apply loose strokes of #2 value

to walls as shown to suggest light play. Paint quickly and directly to prevent disturbing first coats of paint.

6. Add tree foliage with #6 brush and #3 value and planting at base of house with #6 brush and #4 value. Do not indicate foliage higher than the lower branches.

7. Apply shadow to walls under eaves with #3 brush and #5 value. Float on color in continuous tone from one corner of the building to the other, tilting board to keep wet edge moving. When through, pick up surplus material with empty brush. With #3 brush and #5 value, add shadows to fence, draperies, entry, and garage doors. (Note highlight left on entry door trim.)

8. Shade underside of tree foliage with broad strokes of ½″ brush and #4 value. Indicate shadow under ground planting with #3 brush and

Steps 2, 3, and 4.

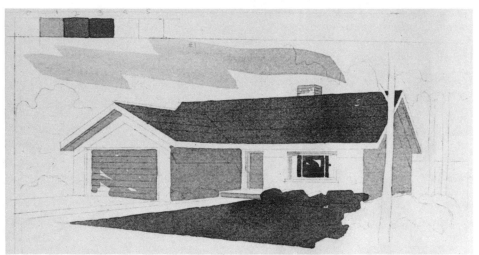

Steps 5 and 6.

Steps 7 and 8.

Steps 9, 10, and 11 and value scale.

#5 value, keeping base of shadow *flat* on ground. Add cast shadows from trees on lawn with #5 value. Use bridge rule as guide to keep shadows flat.

9. Indicate courses of shingles, bricks, textures, and other architectural detail with croquil pen and India ink. Use straightedge for outlines if needed, but freehand as much of the work as possible. Do not define a changing plane or a shape with an ink line if a tone has already done it.

10. Outline foreground shapes, suggest foliage and grass texture with croquil. Use speedball pen for background foliage. After color is thoroughly

dry, remove any visible pencil lines by lightly rubbing with an artgum eraser.

11. Straighten edges and correct mistakes with brush and tempera. In toned areas, mix tempera and lampblack to proper value for corrections.

Numbered value recommendations are not hard and fast rules, of course. They help in tonal comparisons, but may vary according to local color or light effects. Any illustration should maintain the proper relationship of strong darks, clear whites, and middle tones to avoid a too somber or too pale overall effect.

Steps 2, 3, and 4.

Step 5.

FLOW PEN AND FELT-TIPPED MARKER

The medium is different, but the procedure for this technique is similar to that of wash and ink. First values are applied with markers, and then penline is used for detail and texture.

Unlike watercolor wash, whose value varies with the ratio of water to pigment, a marker lays down a constant value during its contact with the drawing surface. Changes of tone are made by using a different marker, or by repeating the application of the same marker.

For an even coating of the area, bands of tone must be applied carefully to prevent the appearance of overlap lines. However, regular overlap lines can often be used for interesting textured effects.

Markers are available in black and nine shades of gray, in either warm or cool shades, and in a wide range of colors. Most useful pens are fine-tipped for detailing and medium for accent.

For a straight, even edge, mask an area with drafting tape before applying the tone. Marker fluid does not erase, but it can be corrected with

tempera to a certain extent. Lines from the flow pen tend to bleed through the correction, so use the instrument carefully to avoid mistakes.

Rendering surface: 1000H technical paper, medium surface illustration board, Bristol board.

Medium: Flow pen and felt-tipped markers.

Equipment: T-square, triangle, bridge rule.

Procedure:

1. Transfer layout to drawing surface.

2. Apply first layers of tones to all areas (use values corresponding to pen and wash technique). Marker fluid dries immediately, and adjacent tones will not bleed into each other. Textures such as shingles, bricks, and wood siding can be suggested by the direction of the strokes.

3. Add tones suggesting lightplay and other variations.

4. Lay in foliage and planting.

5. Apply shadows.

6. Add architectural and landscape detail with flow pen.

Step 6 and value scale.

TRANSPARENT WATERCOLOR

A full wash illustration completely depends on brushwork for both tone and detail. More tonal buildup may be required than by pen and wash technique, but applications still should be as direct as possible. For a crisp and professional appearance overlays should be held to a minimum.

Watercolor is one of the trickier techniques. Certain effects are often achieved accidentally, but more come through careful planning and skillful handling of the medium. Some of the following pointers can be applied in the rendering of the simple example in this chapter; others will be helpful for more complex subjects.

To hold a white surface:

1. Paint around the area.

2. Mask area with drafting tape or masking substance (such as a layer of thin rubber cement), paint over it, lift mask when wash is dry.

To recover a white area:

1. Scrub off paint with a damp sponge.

2. Scrape out highlights with razor blade or frisket knife.

3. Paint over with tempera.

Application and variation of washes:

1. For a smooth, even tone, soak surface with sponge, wait until almost dry, apply color with a full brush.

2. For a wash with sparkly highlights, paint on dry rough illustration board.

3. To vary tone in a wet wash, tilt board toward the section to be darkened. Or, increase ratio of pigment to water during application.

4. For textural effects, use a "dry brush" with very little water in the medium, or dab the medium with a sponge.

If an illustration is proceeding badly and seems to be beyond salvation, don't give up. Hold it beneath running cold water, gently scrub off the entire surface with a sponge, and rinse. Some of the color residue will remain, but not enough to prevent using the same drawing for another start.

Rendering surface: Rough cold press or hot press illustration board (CP for a crisp effect, HP for a softer).

Medium: Transparent watercolor, tempera.

Equipment: Bridge rule, ½ʺ flat brush, #6, #3, and #1 round brushes, fine sponge, masking tape, razor blade.

Procedure:

1. Transfer layout to drawing surface.

2. Mask (or brush around) structure, soak sky area with clear water. When almost dry, tilt board and paint from zero value to darker value at the top. While still wet, pull brush charged with darker value across the sky, let dry for cloud effect.

3. Paint chimney, walls, driveway, fence, and walk. Use similar value range as in pen and wash sketch, with variations as indicated, and same sized brushes.

4. Apply wash to entire roof area, varying value by tilting board and adding slightly more pigment to medium. Leave fascia white. Add lawn area, darkening grass slightly toward house. Paint glass area, varying tone from light to dark.

5. Add second wash to receding roof plane. Suggest light variations on walls and roof. Add foreground tones.

6. With #3 brush, #5 value wash, and bridge rule, delineate courses of shingles and bricks. Add shingles (be sure they are aligned in perspective).

7. Brush in foliage and ground planting. Refine foreground areas with light washes and dry brush.

8. Add shadows to architecture.

Steps 2, 3, and 4.

Step 5.

Steps 6, 7, 8, 9, and 10.

Step 11 and value scale.

9. Paint tree trunks and branches. Shade under-surface of foliage. Add remaining fine detail.

10. Cast shadows from trees and ground planting; add dark accent planting in background.

11. Clean up or correct white areas and add window mullion with tempera and #3 and #1 brushes. With #2 value tempera, paint receding roof trim. Paint underside of roof surfaces, door and window trim in shadow, with #3 tempera. Shape and emphasize tree trunks with tempera as indicated.

TEMPERA AND ACRYLIC

Rendering procedures are basically alike for both mediums. Both are thinned with water, have the same finished appearance, and usually cover a surface with an opaque coating.

Unlike transparent watercolor, whose values only can darken with further wash applications, overpainting with these opaque mediums can go in either direction on the tonal scale. Areas are covered directly in their base values; variations may be added in lighter or darker shades.

Tempera and acrylic are brushed on with individual strokes. They may not be floated and allowed to run like transparent color. The process is a bit slower for this reason; the results are a little less dashing but more solid in appearance.

Acrylic dries to a hard, durable surface that can take unlimited overpainting. Tempera is less likely to damage brushes than acrylic, although both should be rinsed from the bristles immediately after use. An artist experimenting with a new technique usually finds tempera, with softer surfaces and drying qualities, the easier medium to handle.

A white background is used for more conventional illustrations. For a striking, poster-like effect, try a vignette on toned or colored mat board with some of the background exposed.

Rendering surface: Medium surface illustration board, mat board.

Medium: Tempera (in jars) or acrylic (in jars or tubes).

Equipment: Bridge rule, ½″ flat brush, #6, #3, and #1 round brushes, masking tape.

Procedure:

1. Transfer layout to board.

2. Paint sky and foreground (structure may be masked with tape).

3. Paint major areas of architecture in flat base values, leaving white highlights as indicated. Use bridge rule or mask for clean, straight edges.

4. Add shadows, shades, highlights, reflections to architecture; clean up or correct irregularities.

5. Broadly brush on foliage, tree trunks, and other elements.

6. Shape these elements with highlights, shadows, shades, and linear detail.

A different procedure is followed when working on a dark background. Its value may be planned for use as sky, foreground, walls of the structure, or other areas. Paint in lighter or darker sections for proper contrast with the background, and then add detail.

Steps 2 and 3.

Steps 4 and 5.

Step 6 and value scale.

AIRBRUSH

This slick technique is usually reserved for massive shapes of large commercial projects and is unlikely to be used on a subject as simple as this example.

However, it is as useful as an exercise to acquaint you with the potential possibilities as well as with the tricky characteristics of the airbrush.

This is the most mechanical of the techniques described. Values are controlled and areas defined with masking devices and fine, delicate sprays. Brushwork is minimal.

India ink, in black or color, tempera, or transparent watercolor may be used as the medium. Ink is free flowing and less likely to clog the instrument. It is delicate and spots easily.

Tempera can be mixed to a wider range of tints and values. It must be thinned to flow properly. Transparent color is suitable when properly thinned, but value intensities are slower to build up.

First the drawing is covered with frisket paper. Next, areas are cut with a knife and peeled away, and the exposed area is sprayed. Darkest sections are sprayed first to less than final intensity; they are deepened in value as successive areas are uncovered and sprayed.

Frisket paper can be applied again to protect a painted surface, but plan the rendering to keep remasking at a minimum. Cardboard scraps may be used as temporary screens.

Keep the brush moving in sweeps rather than aimed at one point during applications of the medium. Do not spray so heavily that paint puddles and runs on the board. Instead, develop the tone with several light applications, each of which is allowed to dry between coats.

Use the medium, in black or color, at the intensity of its final tone. Less spraying lightens its shade to any desired degree, but it cannot be darkened beyond its full strength value. If an area becomes too dark, reduce it with a spray of a lighter color. Careful erasure can also lighten small areas.

Airbrush is usually combined with other techniques, such as tempera or pen line, to vary the texture or simplify definition. For this demonstration it is used as purely as possible, with only a few pen strokes for detail.

Rendering surface: Medium surface illustration board.

Medium: Ink, tempera, or watercolor.

Equipment: Airbrush, frisket paper (masking tape, liquid frisket, or rubber cement can be used for small areas), scraps of light cardboard, #1 pointed sable brush, bridge rule.

Step 2.

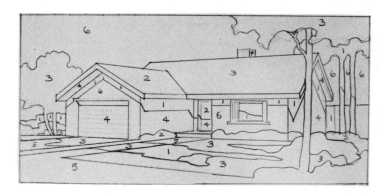

Steps 3, 4, and 5. (Note: It is helpful to cut all areas with the knife before starting the spray, as lines will soon be obliterated.)

Step 6.

Steps 7 and 8 and value scale.

Procedure:

1. Transfer layout to illustration board.

2. Mask entire surface with frisket paper.

3. With knife, cut the outline of all #1 areas and peel away the frisket paper.

4. Spray exposed areas.

5. Uncover and paint remaining areas in sequence. Numbers are steps in procedure only, not color values. Vary the values in an area to take advantage of the fine gradations possible with the airbrush.

Check your work against a value scale frequently, as tones can be very deceptive when adjacent areas are masked.

Short controlled bursts from the airbrush localize the spray to a particular area. If a finished section needs further protection, remask or shield with cardboard.

6. Spray against a cardboard mask to suggest lightplay on sunlit planes.

7. Remove remaining frisket paper, add linear definition. Use pen and ink over ink or transparent water color medium; a small sable brush and tempera over a tempera medium.

8. Add highlights or clean up blurred edges with tempera.

The possibilities of airbrush rendering are exciting, unlimited, and we have barely touched on them in this demonstration. Each drawing presents its own problems to be solved by the experience and ingenuity of the artist.

Environment and Activity

A minimum of landscaping and a suggestion of environment is sufficient nonarchitectural detail to dress up the simple structure shown in the preceding chapter. For the average illustration of a single model home, not much more is necessary.

Larger, more complex subjects usually require a fuller background to convey a sense of scale, function, and realism. In some cases, these descriptive elements become as important as the architecture. Sometimes they may even be the major interest of a drawing.

The purpose of the illustration helps determine the extent of the usage of these elements and how prominently they will be featured in the composition.

Landscaping: Trees, shrubs, groundcover, paving, and other surfacing are essential to soften and point up the architecture.

Secondary Structure: Patios, fences, steps, benches, pools, recreation areas, and other functional or decorative items are common in both residential and commercial developments.

Figures: The method used most for indicating scale; figures may be very suggestive and stylized when the architecture is the important function. In advertising or editorial work, they may move into the foreground as a dominant part of the composition. They are usually omitted in drawings of single model homes and detailed interiors whose furnishings give adequate scale reference, but figures are useful in any other type of illustration.

Vehicles: Cars, trucks, buses, trains, or other forms of transportation suggest scale equally well in any type of drawing, but are used most commonly in commercial or urban subjects.

Environment: Mountains, lakes, seashores, neighborhoods, and other backgrounds or foregrounds are important when a subject must relate to or identify with its surroundings. Bird's-eye views, advertising and editorial art, and large architectural or engineering projects, which must be compatible with the environment, include these features.

Activities: Popular contemporary interests are included prominently in advertising and editorial illustrations, presentations of large housing or resort developments, and land use studies. Recreational facilities are often the center of interest in the composition.

You must be extremely versatile to become proficient in all these areas, but you need a reasonable competence in many to progress beyond the elementary levels of architectural illustration.

Despite the great difference in shape between architectural structures and these other elements, many of the same drawing principles apply to both categories. A few suggestions can make drawing them easier and the overall illustration more pleasing.

1. Use your reference for authenticity.

2. Analyze and sketch an object in its simplest geometric shapes before detailing.

3. Suggest as well as define detail.

4. Determine its major features (architecture, environment, way of life), and compose the illustration accordingly.

5. Keep all objects in the same perspective as the main subject.

6. Unless they are primary, other elements should not be detailed to the point where they detract from the architecture.

7. Play down or omit detail in shadowed or brightly lighted areas.

8. Mass individual objects like trees or figures into massed groups when necessary to avoid spottiness.

9. Avoid the use of foreground features that you can't draw well.

10. If feet, hands, or other difficult-to-draw features give trouble, mask them with a strategically placed clump of foliage, or use another device to hide them.

11. Compose figures, or other objects indicating definite direction, to "look" into, rather than out of, the illustration.

LANDSCAPING

TREES

Trees—and many other plants—are not difficult to visualize as geometric forms. They are conical, spherical or hemispherical, cylindrical, or a number of other shapes.

This simplification is adequate for blocking the plant masses into the composition. But, as in the delineation of a building, you must understand the structure beneath the form to draw the subject well.

Trees take many configurations, but a common growth pattern is common to most. Main branches grow up and outward from the trunk. These divide and redivide until terminating into a network of twigs. Each division is a lighter structure than the preceding, an important point in the indication of the tree's natural gracefulness.

Notice that branches grow in all directions from the trunk—to front and rear as well as the sides.

To draw a tree, first visualize its simple shape and size. Roughly block in the trunk, main scaffold branches, and major foliage clumps. As a three-dimensional form, it is subject to the same perspective as the rest of the drawing.

Render the foliage broadly, shaping it with shadows and highlights. Open its structure to look through to branches or leaf masses in other parts of the tree. Keep all detail in scale. Don't try to draw individual leaves unless they appear in the immediate foreground—and just suggest them for the most part even then.

Shadows cast on the ground or on the architecture should indicate the size and shape of the plant.

Trees lose detail with increasing distance from the station point, until they are drawn more as general masses than as individuals.

Their tonal values may vary to indicate local color, shadows, or highlights, to break up monotonous masses, or to better define architecture.

SHRUBS

On a smaller scale, shrubs are similar to trees in structure. They sometimes grow so close to the ground, however, that their shapes are shown only by the shadows at their bases.

Hedges and border planting usually are drawn as continuous foliage masses rather than individual plants.

A grouping of shrubs or flowering plants is often used as a foreground element, to add depth or help frame a composition. This device is well worn and often trite but effective nevertheless. If you employ it, plant material must be drawn carefully and to scale, detailed enough for identification and interest but not to the point of monotony.

Foreground plantings may also be treated as silhouettes in light or dark values, depending on their backgrounds.

GROUND COVERS

Grass, ivy, and other ground covers are usually treated as tones, varying according to the needs of the composition. Texture and detail may be indicated, but should be subdued and nonobtrusive.

The irregularities of a shadow cast on ground cover can help suggest its texture.

Graceful tree shapes in a project at Valencia, California.
Drawn by Louis Angelikis *for* Gruen Associates.

Structure of a tree, foliage masses, and their detailing.

A few of the plant forms that may be used for variety in an illustration.

From a normal eye level, more of the underside of the leaf canopy is seen when the tree is closer to the viewpoint. Groups of distant trees are treated as a single massed shape in **A.** *Perspective of a tree from above is shown in* **B.**

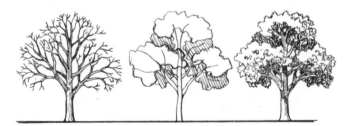

A desert home with plants suited to the location.

Suggestive treatment of ground covers.

130

Container plantings.

CONFINED PLANTINGS

Potted or indoor plants are frequently featured in illustrations of patios or interiors. More specific in shape, prominently placed, and related to the architecture more than general outdoor planting, they must be drawn carefully.

FIGURES

Some illustrators take naturally to figure drawing, delineating their subjects so skillfully that they are important assets to a composition. Others find the action and looseness of a well-drawn human always a difficult problem.

If you find yourself in the latter group (along with the majority of architectural illustrators), play down the prominence of the figures. Don't try to draw them too naturally: learn to stylize them well enough so that they are not jarring notes in otherwise competent artwork.

Professional figure illustration is a complex and demanding talent, involving many preliminary studies and often posed models. Their depiction for architectural purposes must be more direct.

Observing a few general principles can help minimize the effort and time for their layout and rendering.

PROPORTION

A standard architectural figure is six feet tall, give or take a reasonable variation for sex, age, or ethnic differences.

The average body is proportioned to a height of eight head lengths. Legs are four head lengths, shoulder width is two lengths, and hip width one and a half head lengths.

Childrens' heads are slightly larger in proportion to their bodies.

From proper proportions, the figure can be laid out as a series of simplified shapes.

ACTION

Interplay between different parts of the body give a figure the animation to prevent a stiff, stilted, appearance. (Note the reaction of the shoulders as the hips move from a horizontal to a tilted position.)

The action can be worked out first with a stick figure before further drawing.

FORESHORTENING

Parts of a body are not always viewed in a straight head-on or profile position.

The foreshortening occurring in other poses is more easily captured when the parts are thought of in simple, jointed forms.

Proportions of average adult figure—action when in motion.

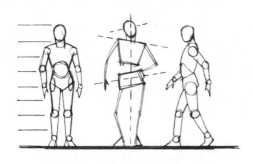

Foreshortening in a figure.

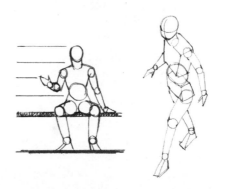

Heads are basically oval shapes viewed from any angle. Eye sockets are located midway in the skull, and other features divide the lower half into thirds.

Figures in perspective from a head-height eye level, below head height, and from above. Distant figures are massed shapes.

HORIZON

HORIZON

HORIZON

HEADS, HANDS, AND FEET

These normally are the most difficult areas.

For faces, block in the position of the features according to the angle of view. (Unless they are in the foreground, features are often omitted.)

Drawing hands and feet takes practice, patience, and observation. However, in stylized figures these members are often played down almost to the point of nonexistence. If worse comes to worst, well-placed clumps of leaves or furniture can screen problem areas.

CLOTHING

No matter how simply drawn, attire should be indicated clearly enough to be in character with the rest of the illustration and explain its function.

Keep styling contemporary. A current mail-order catalog can afford reference for a variety of men's, women's and children's costumes.

Study the directions of wrinkles and creases from stresses of the body in different positions, to drape clothing naturally on the figure.

PERSPECTIVE

Because of their importance to the scale of an illustration, even the most stylized figures must be drawn in accurate perspective.

This is easiest at a normal six-foot eye level. Tops of all the heads in the picture line up on the horizon, whether a figure is six or sixty feet from the station point.

Below eye level, positions of both heads and feet must be plotted according to the figure's distance from the station point.

Overhead views can be the most complicated, involving different placement of head and foot positions as well as foreshortening of figures in the foreground.

HELPFUL HINTS

A clipping file of all types of figures, in different poses, sizes, costumes, and angles of view, singly and in groups, can be one of your most helpful references.

If pose, angle, and scale are right, they may be traced and transferred. If their size is wrong, you can enlarge or reduce them photographically or with a camera lucida.

With a Polaroid camera, you can pose a figure yourself for quick reference or tracing.

Groups of figures in the distance should be massed and indefinite as to individual shape. Trying to draw each separately can suggest an ant colony in the background.

Well-drawn figures in a rapid transit station, by George Bartell *for* Daniel, Mann, Johnson, and Mendenhall.

Figures handled in a poster-like style in tempera, by Barry Zauss *for* Gruen Associates.

Figures in action, in pen and wash.

Loosely handled figures in a quick pencil sketch.

Good figure action in tempera rendering, by QA Architectural Arts.

VEHICLES

Automobiles, boats, and other vehicles are as important to architectural illustration as figures. Their type of delineation depends on the purpose they serve.

For scale and activity only, they may be noncommittal representations. An illustration of an auto salesroom requires identification of the cars' make and models. Automobiles seen in a luxury development will be more opulent in style than those of a small suburban subdivision.

Detail the vehicle, if desired, up to the same point as the architecture it complements, but don't go beyond. An intricately delineated sports car in front of a casually rendered small home will overpower the main subject.

However drawn, the scale relationship of the vehicles to the figures and architecture must be accurate. The chart indicates the relative sizes and general conformation of the most commonly used machines.

Your reference file should contain examples of all types of transportation. A busy and versatile illustrator may draw all the usual forms, plus such exotic conveyances as vintage locomotives, ocean liners, space capsules, or ski lifts.

Most vehicles are easy to draw, providing

Basic shapes are relatively easy to determine in automobiles, but realistic drawing of boats takes observation and practice.

Figures give an idea of the scale of vehicles commonly used in architectural illustration.

their basic shapes are blocked out first in proper proportion and perspective. Make sure the wheels or other elliptical forms are aligned correctly, then refine the outline of the body and add detail.

The compound curves of the hulls of boats can be tricky to handle. Study them from photographs taken from all angles. Better yet, spend a few hours sketching them at a harbor.

Bicycles, too, can trip up an artist unless he approaches them with an analytical eye. First, establish the perspective of the vehicle and the

space it will occupy, and sketch in the frame. Then add the wheels, with their all-important elliptical alignment, then the remaining detail. Last, fit the rider to the completed machine.

Large groups of vehicles, such as traffic on a busy street or in a parking lot, or boats in a marina, call for a massing and very suggestive definition of individual shapes. Emphasize the detail in a few foreground elements, but let the background forms merge and lose separate outline.

City traffic requires drawing automobiles from all angles.

ENVIRONMENT

Large architectural projects must often show their relationship to their environments for their best presentation. Clients react more favorably toward subjects set in recognizable backgrounds.

With increasing concern for environmental preservation, the impact that a new development will have on the land is an important factor to its acceptance. A good illustration must show proof that a project will not blight the neighborhood or the landscape.

The surroundings of such a drawing may demand rendering as elaborate and detailed as the subject's. In other instances, sketchy indications of mountain ranges, lake fronts, or adjacent buildings may suffice. Or it can fall anywhere in between these extremes, depending on the client's requirements.

Whatever its technique or emphasis, the background must be a reasonable depiction of a particular area. Its atmosphere is captured best by a visit to the site, although more often you will depend on photographs and maps for authenticity.

Nature's forms are freer and less confined than those of architecture, but understanding their structure is necessary in order to represent them convincingly.

MOUNTAINS

Peaks, ranges, and hills are solid, distinctive identifications of a particular site or region. Their specific shapes are usually the most dominant natural features of a composition.

If an impressive environment is an important selling point, the mountains may overshadow the architecture. Careful delineation must explain their character as rugged and steep, gentle and rolling, or whatever else their contours may be. Ravines, ridges, rocky outcrops, snowfields, and stands of trees all help the topographical description.

Distinctive features should be recognizable even when they are treated in a less graphic manner. Properly outlined, a few casual lines or flat tones can adequately suggest the type of terrain.

From the major linear direction of a mountain range, secondary ridges and canyons advance and recede, to establish a complicated pattern of movement. Study and sketching, from photographs or from nature, is the best way to learn the anatomy of this terrain.

Successive ranges of mountains can suggest depth and space. Contrasts of light and shadow are rendered more distinctly in the foreground; detail is subdued gradually and lost in the more distant planes.

Developments for winter sports are almost invariably in mountainous regions, as this lodge at Mammoth, California. Landscape drawing is essential to the illustration.

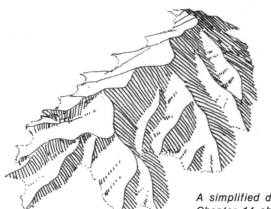

HORIZON

As a mountain is moved farther into the background, the distances from the horizon are lessened for both its base and crest.

A simplified diagram of the mountain range illustrated in Chapter 14 shows the ridges and valleys of its anatomy.

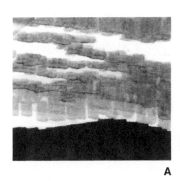

| A | B | C |

*Cirrus (**A**), stratus (**B**), and cumulus (**C**) clouds.*

Normally, the overall tonal value is darkest in the mountain range nearest the observer. You can notice the effect on hazy days particularly. This pattern is generally followed in illustrations, but sunlight and cloud shadows can alter conditions sufficiently to justify liberties you may take to improve or emphasize a composition.

Their perspective will locate mountains in correct relationship to an architectural subject, a critical point in the suggestion of space. With increasing distance from the viewpoint, both bases and summits move closer to the horizon line. Adjusting only one creates an improper effect.

SKIES

The sky in an architectural illustration can be handled in several different ways.

It may be a restful area of no detail, white or toned. It may be a strong abstract pattern to accentuate the architecture, or it may be only suggested by a few quick pen or pencil strokes. Or a sky can be a realistic representation of cloud types and shapes.

Some of the boldest, most dramatic skies set off the architecture of high-rise buildings. Very dark backgrounds accent the generally light tones of sparkling glass walls.

However drawn, and in whatever medium, the sky should be recessive. It may be strong in tone and pattern, and a powerful contribution to the mood of a composition, but it must not dominate the solid and unchanging elements that are the centers of interest.

Study the cloud patterns under different weather conditions, or from photographs in a meteorology book, before trying to render realistic skies.

Cloud varieties are numerous, but three basic types will suffice for most illustrations. They occur singly or in combination in nature, with numerous variations.

Thin and streaky cirrus clouds ride the upper reaches of the atmosphere, and may be indicated with a few wispy strokes or fine lines.

Stratus clouds blanket mid to lower levels, their bases appearing as a series of rolls receding in the distance.

Fluffy, billowing cumulus clouds suggest pleasant weather, may appear at lower and middle altitudes, and commonly form above the ridges and peaks of mountains.

As cloud formations are determined by atmospheric conditions at certain elevations, the bases of any type are located at a uniform height. As a result, the drawing of them must conform to rules of perspective.

WATER

An expanse of water is another element that lacks any particular individual distinction, and it is subject to several types of rendering treatment.

Its surface may be quiet and free of detail, or rippled and busy with reflections. The tonal values may range from blank white to dead black, whichever better complements the subject or unifies the composition.

Perspective is all-important to the drawing of any body of water. No matter how uneven the surroundings are, its surface must be absolutely flat. Faulty drawing of its junction with the shoreline can result in a tilted effect, which can throw the entire illustration out of kilter.

Ripples lose scale unless their perspective is correct. Spacing is closer as they recede toward the background.

A tumbling mountain stream also must follow the rules. Stretches of quiet water may punctuate a rough and rocky descent. As in a flight of steps, the perspective of each flat pool projects from the same horizon as those above or below it.

ACTIVITIES

Sports and recreation possibilities available in contemporary residential or resort developments are often as important to their planning and promotion as their architectural design. Illustrations of these projects may feature entertainment centers, golf courses, marinas, and other facilities as focal points.

Familiarize yourself with equipment, procedures, and accessories relative to the more popular activities, and keep a file on their details. One or more of the following are most likely to be featured in an illustration:

1. Swimming pools and recreation centers.
2. Tennis courts, shuffleboard, and other game areas.
3. Golf courses and club houses.
4. Boating and water sports.
5. Horseback riding and equestrian trails and centers.
6. Bicycling.
7. Skiing, snow sports, ski lifts, and lodges.
8. Gardening and outdoor living.

Wash tones emphasize the architecture of this vacation home. Recreation potential is suggested by line drawing only.

The foreground sets the mood for this recreation-oriented lakeside project. Scale and definition of the ripple lines, indicating the water surface, decrease with distance.

In this quick pencil sketch of lakeside activity, shapes of boats are simplified and often massed for rapid execution of their drawing.

Architectural development in the middle distance is secondary to the activities and environment at this site in San Diego County, California.

9. Stores and shopping.
10. School or park playgrounds.
11. Mobile home and trailer parks.
12. Camping, hiking, and fishing.

Drawings of some of these activities are more likely to supplement land use, engineering, or park studies than projects that are strictly architectural.

In an overall concept of a large development, an activity area may be only a more or less diagrammatic representation. Figures will be too small for any more than suggestive drawing, but game courts, courses, or other facilities must indicate proper proportion and scale.

Details of the activities are more prominent in eye-level views; figure drawing is more demanding.

A recreation area need not always be a center of interest. If attention is concentrated more on architecture, a suggestion of a tennis court or a golf green, at the side or in the background of a composition, is sufficient to indicate the presence of the entire facility.

Around a residence, activities are likely to be more intimate and drawn on a larger scale. Delineation of figures and individual objects requires care and attention. Be suggestive with details in some areas to avoid too finicky a composition, but those that are accentuated must be drawn well.

The recreation center is an important asset in any multiple-housing project. It often is featured more prominently than the dwelling units for advertising and publicity illustrations.

Figures are essential to the animation of any activity scene. These, by QA Architectural Arts, are particularly well-drawn.

Activity outside the sales office of a housing development.

142

9

level three

Complex Residential Structures

Analysis of the basic shapes of a large mansion, a townhouse group, or an apartment building shows them to be no more than elaborate extensions of the simple residences described in Chapter 7.

The greater number and variety of geometric forms may cause the entire structure to seem more complicated than it actually is. Careful study of plans and elevations, however, is necessary to maintain proper scale and relationship of the many forms.

A more pretentious building often offers a greater choice of viewpoints. Experiment with several possibilities, to play up its most favorable, interesting, or dramatic features.

The best angle for one structure may not be so for another. Style and construction of the architecture, orientation to the site and environment, and the direction from which it will be approached all help determine whether it is best viewed from a normal, lower, or higher eye level.

The majority of conventional houses on flat sites are drawn from normal eye levels, looking into major entrances or the angles of the front facades. But an exciting design—or an unusual site—need not be treated in a conventional manner.

When a suitable stationpoint is selected, fit a rough blockout of the total structure onto the paper before trying to break it up into its separate geometric shapes. Unless the final size is established in advance, larger dwellings laid out a room at a time have a habit of running off the page before completion, or uncomfortably cramping the composition.

The blocky general conformation of one house is very similar to another. Distinctions and styles come from varying rooflines, door and window arrangements, material textures, and other architectural details. Don't add any of these until the properly related outline of the entire building is blocked out to your satisfaction. Their scale and proportion are easier to maintain when visualized in relation to the whole complex than when they are drawn in as each separate section is completed.

Although plans and elevations are generally provided for guidance to the architectural concept, you may have to depend on your imagination and design ability to fill in the fences, walkways, landscaping, and other secondary elements necessary to a well-finished illustration.

An assignment may require that more than one dwelling be shown in a single drawing, as in a grouping of model homes, apartments, or condominiums. Plan the composition of the individual units to show their architectural variety, yet retain a continuity through the whole drawing. Judicious placement of landscaping and secondary structure can tie them together, thus avoiding a scattered and spotty appearance.

If multiple units are in a regular alignment, with all wall planes parallel or at right angles to each other, their layout in perspective is no more complicated than that of a single unit. Two vanishing points on the horizon line will serve all the buildings. Once a module is established for horizontal and vertical scale, all structures in the composition can be projected from it.

Other subjects may not be arranged in such a simple, grid-like pattern. A cluster of houses may be set at various random angles, or a row may be lined up along a curving street.

Each change of angle requires a different set of vanishing points, each pair spaced the same distance apart on the horizon. A nonuniform spacing will result in a distorted appearance of some of the buildings.

Vanishing points above the horizon, for peaked roofs, must also be changed for differently aligned structures.

The same dimensional module, however, can be used to determine the scale of all the buildings. With practice, you will be able to speed up layout procedures by eyeballing more and more of the perspective.

A nonrectangular element, such as a hexagonal or octagonal room, can be plotted by first determining the space it would require as a rectangle on the ground plan. Then modify its form to the required shape.

When the layout is satisfactorily completed and transferred to the final drawing surface, its rendering procedure is a more extensive application of the same techniques described in Chapter 7, and the inclusion of the elements introduced in Chapter 8.

Whatever rendering technique is introduced,

A low angle is a dramatic choice of view for these stilt houses.

144

The structures are complex, but their basic shapes are easily identified in this project in Idaho.

Scale of details must be watched carefully in this large multiple structure styled like a single-family residence.

This apartment grouping follows the contours of a Sardinian hillside. Perspective changes are subtle but must be considered by relocating vanishing points for each series of units.

Perspective projection of an irregularly shaped structure.

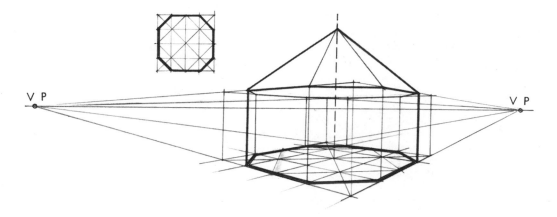

V P   V P

apply the medium as directly as possible. Plan light, dark, and medium value areas in advance on thumbnail sketches. A fresher and more professional appearance results when you have first visualized the final effect in your mind than when an excessive number of tonal layers—which cause a tentative and timid effect—have been applied.

A stage-by-stage rendering of the entire illustration is best for most mediums. The cohesion of the overall composition and the proper relationship of its various elements are achieved more easily by this overall approach than by finishing up one small area at a time.

An exception may be made for a drawing in pencil, charcoal, or other mediums that are subject to smearing. For cleaner results, a section may be completed and sprayed with fixative—or otherwise protected—before proceeding with the rest of the sketch.

DOORS AND WINDOWS

Types, sizes, trim, and installation of doors and windows for a residential structure are provided in its plans and elevations. Draperies or other decorative treatment must be added by the illustrator.

These details show how various styles look in perspective and suggest methods of delineation.

Vignettes show details and rendering of entryways, windows, and secondary architectural features.

Most highrise apartments feature balconies for their living units, in America as well as this example in Chartres, France. Avoid monotony in their rendering by varying their tonal contrasts.

Terraces extend the living areas of homes situated in milder climates. This editorial drawing prominently features a small terrace yet relates it to the rest of the project.

BALCONIES AND PORCHES

Balconies and porches are popular design elements in many contemporary single-family and multiple-residential units. They may project or recess into the structure, but their common delineation is a strong shadow pattern.

A large shadow should not be so opaque as to obliterate all of the detail within it.

SECONDARY STRUCTURES

Fences, terraces, planters, walkways, and other features used to set off the house must be included in the rendering for effective and attractive product presentation.

Sometimes architectural specifications are accompanied by a plot plan of the building's surroundings as a guide for the layout of land-

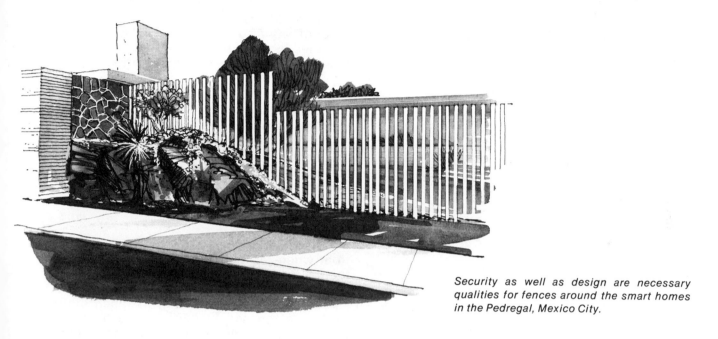

Security as well as design are necessary qualities for fences around the smart homes in the Pedregal, Mexico City.

A pavilion is a center of interest in a California garden. Secondary structure illustrations are usually for editorial purposes.

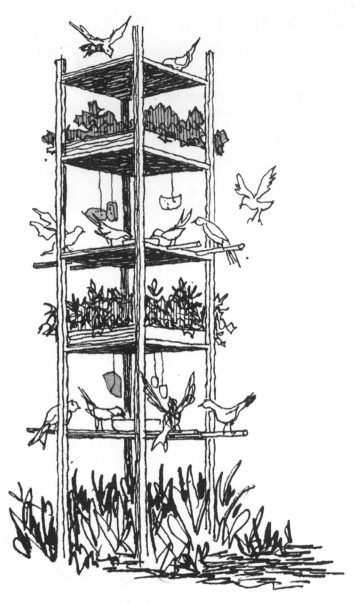

A combination planter and bird feeder. Playful structural additions can add life and interest to a sketch.

POOLS AND PATIOS

Increasing emphasis is placed on outdoor living and home recreation areas.

Patios are often extensions of the living areas of the house itself, and they should relate logically to the architecture. Dining, entertaining, relaxing, and sunning are among their more popular uses.

Swimming pools are included more and more in single-family dwellings and are virtually essential to the recreation areas of multiple units of any size. Their hard outlines are often softened by free-form designs, landscaping, and outdoor furniture.

LANDSCAPING

Landscaping features add necessary interest and activity to certain types of illustration but are not visible from all angles of view. A pool or patio, for example, would be an unusual addition in the front elevation of any type of building.

Its gardens and plantings are in evidence from wherever a house is seen. Next to architecture, they are the most important part of an exterior rendering.

A landscape architect gives much thought to the design and function of the gardens. A good sketch should incorporate these ideas as fully as possible. If you do not have his plan to guide you, you will have to rely on your own concepts. Studying photos from your files will help.

Try a little innovation in your thinking. Remember that raised beds and planters, reflecting pools, and cascades can be as much a part of the modern garden as plant material.

Relate the features and planting to the section of the building that shows. A rear area would be more casual and private in its plan than the more formal landscaping of the front facade.

Consider the region and terrain of the site in selecting trees and plant material. Use those suited to the climatic conditions of the area.

The building is the main product to feature in a sketch: don't smother it with planting. Even if a given plan calls for a particularly dense setting of trees and shrubs, thin them out enough for good exposure of the architecture.

scaping and secondary structure. More often these details are not described in working drawings of the average residence, and the illustrator must fill them in from his files or from the top of his head.

The terrain will suggest secondary elements to complement the house. Fences and walkways occur on level lots; steps, retaining walls, decks, and terraces are more likely to occur on sloping sites.

A strong pattern of dark and light tones is used for a nighttime view of a patio. Patterns of lighted areas and their reflections in the pool are specified in a benday overlay.

Dark washes and tempera highlights are used for a festive night effect.

Contoured grass slopes and informal tree groupings create a tranquil environment for condominiums and a recreation center.

Raised planter, pools, and exterior stairways give interest to a flat building site.

152

10

Commercial Buildings

Commercial buildings include a wide variety of architectural construction. Unless designed for continuous living occupancy—such as single-family homes, condominiums, or apartments —nearly every other type of building may be catalogued as commercial. High-rise office buildings, hotels and motels, shopping centers, hospitals, medical centers, schools, churches, factories, warehouses, municipal buildings, theaters, stores, and resort facilities are only a few examples.

Massive commercial projects are developed all over the world. The high-rise office tower is becoming as familiar to the skyline of European and Asiatic cities as it is to an American metropolis. Vast shopping centers sprout in the middle of vacant fields, anticipating suburban growth before the bulk of the population arrives. Giant resort complexes appear on the beaches of remote islands. The municipal cores of new cities spring up. The design of such architecture often tends toward an international sameness, and its distinctiveness comes from the setting.

Variations of commercial buildings cover a broad range of sizes, styles, and functions. Some are flat, slab-sided monoliths of glass or con-crete confined to rectangular configurations. Others feature facades of recesses, projections, and intricate fenestrations. Some designs experiment with curvilinear outlines and imaginative geometrical shapes.

All can present problems to their delineators. Because they are generally more massive than the average residential structures, indicating their scale can be more difficult. Proportions and detail must be accurate and precisely drawn. Carelessly measured, undersized, or oversized elements will destroy the effect planned by the architect.

The flat planes of a boxy glass office building may seem to add up to a simple design, which was easy to lay out and render. They can be deceptive. Surfaces must indicate its transparency and enough detail to explain construction, but they must be rendered so subtly as not to detract from the glistening, uncluttered elegance of the entire form.

More heavily ornamented structures, as might be found in theaters, resort facilities, or shops, challange the artist. He must include sufficient detail to suggest the richness of the structure without overpowering the lines and proportions of the overall mass.

The composition of an illustration of a commercial building is usually (although not always) suggested by its type. A forty-story tower, for instance, will be more favorably depicted in a vertical layout. A more linear shopping center, even with a few multistory elements, would be difficult to present in anything but a horizontal composition.

Perspective in the taller buildings tends to be more angular and dramatic than that of residential construction. This effect can be accented by moving the station point closer to the subject, or decreased by backing farther away (locating vanishing points farther apart).

In most cases, the closer and more striking position is more likely to be used in a delineation of a single building. In a complex of tall buildings, however, a more distant viewpoint may be preferred. Emphasis will not be centered on any one structure but instead spread over the whole group.

Raising or lowering the eye level causes considerable variation in the effect achieved. A low level gives more importance to the foreground. This is useful for giving depth to the composition and allowing trees or other objects to break and soften the lines of the architecture.

At higher positions, the foreground will be minimized but the details of landscaping, malls, or plazas will be more clearly explained.

Because of the many layout possibilities, explore the potential of a commercial structure with rough sketches from several angles before the final layout.

Experiment with several value studies before starting the rendering. The more thoroughly the procedure is planned, the less doubtful the results will be.

A difference in the value pattern can radically change the character of the illustration. A light building against a pale sky may be too weak; a dark building backed by a dark sky may be too heavy: contrast will be difficult with either. Against a dark background, a light-colored structure has an airy quality. In front of a light sky, the somber massiveness of a dark building is accentuated.

A wide range of tonal variations show in the buildings themselves. Because of their mass, walls are monotonous when they are rendered in the same values overall. Cloud shadows, reflections, and other external factors create differences. On facades in the shade, reflected light from below can vary the dark

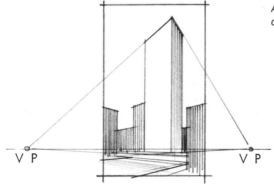

A close station point emphasizes a single building; a more remote one spreads the center of interest.

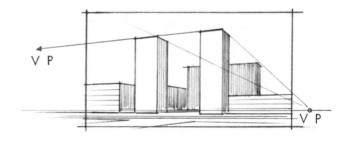

A Building dramatized by low horizon. B Ground features are more prominent from a high angle.

Value patterns can change the mood of an illustration.

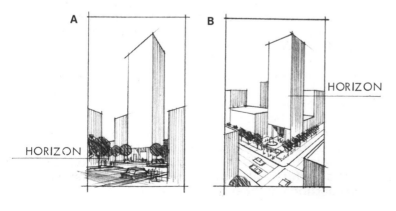

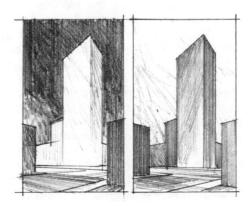

154

Pen and wash sketch of a large retail store. Vehicles are suggested with minimum drawing as massed patterns on the parking lot.

A felt-pen sketch by Carlos Diniz *is a loose, free-flowing interpretation of a hotel designed by* Daniel, Mann, Johnson, and Mendenhall.

tones at top; these will lighten as they descend. Interior conditions within the building can cause changes from floor to floor.

Cast shadows from openings or projections can create strong patterns on a facade but not necessarily over the entire surface. Some may be lightly suggested or omitted altogether in areas of strong light or shade to relieve the monotony of identical overall treatment.

Most rendering techniques are suitable for delineating commercial subjects. Pencil, because of its rapidity and flexibility, is useful for sketches and studies. Pen and ink, watercolor, tempera, and airbrush are favored for presentation drawings. Straightedges, bridge rules, French curves, and other mechanical aids are used extensively to lay out and render the long clean lines of commercial structures.

Tempera renderings can suggest the mass and solidity of their subjects. The delineation of the windows and brick wall surfaces in this illustration by QA Architectural Arts also shows the meticulous attention to small detail possible with this medium.

Fine pencil lines suggest the brick construction of a cooperative housing project, designed by architect Chris Wojciechowski.

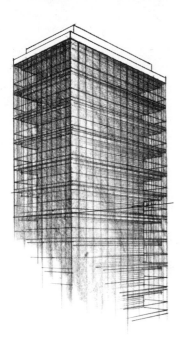

Unless they are made of mirror glass, large glazed areas are rendered to show their transparency.

The visibility of the stairways adds interest to a large corner expanse of glass in a QA Architectural Arts *tempera* rendering.

Felt-pen sketch by Jay Vance *for* Daniel, Mann, Johnson, *and* Mendenhall subtly indicates the transparency of the buildings.

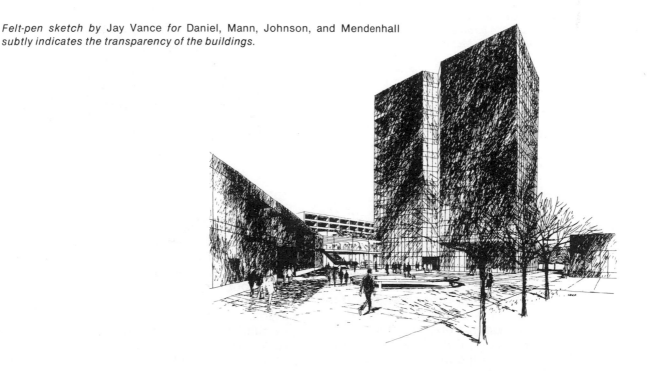

GLASS TREATMENT

As a rule, glass areas are more prominent and extensive in commercial than in residential subjects. Office buildings may be sheathed with curtain walls of the material. Transparent windows display the products featured inside shops.

Unless rendered to suggest the qualities of glass, these areas can be read as flat, nondescript walls or uninteresting black holes. The viewer should be able to look into them to see construction details, furnishings, and activities, or even beyond them to see objects on the far side of the building.

Avoid too busy and spotty an appearance by treating many of the details suggestively, ac-

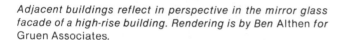

Reflections on glass and polished stone, and interior details, are skillfully executed in an airbrush illustration by Uri Hung *for Daniel, Mann, Johnson, and Mendenhall.*

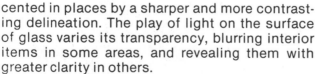

Adjacent buildings reflect in perspective in the mirror glass facade of a high-rise building. Rendering is by Ben Althen for Gruen Associates.

cented in places by a sharper and more contrasting delineation. The play of light on the surface of glass varies its transparency, blurring interior items in some areas, and revealing them with greater clarity in others.

Some buildings are faced with mirror glass. This is not transparent; it is a highly reflective material that picks up images of other structures in sharp detail. Trees, vehicles, clouds, or anything else within its vicinity are reflected.

You must render mirror glass accurately and authentically. Perspective, relative sizes, and a plausible angle of reflection must be maintained in the images.

Floor levels, window mullions, columns, or construction details in other textures will also be evident in glass walls. Unless the area covered by the different material is extensive, treat the entire area as glass during the rendering process. Necessary detail may be added over the surface when the illustration is finished.

SKIES

Skies, used in sharp contrast to define and emphasize a structure, are more important to the rendering of a high-rise building than to one of more modest proportions.

Your preliminary sketches will have indicated the desired effect, so apply the selected medium boldly and directly. With watercolor, particularly, avoid a worked-over appearance. Apply final values in the first wash, adding color to darken certain areas while the preliminary coat is still wet.

Because revisions or reworking can be so obvious, the sky is usually the first area to be rendered in wash techniques. Other mediums are more adaptable to change or correction.

As a contrasting tonal value to set off the structure, skies in delineations of commercial buildings tend more toward abstract than realistic patterns.

A

B

The treatment of the skies in these illustrations differs, but all are distinctly separated from buildings by tonal values. Ben Althen *did* **A,** *the pen and ink drawing;* **B** *and* **C** are by QA Architectural Arts, *in tempera.*

C

159

ADJACENT BUILDINGS

Other buildings in the neighborhood of your subject are important to its scale and to the identification of its vicinity. Don't let them compete for attention with the center of interest, however.

Show their conformation in proper size and relationship to the subject, but play down their detail. Definition of their planes, doors, windows, and ornamentation should show less contrast. Often an outline or a few flat tones will suffice for the more remote flat structures.

Foreground buildings can be silhouetted to frame the subject for a strong composition.

ACTIVITY

Vehicles and figures are included in almost all illustrations of commercial buildings. As important indicators of scale, they must relate in size to the subject, no matter how sketchily they may be drawn.

In your layout, establish their sizes at the measuring point for the structure, and project them in perspective to other areas of the drawing. This relationship can be deceptive and easily misdrawn.

Even if you are a practiced eyeballer, projected guidelines will help to hold correct scale at all points.

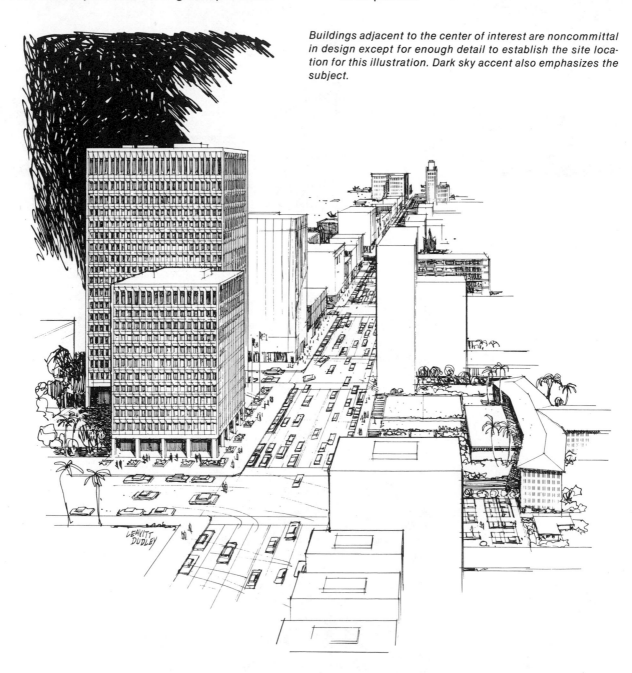

Buildings adjacent to the center of interest are noncommittal in design except for enough detail to establish the site location for this illustration. Dark sky accent also emphasizes the subject.

Though all buildings are carefully delineated in this realistic illustration, they don't compete for interest with the subject at left because of their smaller size and contrasting architectural style. The drawing is by Ben Althen for Gruen Associates.

Figures and cars add bustle to a quick sketch of a shopping center.

Activity abounds within and without this drive-in church.

ENVIRONMENT

From lower eye levels, the bulk of a large project may hide all but its most immediate vicinity. The suggestion of a mountain or a lake, or a city skyline, may be all that is necessary for representing a specific background.

Sometimes the total environment is as much a part of the illustration as the architecture; this situation requires a different approach to the composition. A higher eye level may be needed to include more of the background. Buildings, while still the center of interest, are smaller and less dominant. The character of the surroundings must be reproduced faithfully, which demands some competency in painting or drawing landscapes and an ability to visualize unfamiliar settings.

LANDSCAPING

Office structures, municipal centers, shopping facilities, and other large commercial developments are often planned as building complexes. Green areas and open space are not only visually desirable, but may be stipulated by zoning regulations. Sizable parking areas must

be provided, but must not look like asphalt deserts.

Even single buildings in land-scarce downtown districts often include landscaped setbacks, sidewalk plantings, entry courts, fountains, and terraces softened by greenery.

The landscaping of a large project is planned by professionals who leave nothing to chance. Their working drawings may locate and specify the varieties of individual plants.

In general, the scale of the landscaping is grander and more formal than that of residential developments. Planters, boxes, and other containers are oversized for scale. Trees and shrubs are massed for a more unified effect. Fountains and pools are prominent; seating and rest areas for pedestrians are provided.

Lighting is essential and must be functional as well as decorative. Good traffic circulation and access to offices, shops, and parking are necessary.

For more elaborate presentation drawings, these details are usually worked out for you by the designers. Plans may be incomplete—or vague at best—for studies and quick sketches. If they are, draw the missing information from your files and imagination, basing your concepts on the preceding requirements.

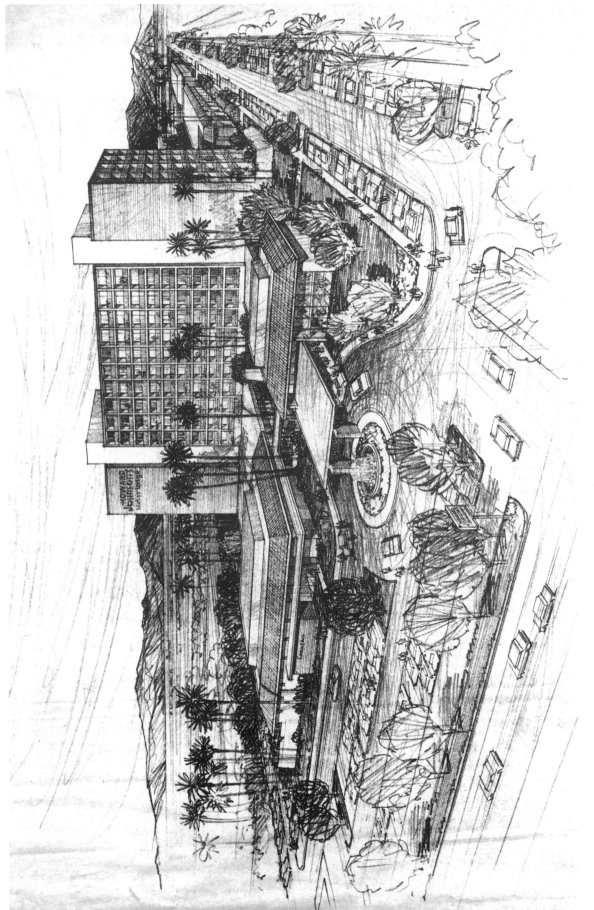

A few mountains in the distant background and the landscaping suggest the Las Vegas background of a motel and restaurant complex.

Nearly the entire sketch is devoted to environment in this design study of the Santa Barbara College Theater, done for Daniel, Mann, Johnson, and Mendenhall.

Despite the large scale of the planters, informal landscaping gives this shopping center an intimate atmosphere.

Landscaping complements the Polynesian design of this architecture.

11
level five

Aerial Perspectives

A bird's-eye view, or aerial perspective, is much more difficult to draw than the view from normal eye level. More architecture is visible, and a greater and more varied amount of background is included. A farther range of depth is usually covered; objects in the distance can diminish to infinitesimal sizes.

Because of the scope of such an illustration, all its elements must maintain proper relationship and scale in order to display the desired effect. Rendering must unify the entire composition while emphasizing its key features.

Unless the view is from a tree-covered hillside, few chances are offered to work in dramatic foreground pieces. There are fewer opportunities for striking compositions than when the illustration is drawn from a normal level.

Despite the problems with delineating them, aerial perspectives are unequaled for showing the extent and planning of large residential or commercial developments or for describing their surroundings. This type of drawing can serve several purposes, the approach to each of which is different.

A bird's-eye presentation must be an accurate depiction of its subject. Complete plans and elevations are usually provided, accompanied by photographs, slides, maps, or other information concerning the background. The material must be faithfully projected and rendered.

Sometimes you may take a few more liberties with the composition of an advertising or editorial illustration. Its story-telling qualities may be improved if a building is shifted slightly one way or another on the plan, or if a mountain is moved a few points on the compass to a more favorable location. Since reference material is not always complete, you must depend on the scant information supplied as well as your general knowledge of the area in order to fill in missing details.

Modifications are not to be carried too far, however. Both subject and background must always be recognized for what they are or what the architect intends them to be.

Study sketches are prepared while the design is in progress and usually in a state of flux. Usually you will at least know what the site looks like. Some preliminary plot plans and architectural concepts may be available, or you may have to proceed with a limited knowledge of the subject.

As these are working visualizations rather than presentations, their purpose is to convey

An apartment complex from a high angle does not include the horizon in the picture. Layout, and rendering in tempera, of a structure this complicated is a lengthy and painstaking process. Delineation is by QA Architectural Arts.

Lower angle shows more of the environment. Notice the simplified treatment of the distant buildings.

On sloping terrain, some structures may be viewed at eye level, while others are in aerial perspective.

ideas rather than to fully describe finished products. Function and massing of shapes are more important than details at this point. Execution must be quick and flexible. With little time for complicated projection, eyeballing the perspective is the rule.

LOCATION OF HORIZON AND VANISHING POINTS

Position of the station point in an aerial perspective may vary in elevation from slightly above roof level to thousands of feet above the ground. The angle of view, the extent of the subject to be featured, and the environmental elements to be included all help determine its location.

The same factors also complicate composition of the illustration on the drawing surface. Unless scale is correctly established in its initial stages, a layout can have the annoying habit of running off the page before essential features can be included.

To settle composition questions before beginning the final layout a good comprehensive freehand sketch is necessary. From it, you can locate the horizon line, approximate positions of the vanishing points, and estimate the space the drawing will occupy.

Angle of view is an important factor in the effect created by the illustration. Directly overhead, at a ninety-degree angle to the ground plane, the subject will appear as a three-dimen-

With thumbnail sketches, you can compare the effects on a subject at high- and low-angle views.

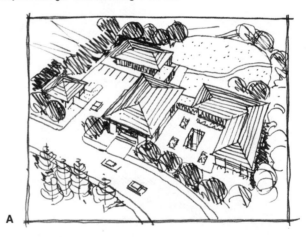

A

B

sional plan. Horizon and background will not be included, but the layout and relationship of the buildings to one another and the landscaping will be clearly defined (see diagram **A**, p. 169).

A view from a shallower ten or twenty degree angle shows the architecture of foreground buildings, the horizon and environmental background, and will be a more pictorial representation. Buildings in the rear are more obscured and indefinitely positioned (as shown in diagram **B**, p. 169).

The purpose your illustration is to serve will influence your choice of a visually pleasing low angle, a graphically descriptive high one, or a compromise anywhere in between. Qualities of the former are well suited for advertising and editorial usage, where an attractive presentation of an interesting key section is more important than a description of the entire development. A lower angle, emphasizing facades or details, is also favored for single buildings or small projects with simple ground plans.

Station points at higher elevations and steeper viewing angles will indicate building orientation better, as well as traffic circulation, landscape planting, and other details essential to a full explanation of a major project.

LAYOUT PROCEDURES

PHOTOGRAPHIC METHOD

This is the quickest, most accurate method of projecting the layout of a complicated aerial perspective. If you have a well-drawn plot plan, a camera, and access to enlarging facilities, the process is relatively simple.

1. Lay the plan flat on the floor or on a large table. A checkerboard grid—drawn to conveniently sized modules and set upright on the plan—is a vertical scale. Small modular blocks placed on several spots about the plan also are good vertical scale references.

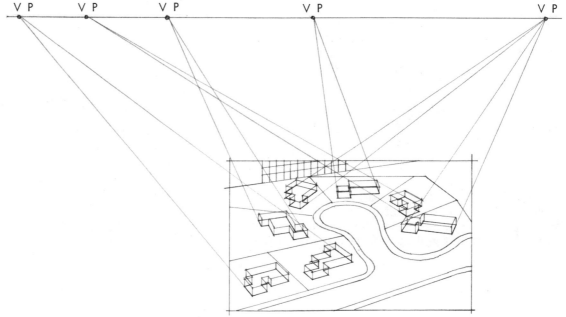

Perspective photo of plan and modular scales, and preliminary projection of the building masses. Projection to second vanishing points can be eyeballed, or the points may be located on the horizon if the drawing board is large enough. A custom grid under the layout also can help keep projection of lines to remote points in proper perspective.

Tracing over an enlarged photo of a study model can save hours of time in layout of a complicated subject.

2. With a thumbnail sketch as a guide, frame the plan in the viewfinder of the camera from the proper station point and photograph it. A polaroid camera can give you a usable print, but a negative from a conventional camera may hold the detail better. The polaroid is useful for trying several shots from different angles before making a final selection.

3. Enlarge the print or negative to the required size of the layout.

4. Place the enlarged print under tracing paper and project the layout of the illustration over it. Extend the lines of the plan to locate the horizon and vanishing points. Height of buildings and land contours are projected from the vertical scale.

This type of projection is helpful when architectural units are irregular in shape or randomly arranged on the plan.

If elevations of a building are available and in proper scale you can mount the visible facades on illustration board and prop them vertically on the plan. The photograph will include many of the architectural details and further cut down on layout time.

Architects often use small-scale study models—showing main building shapes and land contours—while planning a project. Except for small details and background, an enlarged photograph of such a model provides most of the elements needed to solve your layout problems. Tracing over the enlargement, particularly when the subject includes many irregular forms, can save hours of projection time.

GRID METHOD

Despite its advantages, the photo method is not always a practical layout aid. The enlarging process may be inconvenient, not readily available, or too time-consuming for a rush job. It is easier to make changes in building arrangement or take slight liberties with perspective when you are not working over a photograph.

In such cases, project the layout by the grid method. You may find a suitable ready-made grid, but most artists make their own according to the needs of the job. It may require only a minimum number of grid lines. With practice, most building proportions can be eyeballed.

The layout of a development with many irregularly aligned and oddly shaped buildings can be a complicated and tedious job, requiring the location of many sets of vanishing points on the horizon. A project whose elements are in a fairly regular arrangement can be laid out about as quickly by the grid as by the photo method.

1. Rule a grid of equally spaced lines on the plan. Number them in both directions as checkpoints to the perspective grid. More lines and smaller squares increase the accuracy of building proportions, but it takes longer to match them up with the other grid.

2. Lay out the same grid in perspective on the drawing surface, locating horizon and vanishing points as determined by the thumbnail sketch. This grid need not be drawn to the same scale as that on the plan, but the number of lines on it must correspond.

3. Transpose the buildings from the plan grid to the perspective grid. The floor plans should occupy the same proportionate spaces in each grid.

4. Add a vertical scale in the foreground, preferably on the corner of a building. Extend it high enough to cover all the architectural features.

5. Project the shapes of the structures, then finish and detail the layout according to plans, elevations, and topography. Add environmental elements and activity.

Rules of perspective are sometimes stretched a bit in this method. Particularly at lower angles, a grid shrinks and tightens up at a rapid rate as it recedes.

If much of the interest is located toward the rear of the plan, actual space may be too restricted to give it sufficient prominence, and the foreground may be too spacious. Reduce the depth of the front grids and increase those to the rear to help equalize the emphasis.

Approach these adjustments cautiously. Cheating too much on the rules is worse than not tampering at all. Sometimes the best correction is raising the horizon and the angle of view to achieve desired results.

EYEBALL METHOD

Each method of aerial perspective involves eyeballing to some degree. Without using eyeballing, an artist is bogged down in tedious projection of every small detail.

Some illustrations are almost completely dependent on the eyeball method—for the entire concept as well as the secondary detailing.

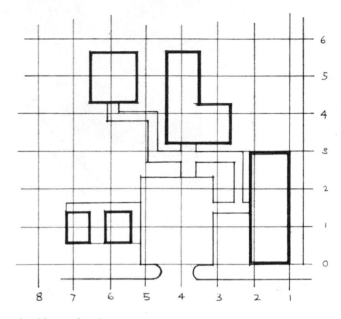

A grid over the plan.

Same grid in perspective, with buildings blocked in.

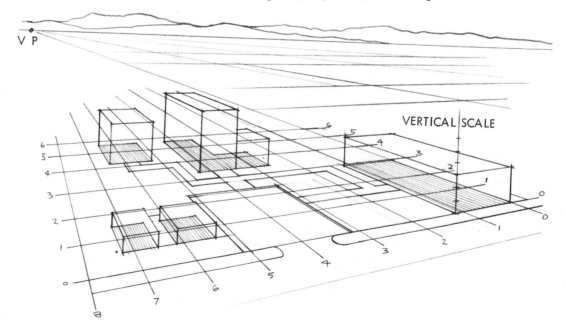

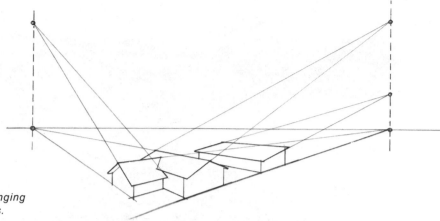

Location of vanishing points for roof planes. Changing slopes of roofs move the vertical positions of points.

A plan, for instance, may be visualized no more specifically than as a loose arrangement of architectural elements, with no definite descriptions other than relative sizes and a suggestion of style. Or an advertisement may require that buildings and environment be repositioned drastically in order to present a subject properly or open up avenues of view.

Though the eyeball approach to these problems varies with individual artists, the general procedure is similar. The thumbnail, rough sketch is the important beginning.

1. From available information, draw the main architectural and environment shapes quickly and lightly in freehand. Work to the size of the finished drawing.

2. You may try several starts before hitting the right solution. When satisfied, locate a horizon and vanishing points, which will retain the same general composition as the drawing firms up. Establish a vertical scale.

3. The remainder of the process is similar to that of other methods, projecting to vanishing points to construct the architecture. However, you are more free to rearrange buildings for pictorial advantages. Unless you have been provided with elevations or given a free hand with design concepts (it does sometimes happen!), you will have to consult with the architect before adding details.

THE THIRD VANISHING POINT

Even though three-point perspective is employed infrequently, its most likely use is in aerial projection. Taller buildings, especially when in the foreground and viewed from an overhead angle, may sometimes need a slight taper toward the third point to create additional realism or a dramatic effect.

To position this point, drop a vertical line from the station point. The point will fall somewhere on this line. The closer its location to the station point, the sharper the taper; the farther from it, the less it will be. Unless used for an extreme effect, the point will be so far off the bottom of the drawing board that it will be only a general guide to eyeballing.

If you do need it, remember that:

1. If the point is used for one building, it must be used for all.

2. All verticals converge to the same point, regardless of different building alignments on the plan.

3. You should work from outside buildings toward the center, gradually lessening the slant to avoid overdoing the taper.

A different type of third vanishing point (VP), for the projection of peaked roofs, is often used in illustrations of residential developments. Its exact location is determined by projecting a known roof pitch on any convenient structure in the plan, to a vertical line above the vanishing point on the horizon. The upper VP can be above either the left or the right horizon VP, according to the direction of roof pitch.

All similar roof pitches from buildings in the same alignment are projected from this point. However, if the alignment of another building changes, the third point must be relocated above the new VP.

A shallower or steeper pitched roof, of course, will require a point at a smaller or greater distance above the horizon VP.

ENVIRONMENT

Mountains, lakes, adjacent buildings, and other background features are not usually included in the plot plan of a project. For reference you may have to depend on photographs, topographical maps, or general maps of an area.

As such, they will not be scaled in the manner as the plans and elevations of the subject. But every element appearing in a drawing must be proportionate to the rest.

If a nearby building is shown on a map,

The importance of the environment overshadows the subject in this sketch of Elkhorn Village in Idaho.

figure the space it will occupy by transposing the scale to that of the plot plan. If shown only in a photograph, count its floors and multiply them by twelve feet (an average spacing). Other dimensions can be estimated from this approximate height. If a photograph is shot straight down and doesn't show the floors, cast shadows can give a general idea of building heights.

For more distant features, project a known vertical dimension toward the horizon and use it as a guide to estimating heights at different background depths.

RENDERING TECHNIQUES

Any medium lends itself to good rendering of an aerial perspective.

For studies and quick sketches, pencil is recommended because of its flexibility. Pen and ink is superior for reproduction drawings, and will hold detail and quality when reduced to a small size. Transparent watercolor, tempera, and airbrush are most commonly used for presentation work.

While other mediums are broad enough

First step of a pen and ink bird's-eye —a quick pencil sketch of the composition, approved by the client.

Step 2—a careful pencil drawing of the subject.

Step 3—architectural definition in ink with straightedge.

Step 4—freehand drawing to complete the illustration.

LEAVITT
DUDLEY

175

These pen and ink illustrations are from a moderately low angle. In large projects, don't take an angle so high that architectural facades are lost beneath a sea of roofs.

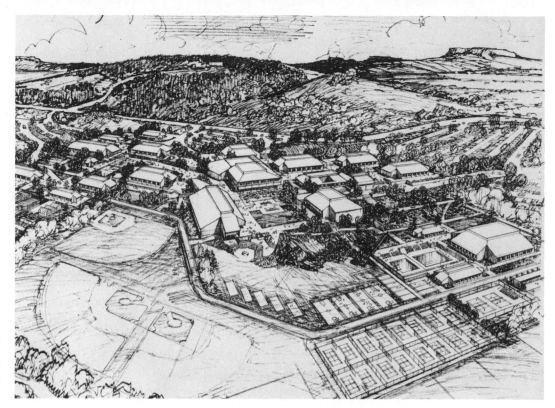

A quick pencil sketch of a northern California college, done for Daniel, Mann, Johnson, and Mendenhall. *For speedy rendering, major elements were drawn first in non-photo-reproducing blue pencil; then drawing was completed over it with No. 2 graphite pencil.*

for relatively quick application to larger sized illustrations, pen and ink drawings are best kept to a smaller format. Filling an overly large area with fine pen strokes is a long and tedious process. The original can always be photographically enlarged for presentation, and reproduction quality is better if the reduction is not too great.

Whichever technique you use, maintain a continuity between the subject and the foreground, lateral, and background elements. With so much depth shown in the illustration, a mountain range or a group of buildings appear detached and spotty without tonal or linear connection to the center of interest.

This serpentine French hotel presents a layout problem; it depends heavily on eyeballing the perspective. The ground plan was laid out first; then a series of vertical scales was established along its curves.

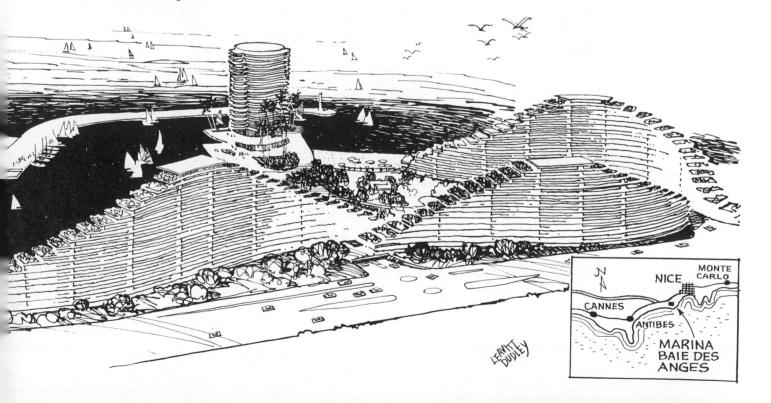

VERY LARGE PROJECTS

Some projects are so vast that they are measured in square miles rather than acres. Pockets of development may be scattered about a mountainous terrain, and nearby communities may be included as reference points.

An accurate descriptive drawing of such a subject is impossible unless rules of perspective and scale are bent considerably. In true proportion, architecture far in the background will be unrecognizable as such, if seen at all.

Key areas, such as civic or recreation centers, need a "cartoon," or overscale, treatment for identification. Buildings must be reduced to their simplest basic forms, with only a hint of window or other detail. Massed structures, as in a development of small homes, are best shown as a texture.

Drastic liberties may have to be taken with the terrain as well. It is usually compressed to include major features in the composition.

Despite these violations, perspective must be maintained and the character of the environment must be preserved. "Cartooning" should be carried only to the point of recognition rather than gross exaggeration.

An assignment of this type may seem difficult. It is. The environment often dominates the architecture and demands considerable ability in landscape delineation.

Eyeballing is the only approach to such a layout, but establish the horizon and vanishing points for reference and guidance. If they are too casually indicated, buildings may appear to be sliding down a mountainside or toppling into a lake.

Road maps, topographical maps, land use and plot plans, and photos are the usual reference materials.

Rancho California, a huge development of homes, estates, ranches, shopping facilities, and recreation areas, was too vast for true-scale drawing or architectural definition. The whole layout was eyeballed, with the aid of a few grid lines to keep the various areas in proper relationship.

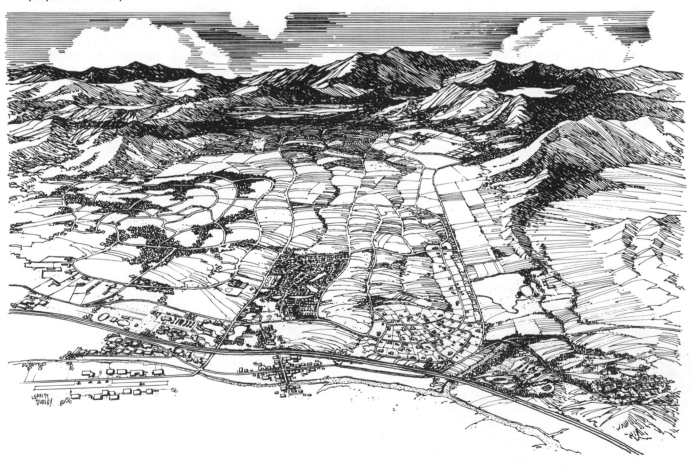

12
level six

Cityscapes

A city scene may be illustrated from a normal eye level or a bird's-eye view. Layout and rendering procedures are similar to those already described. The difference lies in the greater number of buildings to be considered and included.

Surroundings about the center of interest are mostly or totally made up of architectural units in a wide variety of shapes and sizes. In many such illustrations, particularly aerial perspectives, rendering the background is a longer and more difficult task than drawing the center of interest.

The setting, existing and of controlled shapes, requires more careful drawing than the freer forms of the mountains or lakes of more rural sites.

Structures in the city tend to be massive and powerful in concept and construction. Scale must be observed rigidly to preserve this effect. A common mistake is rendering windows, pilasters, cornices, or other fine details too large. Careful layout, straightedge guides, and the use of more delicate tools in delineation help overcome the problem.

LAYOUT PROCEDURES

PHOTO METHOD

Since cityscapes include so much, use all the help you can get in laying them out. Photographs taken from the same angle as the illustration are the best reference, even if they mean taking additional time and effort to track them down or make them.

Any readable print can be enlarged and used as the basis for the layout. Print quality of the blowup is not important, as long as outlines and major details of the buildings are discernible.

Place the enlargement under the thinnest tracing paper you have, and establish the horizon and vanishing points (VP) by extending building lines. Trace the structural shapes and prominent or important features. Minor details, often fuzzy or obscured by shadows, are hard to read through the paper and are better when they are added after the layout has been transferred to the final drawing surface.

Quick pencil sketch of Baltimore. Existing portions of city rendered directly on tracing paper laid over a photo enlarged to drawing size. Proposed college was added at right; future high-rise development is in outline only.

When the background is blocked in, remove the photograph from beneath the tracing and add proposed structures to building sites. Project them from the photographic horizon and vanishing points, and determine their vertical scale from adjacent buildings.

All photographs are in true perspective. The effect of the third vanishing point will be evident, particularly in aerial shots. If you trace the photo exactly, the third VP will also have to be included in the projection of proposed structures.

Taper of the buildings in three-point perspective can slow down and complicate your layout and subsequent rendering. If the third point effect is not too pronounced and the buildings are small in scale, you can trace the photo as a two-point perspective—with all vertical walls parallel—and save much time and effort.

As a time-saving alternative to tracing paper layouts, the print may be enlarged to size on the thinnest possible photographic or photostat

paper. Tape it firmly to illustration board, with a sheet of transfer paper between. Firm pressure with a 4H pencil will transmit the image directly from the print to the drawing surface.

If you are sure of your subject and confident of your abilities, pencil or pen and ink rendering is possible on 1000H technical paper, working directly over the photo. Eye-level views—with buildings in silhouette—or structures in large scale are best for this method, as the semi-opacity of the paper limits the photograph's visibility.

GRID METHOD

If a suitable photo for tracing is difficult or impossible to obtain, construct the layout from available reference. As the heights of city buildings obscure each others' bases, photographs from several angles help clarify details and ground plans. A straight-down aerial shot,

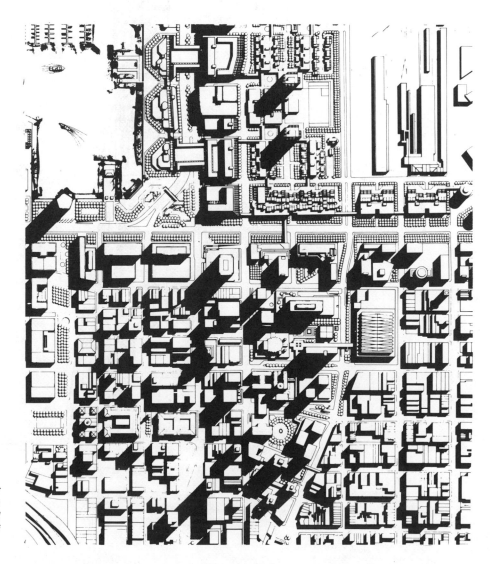

If an oblique view is not available for reference, cast shadows on a rendered plot plan or an aerial photo-map can give you an idea of comparative heights of buildings.

This quick sketch of a city street was done from photographs as reference and is livened by the clutter of signs and other sidewalk features. Shading on the buildings was produced by the flat side of a pencil lead, guided by a triangle as a straightedge. It was prepared for Gruen Associates as a background for a transit study, and versions of different rail systems were superimposed over it.

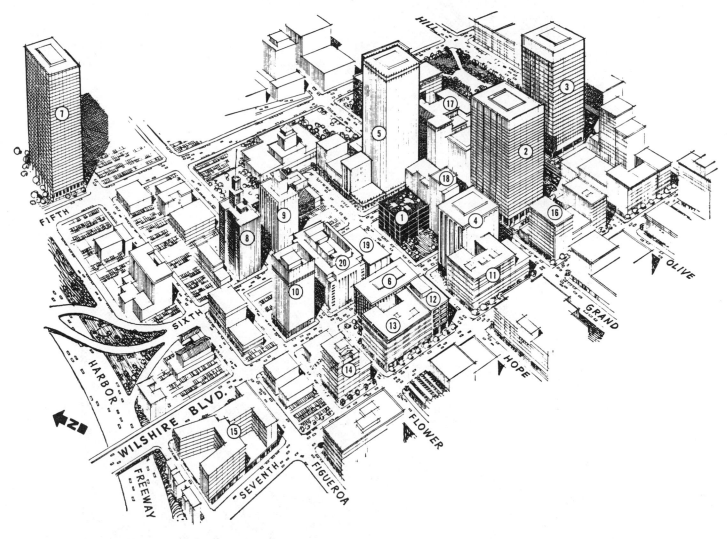

Bird's-eye view of downtown Los Angeles in the mid-1960s. Street grid was first laid out; buildings were positioned from maps and photos. A straightedge was used extensively for rendering the architecture quickly with pen and ink. Composition was simplified and delineation speeded by the elimination of many existing but unimportant small buildings.

though offering little description for facades, describes building relationships and street patterns accurately. Comparative heights can be reckoned by cast shadows.

Good city maps also provide information on street and building layout. Supplemented by oblique photos, they furnish sufficient reference to start a layout.

The grid method used for other bird's-eye views will plot the city street layout in perspective. The dimensions of a block are known or readily available, and can be used as the basis for the construction of a vertical scale.

Establish the position of the tallest buildings first, then block in the layout from the foreground to the rear. As you fill in the structures, you will notice how they obscure each other. Detail only what is likely to be seen.

RENDERING

A cityscape is an illustration heavily dependent on suggestive rendering. Complete delineation of every building would be an endless job; the centers of interest would be lost in a mass of confusing detail.

Usually the intricate drawing is concentrated in the major structures and dwindles with increasing distance from the centers of interest. More remote buildings may be incomplete in outline and treated as single massed shapes.

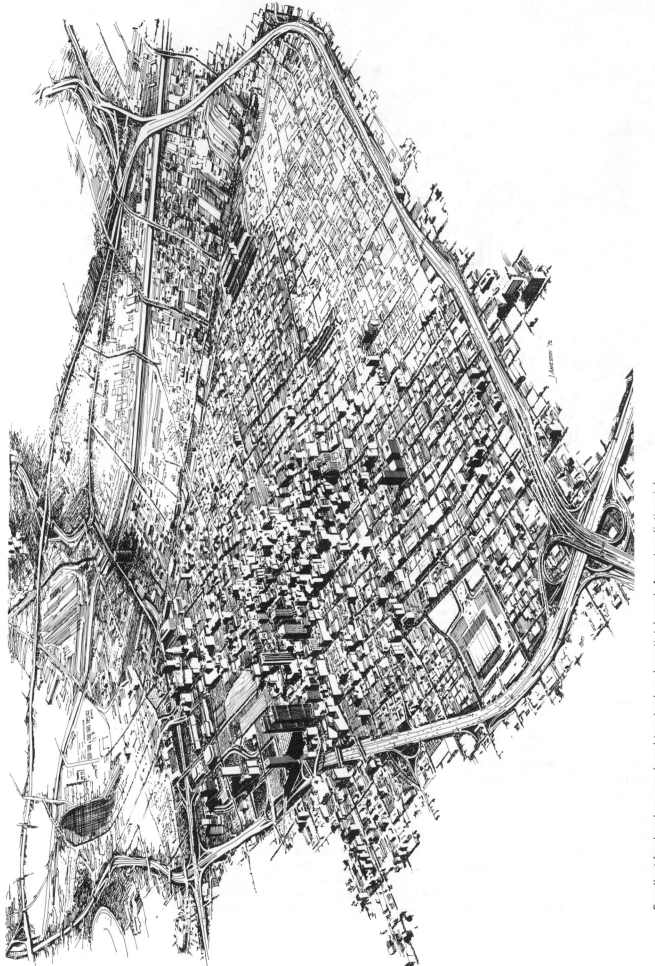

Excellent freehand pen work and tonal values by artist Joseph Amestoy distinguish this illustration of a look into a city's future. Plan was prepared by Wallace, McHarg, Roberts, and Todd for the Committee of Central City Planning and the City of Los Angeles.

Tempera rendering by QA Architectural Arts shows the precise value control possible with this technique. Though the drawing throughout is carefully done, areas of particular interest stand out because of higher-keyed tones and greater contrasts.

A quick one-point pencil perspective of a proposed retail center backed by the metropolitan skyline. Straight-edges were used to speed the job. A look too mechanical was avoided by varying the line values and adding a few freehand strokes.

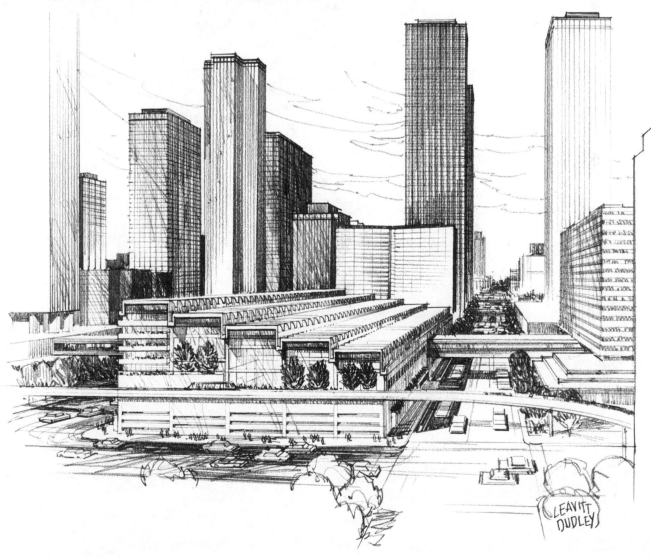

185

Design study for Daniel, Mann, Johnson, and Mendenhall simplifies the city to a few lines and shapes. Portland Plaza, the subject of the sketch, is distinguished by contrast of towers against darkened background.

PHOTO-ART COMBINATION

For presentation in the most realistic setting, a drawing of a proposed building can be incorporated directly into a photograph of an urban area. A substantial amount of layout and rendering time will be saved, as well.

The negative must be of good quality, sharp in detail, well lighted, and contrasty. A print, enlarged to convenient working size, is first dry-mounted on a backing of heavyweight illustration board.

On the mounted print, the area of new development is blanked out carefully with tempera or acrylic in a light medium gray value.

As shown in the overlay, streets are projected to locate horizon and vanishing points for this composite view of an Oklahoma City development. Proposed new buildings are added with meticulously applied tempera. Structures at upper left of painted area are at different stages of rendering. Microscopic examination is needed to differentiate between additions and existing buildings. Delineation is by Ben Althen for Gruen Associates.

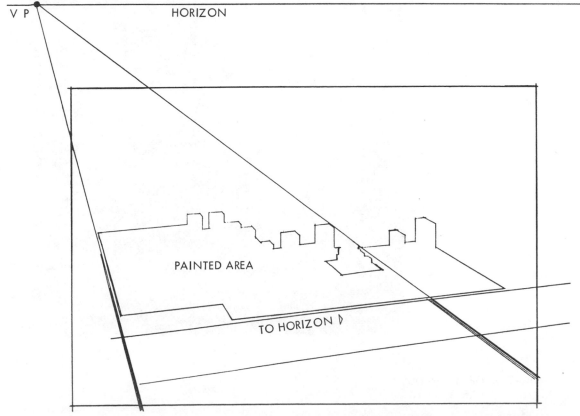

On a tracing paper overlay, locate the horizon and vanishing points. Project the proposed architecture in the same scale as the existing buildings, and transfer the drawing to the print with a sharp hard pencil.

The buildings are then rendered in tempera or acrylic. As the detail is usually in small scale, delineation requires a precise touch with delicate brushes. Maintain the same light direction and shadow patterns shown by the existing buildings, and the same general range of tonal values.

For a quicker, alternate method, proposed structures may be rendered in pencil. Although the realistic quality is less than that of tempera painting, it is a very useful technique for preliminary concepts and variations because of its efficiency.

Blanking out the project area on the print is not necessary. On an overlay of 1000H technical paper, outline the area, locate the vanishing points, and block in a couple of nearby buildings for scale reference.

Remove the print, draw the new architecture, and render it as closely as possible in the values of the print.

When completed, cut out the area and rubber cement it carefully to the print. Some additional pencil toning may be needed to blend it better into the tones of the photograph.

The final step to either of these processes is to copy the finished work to give a uniform texture and smoothness to the entire surface and reprint it to the desired size.

This technique is suitable only on black and white photos.

A low-angle composite by Philo Jacobson *for* Daniel, Mann, Johnson, and Mendenhall *shows a new building drawn on tracing paper over a photo enlarged to desired size and then transferred to illustration board for line and airbrush rendering. Finished artwork was trimmed to shape, stripped to the photograph, and the assemblage recopied photographically.*

A composite by the quickest technique. Pencil sketch is made to perspective and scale of the photograph and is stripped to it; then the whole is recopied.

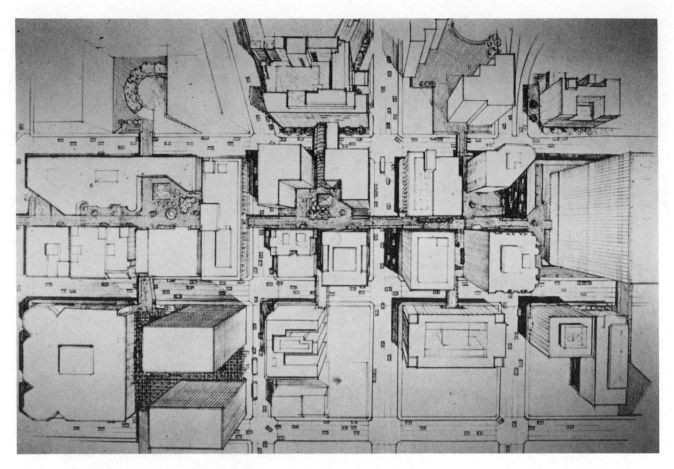

Vanishing point of this 3-D plan had to be located so that the route of the subject, an elevated pedestrian way, would not be obscured by the rise of the buildings.

THREE-D PLANS

By a one-point perspective method, a plot plan of a metropolitan development can easily be projected to a descriptive graphic presentation. Circulation and traffic patterns, building positions, and relationships to adjacent areas are explained.

The procedure is so quick and simple that the layout can be projected directly onto the drawing surface.

From the plan, determine the amount of its area to be included and the final size of the illustration.

With dividers or measurements by a scale ruler, reduce or enlarge the plan to fit the space comfortably with a generous margin for inclusion of nearby property. Draw it lightly on the paper.

The perspective point can be located anywhere on the plan, but it should be placed thoughtfully. Tall buildings expand rapidly in perspective as they rise, so make sure they enlarge in directions which least obscure important sections with quick tracing paper overlays before proceeding with the final drawing.

A pushpin is a good vanishing point, as all verticals can be swung from it with a triangle.

The higher the station point is assumed to be, the lower the heights of the buildings will appear in the drawing.

PERSPECTIVE MAPS

Editorial or promotional publications often use a stylized, overall view of a metropolitan region to locate points of interest, areas of development, routes of proposed freeways, or other properties whose relationship to existing areas must be explained. Approach such an illustration in the same manner an an aerial perspective of a very large development.

A vast expanse is compressed into a small drawing, and true scale is impossible to main-

This perspective map of the Los Angeles basin emphasizes particular points of interest.

LEAVITT DUDLEY

191

tain. Geography, and the proportions of size and distance between different areas must be reasonably accurate, however, and roadways must generally follow correct compass courses.

Important structures are "cartooned" to recognizable sizes, and larger districts are simplified to dense clusters of buildings. Thousands of residences and small shops between are represented by scattered, blocky shapes. Major traffic arteries are shown, but only a few lines can suggest the network of secondary streets.

Perspective and layout must be eyeballed, from maps and photographs.

Labels may be needed for identification. These can be included in the drawing but may complicate the rendering. They are difficult to change and may suffer if the art is reduced by reproduction. A typographic overlay is a more professional method of addition, and the illustration is adaptable to various purposes rather than limited to a single use. (See Chapter 18, for "Overlays.")

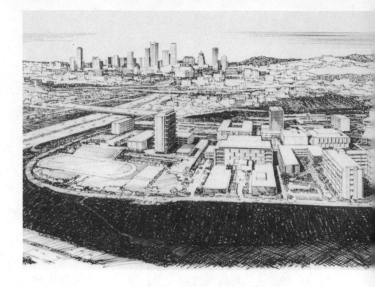

This illustration relates the location of the California State University at Los Angeles campus to the city. To stress the proximity, the downtown area was moved closer to the school and quite a few liberties were taken with the city skyline and the intervening territory. The drawing was used for the cover of a brochure.

"Cartoon" treatment of map of smaller community.

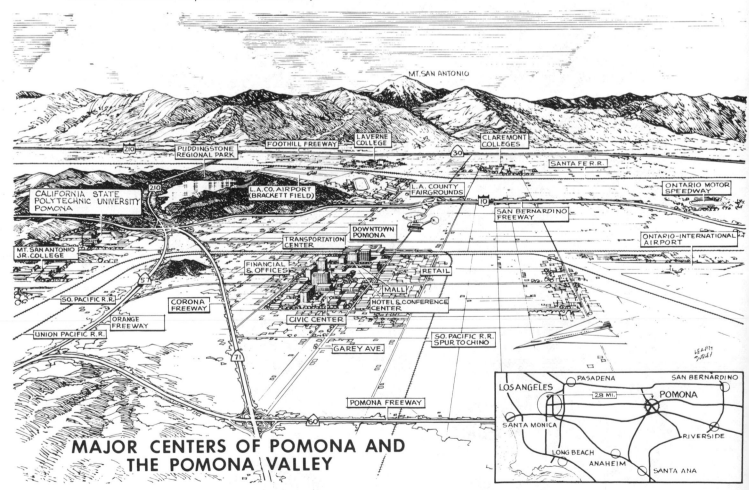

MAJOR CENTERS OF POMONA AND THE POMONA VALLEY

13

level seven

Interiors

An interior illustration, either of a residential or a commercial project, is interpreted in different ways according to the purpose it serves.

The type most commonly assigned to an architectural illustrator is a depiction of a particular room or section of a building. It may be a colorful, highly finished presentation to sell a design concept to a client, reproduction artwork for advertising and editorial promotion, or a quick sketch for interoffice communication and study.

Although furniture is necessary to complete the illustration, it is secondary to the form and function of the architecture. The structural design will be more or less prescribed, depending on the required degree of finish, but the interior decoration is often left to the artist.

Drawing chairs, tables, and other pieces to complement the room is not an easy job. A good reference file of all types and styles of furnishings is a must for even the most experienced illustrators.

Other drawings are primarily displays of particular lines or styles of furniture. Specified pieces or groupings are featured, and the architecture is suggested only enough to establish a background.

This artwork is used by interior decorators or in ads selling furniture store products. Delineation of the furnishings must be extremely accurate and skillful. Rendering, in a controlled loose style with sparkling highlighted areas, is usually handled by specialists in this field.

Motion picture and television studios also make use of many interior sketches. Architecture and furnishings are usually designed and designated by art directors.

In any interior illustration, the structure is generally the simpler part. Lines are definite and regular. The complex shapes of furniture are more difficult to draw. Angles of alignment are varied. The vanishing points required for their layout are scattered the length of the horizon. Each item must relate to the room at correct scale.

Delineation is simplified by the initial layout of each piece by geometric shape analysis. When the space occupied by the total form is blocked out properly in size and perspective, its legs, cushions, or other details are much easier to add.

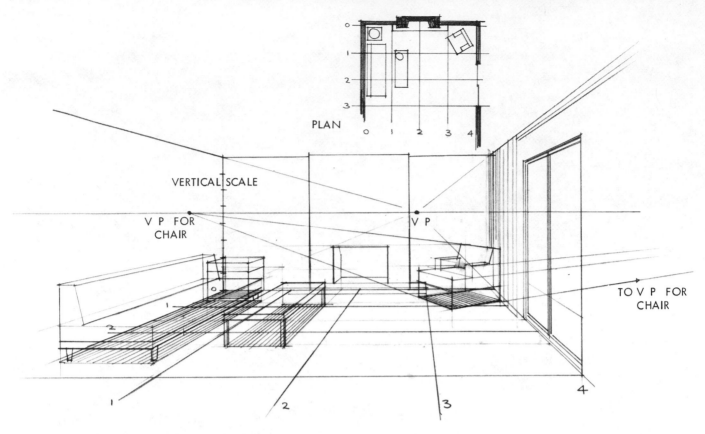

PLAN

VERTICAL SCALE

V P FOR
CHAIR

V P

TO V P FOR
CHAIR

Interior layout in one-point perspective. Corner chair is in two-point. Grid is used to locate furniture.

PERSPECTIVE LAYOUT FOR ARCHITECTURE

The one-point (parallel) perspective is a favorite layout method. It can be measured and projected quickly and has the advantage of showing three walls in a single sketch.

All horizontal lines on elevations facing the station point are drawn on a parallel plane with the T-square. The station point can be located at any point on the horizon, but it is usually set off center to avoid a too-symmetrical composition.

The room may be laid out by a mechanical projection if you are sure of the amount of depth to show in proportion to its width.

Approximation of depth by eye-balling is the quickest layout method. Measurements of the rear wall elevation are simply enlarged or reduced to a suitable working size, and the side walls are projected from the vanishing point.

A two-point perspective, showing only two interior elevations, represents a view into a corner of a room. The layout can be projected by a conventional method, or eye-balled from a vertical scale at the corner.

Ready-made perspective grids as layout aids are easily adapted to the average interior illustration.

A particular perspective method is employ-ed for motion picture sketches, which must reflect the exact area that will be seen through the lens of a camera. A special angle, in thirty-five or fifty millimeter sizes to correspond with the lens used, is laid over the plan to determine the section of stage set that is covered from a specified station point. (See the Appendix for details of the process.)

PERSPECTIVE LAYOUT FOR FURNITURE

The walls in a sketch of a room may be laid out in one-point perspective. If furnishings are aligned parallel to the walls and picture plane, their layout is drawn by the same method. All lines of projection will radiate from a single vanishing point. Individual pieces will be less subject to faulty drawing, and your task will be comparatively simple.

Such a condition is unlikely unless the interior decoration is unusually formal and rigid. As a rule furniture arrangement is more casual. Each article in a grouping may be positioned at different angles to the walls.

Each piece not parallel to the walls will be seen in two-point perspective, with a different pair of vanishing points for each variation.

Quick renderings of the layout in pencil and ink and wash for a student demonstration.

In a room drawn by two-point perspective, furniture is added by the same method unless a piece is aligned parallel to the picture plane. This exception is seen in one-point perspective.

Before beginning a layout, position the furnishings to scale on the floorplan of the room. A grid drawn over the plan and projected onto the perspective gives reference points for furniture location, helps maintain scale, and simplifies the establishment of vanishing points.

When their bases are placed on the floor correctly, the basic geometric shapes of the furnishings are drawn. To keep true relative sizes, project their heights to different points about the room from a vertical scale on the rear wall. Add separate parts and detailing to complete the layout.

INTERIOR DIMENSIONS

Cabinets, counters, bookcases, and other built-in features are important elements of the room plan. Their sizes and functions may vary because of architectural design or particular usage, but certain dimensions are fairly standard and indicate average sizes of fixtures and installations.

Typical dimensions of built-in interior features.

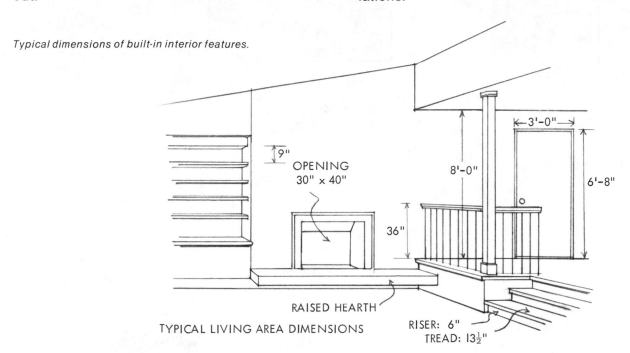

TYPICAL LIVING AREA DIMENSIONS

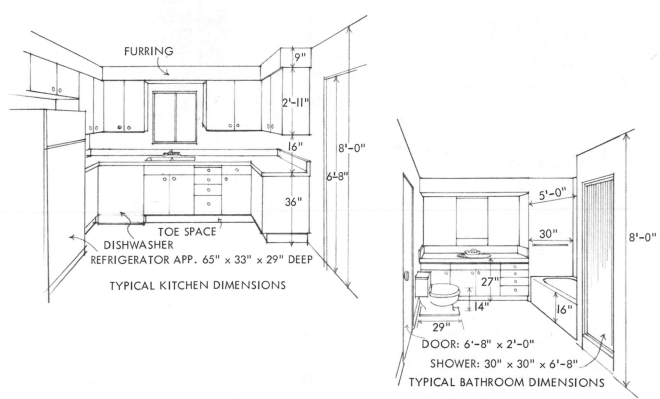

TYPICAL KITCHEN DIMENSIONS

TYPICAL BATHROOM DIMENSIONS

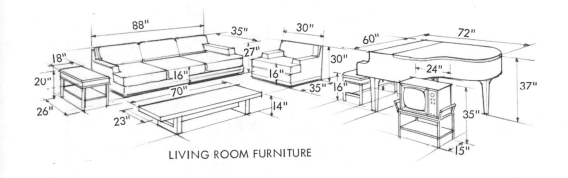

LIVING ROOM FURNITURE

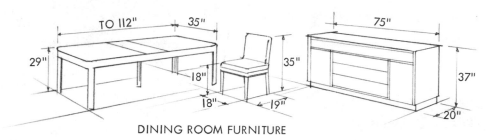

DINING ROOM FURNITURE

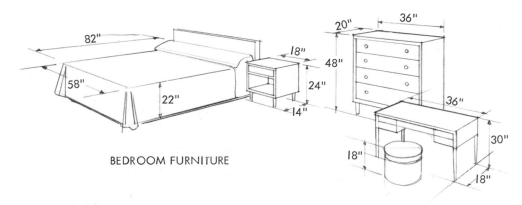

BEDROOM FURNITURE

Typical furniture dimensions. These are subject, of course, to many variations as to size and form.

FURNITURE DIMENSIONS

Furniture is available in a great variety of sizes, shapes, and styles. Innovative designers are adding to the list daring ideas that bear little resemblance to more conventional concepts.

An occasional sketch may include radical departures from the more familiar forms, but a recognizable chair or table is a better sales item in the average illustration. However, the range of contemporary and traditional styling is extensive enough that no drawing need look trite or stilted from lack of choice.

Examples here do not attempt to show particular styling, but are guides to general sizes of furnishings most likely to be found in typical residential interiors.

RENDERING TIPS

An exterior view is lighted by a well-defined source, causing shades and shadows to assume regular and easily calculated patterns. Light may come from several sources to an interior setting. The placement of bright and dark areas in an illustration can be a very confusing task.

A large window or glass doorway will transmit the strongest light, shading the wall through which it passes and casting some shadows in the vicinity of the opening. Other sources within the room, and reflected illumination, will tone down shadow intensities farther from the windows.

Secondary shadows and shades about the

A bedroom in ink line and wash.

Line and wash drawing by Leon Harris *for Universal Studios' motion picture* Pete 'n' Tillie. *Figures are important to composition for this type of use.*

Tempera is the medium for a clean rendering by QA Architectural Arts. Wood grain is suggested on cabinets and doors with dry brush strokes over the background color.

room tend to blur and fade out rather than form regular, hard-edged shapes.

Vignetting, or leaving unfinished areas rather than rendering all the way to the margins of the drawing surface, is a common practice. This allows you to concentrate shadows and shades where they are most effective, and forget about them in the rest of the composition.

The prominence of large furniture in the foreground is also reduced by vignetting. Left untoned and suggestively outlined, pieces appear as interesting, unobtrusive patterns rather than the dominant, distracting elements they might be when completely detailed and rendered.

Foreground furniture in motion picture sketches is often effectively used to heighten the dramatic impact of the composition. From a low eye level, pieces are shown as dark silhouettes with detail lost in shadow.

Figures are worthwhile additions to an interior, adding scale and interest if done well. If your delineation of them is stiff and uncertain, however, you'd better leave them out of the picture or see them in the distance through the window. Normally, furnishings will provide sufficient indication of scale.

An airy, imposing entryway rendered in pencil.

A pen and ink vignette.

Tone is used sparingly but directly in this line and wash drawing to clarify the design of the bookcase and organize its contents.

INDOOR-OUTDOOR RELATIONSHIPS

Even though the station point is within the room, interior architecture and furnishings may not be the all-important elements of a drawing.

A glass wall may look out to a magnificent view, an inviting garden, or an enticing activity. Its environment may be a major selling point for a home. Interior features are used as a foreground and attractive frame to set off the outdoor center of interest.

Inside and outside elements must be drawn well enough for easy identification, but must be separated by technique to avoid confusion with each other. Although artists develop their own solutions to this problem, these general suggestions are helpful:

1. Different emphasis on area: delineate the interior with heavier lines, stronger tones, and contrasts: use a similar but lighter treatment on the exterior.

2. A strong frame: apply a general overall tone to the interior, little or no tone to the exterior.

3. A strong center of interest: apply a tone to glass area to organize outdoor elements; define the interior in line with little or no tone.

The environment and the interior are equally necessary to the story told by this pen sketch.

In this sketch, the interior serves merely as a frame for a small exterior patio.

Indoors and outdoors are separated by contrasting handling of the pencil rendering.

CUTAWAYS

A cutaway drawing is an excellent explanation of a floor plan to someone who is unable to visualize it in two dimensions. At a glance, the layman can read the functions and room relationships of a building.

For this reason, cutaways are valuable advertising and editorial presentations of homes to prospective buyers.

To lay out such a drawing, project the plan by the grid method as in a high-angle aerial perspective. Include enough furniture to identify the rooms' purposes. Extend the walls high enough to separate each room, but not so far as to conceal important features of the plan or furnishings.

Cutaway, drawn in two-point perspective, clearly explains room functions of a small home. Heavy black line identifies cut portions of its walls.

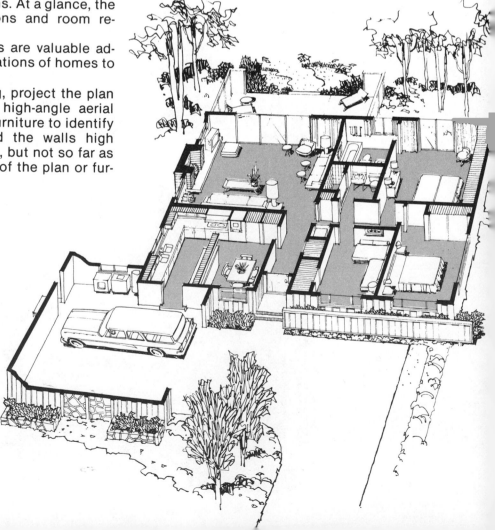

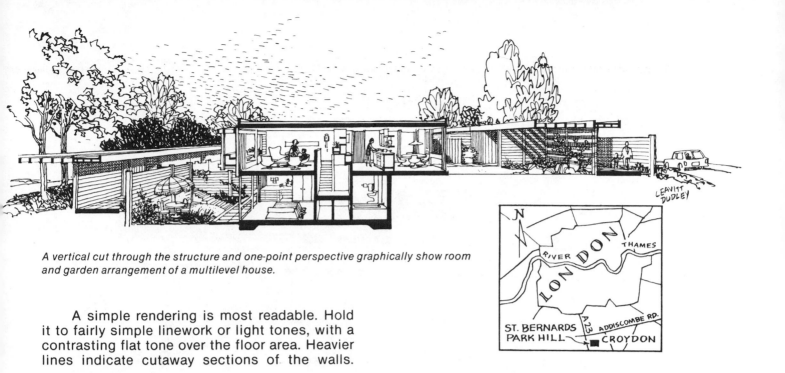

A vertical cut through the structure and one-point perspective graphically show room and garden arrangement of a multilevel house.

A simple rendering is most readable. Hold it to fairly simple linework or light tones, with a contrasting flat tone over the floor area. Heavier lines indicate cutaway sections of the walls.

COMMERCIAL INTERIORS

Interiors of shops, offices, restaurants, and other commercial structures are laid out and rendered in the same manner as those of residences; scale and furnishings are the major differences between them.

Felt pen design study of a hotel lobby, by Carlos Diniz for Daniel, Mann, Johnson, and Mendenhall.

Office waiting room, in tempera by QA Architectural Arts. Rug is textured by stippled dry brush.

Newspaper office clutter is the decor of mixed-media sketch for The Front Page, a Universal Studios picture. Drawing is by Gene Johnson for art director Henry Bumstead.

Pencil sketch of San Bernardino Cultural Center, by Barry Zauss for Gruen Associates. Press-on figures used for animation.

Ceilings in offices can rise ten or eleven feet above the floor. The ground floor ceiling of a building may soar twenty-five feet or more in height, and may be interrupted by mezzanines, escalators, and other architectural features.

Furniture tends toward slick, contemporary styling and includes desks, display cases, and other nonresidential items. Planters and indoor landscaping are popular and attractive additions.

At the large scale of many projects, design and function of the architecture are so important that the furniture is often incidental. It is simplified by stylized treatment, becoming almost another architectural shape.

In a restaurant, tables and chairs are so numerous that a very suggestive rendering is the only practical method of including them all. Foreground pieces should be detailed and carefully drawn. Tables should not be left bare; they create a livelier and richer effect when set with the maximum amount of glassware, cutlery, and napery.

Glass is used extensively in commercial building design. Entire walls from this material are common. An artist is confronted not only with the problems of looking through to the outside, but often wih the reverse situation of viewing an interior from the street.

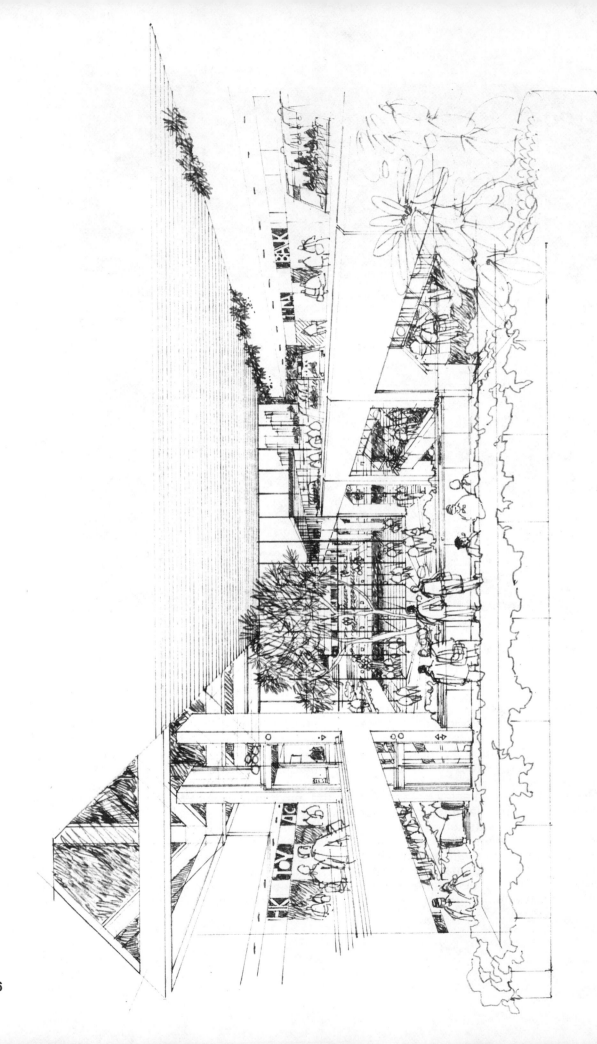

Skillful use of tones in central areas and suggestive treatment of foreground features effectively hold the composition together in this felt pen sketch by Fred Lappin for Daniel, Mann, Johnson, and Mendenhall.

Sectional Drawings, Engineering Projects, and Land Use Studies

A broad field of illustration is covered under this heading. In addition to projects for architects, it can include assignments from engineers, economists, and land planners. You will frequently contribute your own ideas on the subject as well as develop those of others.

Through these commissions, you will become better acquainted with the mechanics of a building as well as the design, ecological restrictions and goals, transportation problems, the physical and social impact of new developments, and municipal or government procedures and attitudes.

Your drawings are the important end products, but you must familiarize yourself with the other considerations to produce competently. Innovation and a capacity to go ahead with minimum direction are essential. Subjects are sometimes too abstract or undeveloped for complicated projections; you must be able to eyeball and draw directly.

Rendering techniques range from loose quick sketching to finely polished delineation, depending on the stage of a project's progress. Preliminary planning requires many concept studies for conveying ideas.

On many assignments, quick sketches solve the problems so descriptively that no other artwork is needed. Others may be finalized with more formal presentations in the more complicated mediums of pen and ink, water color, or airbrush. In such cases, planning has reached the point where more permanent techniques can be used. Each of these might be the result of dozens of quick sketches.

SECTIONAL DRAWINGS

A sectionalized illustration is a cutaway view of a project, explaining its function and general construction. Information and details are included which are impossible to see in a conventional perspective. Although primarily a representation of a building's interior, it can show exterior and environmental features as well.

As its purpose is the display of as much of the inner arrangement as possible, a section is usually laid out by one-point perspective. The composition looks deep into the central space and includes side wall details.

In a multifloor structure, eye level is located at the floor to be given the most emphasis.

If you are provided with a two-dimensional

Sectional view of future traffic routing shows activity above, below, and at the surface in a single illustration.

Interior arrangement of theater at Santa Barbara College, a design study in pencil for Daniel, Mann, Johnson, and Mendenhall.

Two-point perspective was used to illustrate the mechanics of an automated underground garage at Chartres, France.

cross section of the project, you can trace it or quickly scale it up or down to complete the first step of the drawing. Lines are projected from the station point; interior and exterior features are added as in any other parallel perspective.

The section is usually cut on a continuous flat plane, but it may be offset if it tells the story better. A structure is sometimes described more completely when certain areas extend beyond the planes of others.

Floor and roof sections are heavily constructed in large multistory buildings. Be sure their thickness shows in scale to the spacing between levels.

Rendering is similar to other types of illustrations, but interiors are simplified for clarity. Walls, ceilings, and floors are defined with flatter tones; cast shadows are used sparingly.

Pen and ink is a good quick medium for the bold forms of an industrial installation.

The cutaway section must be prominent and legible. It is usually treated as a solid dark mass or a light area defined with a heavy line. No detail is indicated in the cut portion.

ENGINEERING PROJECTS

Highways, transit systems, power plants, dams, bridges, airports, factories, and space exploration facilities are only a few of the types of projects encountered in this field.

Although their mechanics and purposes differ widely, all have points in common. They are highly technical and extremely practical. Functional efficiency is a primary design factor in all, but a pleasing visual appearance is just as important in many.

The slide rule is used as much as the T-square in planning these jobs, and you will team up with engineers as often as with architects.

Despite the emphasis on technology, you need not be a graduate engineer to illustrate these projects successfully. Your main concern is how an installation will look, and usually you can refer to working drawings and photographs for help with mechanical details.

A precise airbrush illustration of an aeropropulsion test facility, by Uri Hung for Daniel, Mann, Johnson, and Mendenhall.

Underwater experimental laboratory, by QA Architectural Arts, *is one of many out-of-the-ordinary engineering projects.*

For preliminary concepts, an initial briefing and some study of dimensions, functions, and structural requirements will provide enough information to start a sketch.

If an architect is not involved in the project, you may have to supply a few of your own ideas to add a little style to an illustration. Engineers, concerned with the problems in their own fields, cannot concentrate on architectural design. Usually they are willing to give you your say—as long as you do not impair the functional properties of a project and have a fair idea of what you are doing.

A vast project such as a superhighway or transit line, can effect a tremendous change on its adjacent environment. Municipal authorities are interested in the directions this will take and its beneficial aspects to their communities.

An illustrated impact study can explain and project future development. For visualizing its sketches, you will know the location and appearance of the project, and the present conditions of its surroundings. Planners will give you an idea of the general type of development they foresee, its extent, size of buildings, and other pertinent information. From these indications you should be able to fill in the design details which, after all, are simply tentative suggestions for things which may be a long way from realization.

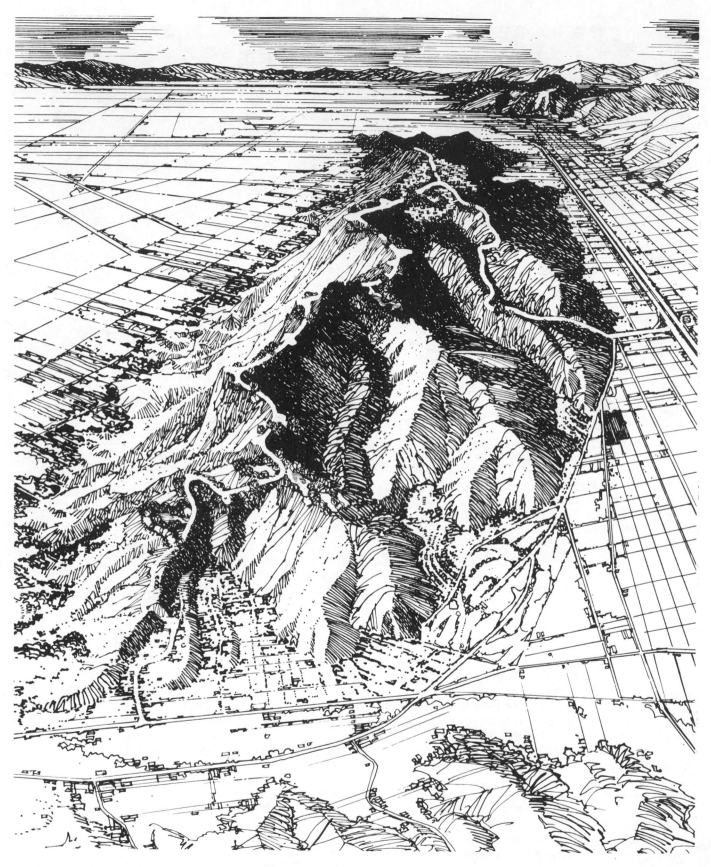

A perspective map shows the route of a scenic highway near Los Angeles, for Daniel, Mann, Johnson, and Mendenhall.

Details of construction for the highway (opposite). .

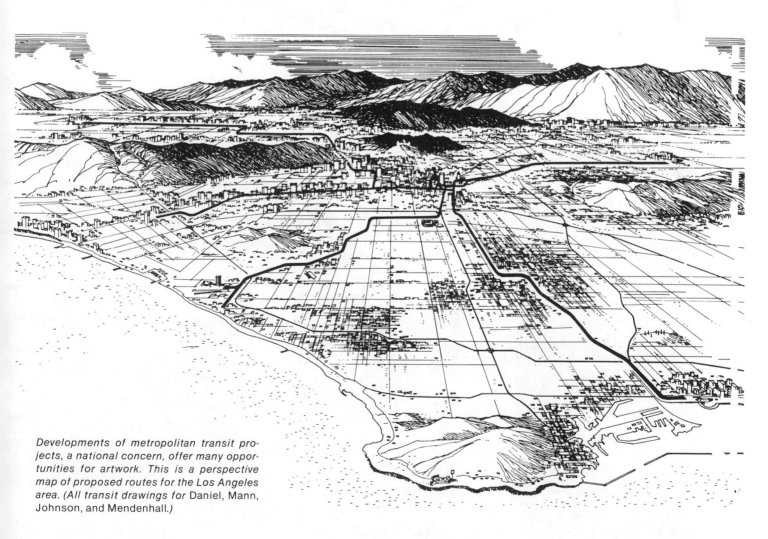

Developments of metropolitan transit projects, a national concern, offer many opportunities for artwork. This is a perspective map of proposed routes for the Los Angeles area. (All transit drawings for Daniel, Mann, Johnson, and Mendenhall.*)*

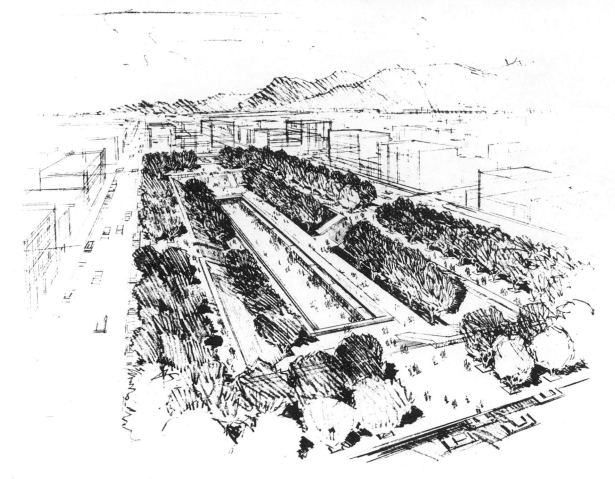

Quick sketch of a Los Angeles station.

Airbrush composite of station and track by Jess Fender.

Pencil section of a station.

Expected future development around a transit station; Minneapolis, St. Paul area.

Quick pencil sketch of land use for major development on Mississippi River, near Memphis. This, and following drawings of particular areas within it, were done for Albert C. Martin Associates, planners of the project.

LAND USE STUDIES

A proposal for an intended development of a parcel of real estate is presented through a land use study.

Private contractors may plan a project of homes, commercial or industrial areas, recreational facilities, resorts, or a combination of several ideas. Emphasis on architecture, and its effect on the surroundings, is stressed in illustration put together for this purpose.

Town center details.

Housing and lakeside development.

217

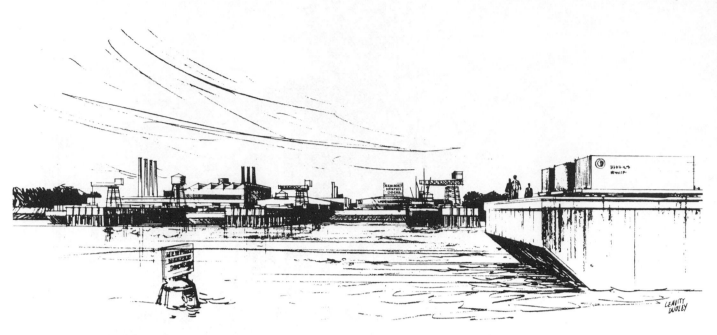

Industrial waterfront development.

In other types of studies, increased or better usage of the land itself, and methods for its conservation, are of primary importance. Campgrounds, hiking trails, scenic roads, and other recreational considerations take precedence over architecture. Government bodies, which are interested in proper utilization of public property, often commission assignments of this sort. An architectural office, or a consulting firm organized for research in this field, may enlist your services.

Whatever its ultimate purpose is, a land use

Ink line and wash, quick sketches of a proposed development in Sonora, Mexico, for architect Robert Sully show concepts for the marina area of the project, a waterfront residential section, and a hilltop hotel.

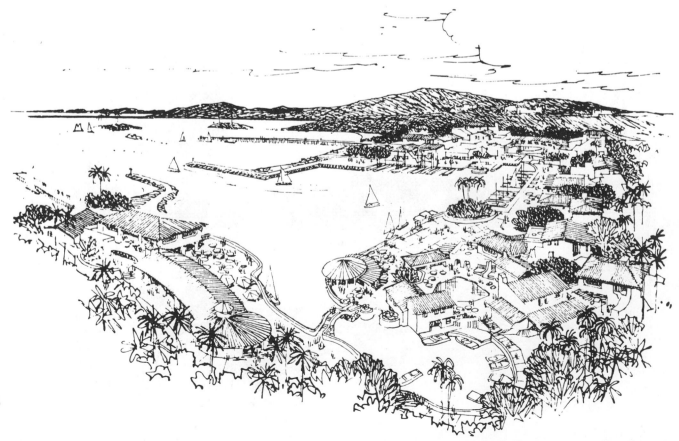

study in its preliminary stages is more concerned with overall concepts than with fine details. Your work may require a bird's-eye view of the entire project, supplemented by quick sketches suggesting particular activities or areas of development.

Reference material is usually limited to maps, photos, and an idea of the proposed usage. This might be a well laid-out plot plan, including street patterns and building clusters, or it may indicate only a general zoning.

Architectural direction may vary from only verbal suggestions to preliminary elevations of the buildings.

In any case, you may find it necessary to fill many gaps of information from your own knowledge. As long as the subject is covered adequately, much of its interpretation will be left to your own judgment.

Initial concepts may not resemble final solutions, but they must approximate fairly closely the type, style, and scale of the development. Detail will be specified and refined after approval of a project or in succeeding studies.

Atmospheric sketch of recreation area facilities at Rancho California.

Some land use studies are not concerned with architectural development. These pencil sketches for William-Kubelbeck planners illustrate types of activities to be made available through improvement of public land.

Freehand Sketches and Vignettes

Freehand sketches and vignettes are direct and casual in execution. Less laborious than most other types of architectural illustration, their rapid drawing seldom requires more than an eyeball type of projection.

Their simplicity can be deceptive, however. Only a few lines or strokes may be used in delineation, but each must count for more than it might in a more complex illustration. Minor mistakes, which might be camouflaged by the amount of detail and distracting elements in more complicated composition, are evident immediately in a less involved subject.

FREEHAND SKETCHING

An artist can learn many of the processes of more controlled or mechanical methods of illustration. With practice, the skill to perform them can be mastered.

Fluent freehand ability is more a natural than an acquired talent. It is a personal form of expression, developed more by following one's own instincts and inclinations than by the guidance from others.

Unless he is gifted with a generous dash of this native capability, an artist will have difficulty in attaining a high level of professional competence in freehand work.

Even for those without a great aptitude, freehand sketches are important aids to any kind of architectural illustration. Whether the drawings are perfect or show a few faults, sketches can still reveal essential facts and information to the artist as well as to others.

Your simple line drawings can record the forms of architecture and environment as reference for finished illustrations. They are excellent supplements to the camera, capturing what it misses if, for example, important detail is lost in a shadow, or supplying the outline of landscape features blurred by bad weather.

A rapid, on-the-spot sketch is a sure method of communication by pictorial shorthand. A few meaningful lines to shape a subject, with just enough detail to suggest its character, are adequate to convey the essence of its concept.

On your travels, there is no better way to sharpen your powers of observation than by quickly sketching impressions of your architectural encounters.

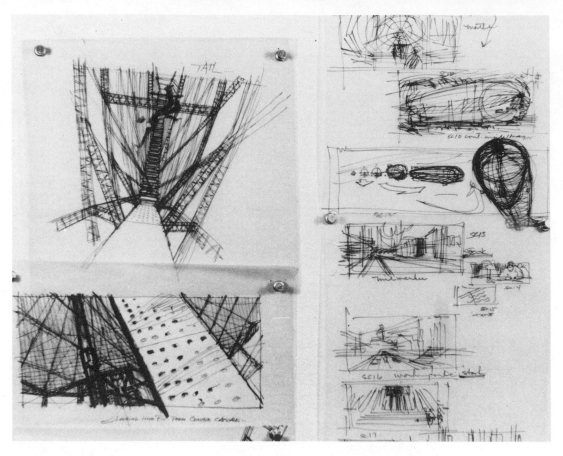

Continuity sketches for Universal Studios' motion picture Hindenburg. *These are primarily for planning the action of the scenes, but artist* Tom Wright *needed a knowledge of dirigible architecture as well as figure drawing.*

When skillfully executed in reproducible techniques, freehand drawings can be an end product as well as a reference or impression. Their loose and casual style is ideal for certain advertising and editorial usages.

The apparent freedom of their delineation may not be quite as spontaneous as it appears, however. Sketches printed in magazines or newspapers may have been preceded by a number of less successful attempts before the artists arrived at these final versions.

Procedures: Many mediums and materials are suitable for freehand sketches, depending on what is closest at hand or most convenient to carry about.

A drawing surface may be anything from an old grocery sack to a scrap of illustration board, but other papers are easier to use than these expedients.

Canary- or buff-tinted bond paper is durable and takes the common sketching mediums well. Cut to 8½″ x 11″ sheets, it can be used with a clipboard as a stiff backing. Spiralbound sketch pads in several sizes are available at art supply stores, work well with all mediums, and keep your work organized for quick reference.

Pencil is the most popular medium because of its portability, convenience, and satisfactory results. Use only the softer grades for effectiveness and legibility. Changes or corrections are easy, an advantage for artists who are more tentative than direct in their approach.

Pencil sketch of a small Mexican Plaza.

Worms *11ᵗʰ Cent. Cathedral in backgr.*

On-the-spot felt pen notations from a travel sketchbook.

Flow pens and felt markers are equally portable and convenient, are capable of strong contrasts, strong linework, and halftone effects. All these qualities are advantages for sketching by artists who are sure of their medium.

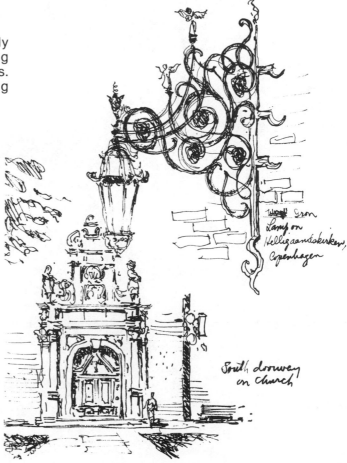

Iron Lamp on Helligaandskirken, Copenhagen

South doorway on church

A felt pen sketch as reference for a later watercolor, by Robert Jackson.

This subject is handled very broadly with felt-tipped markers, by Robert Jackson.

Tones laid in with markers, detail in felt pen, by Robert Jackson.

Felt pen study for an apartment building, by Robert Jackson.

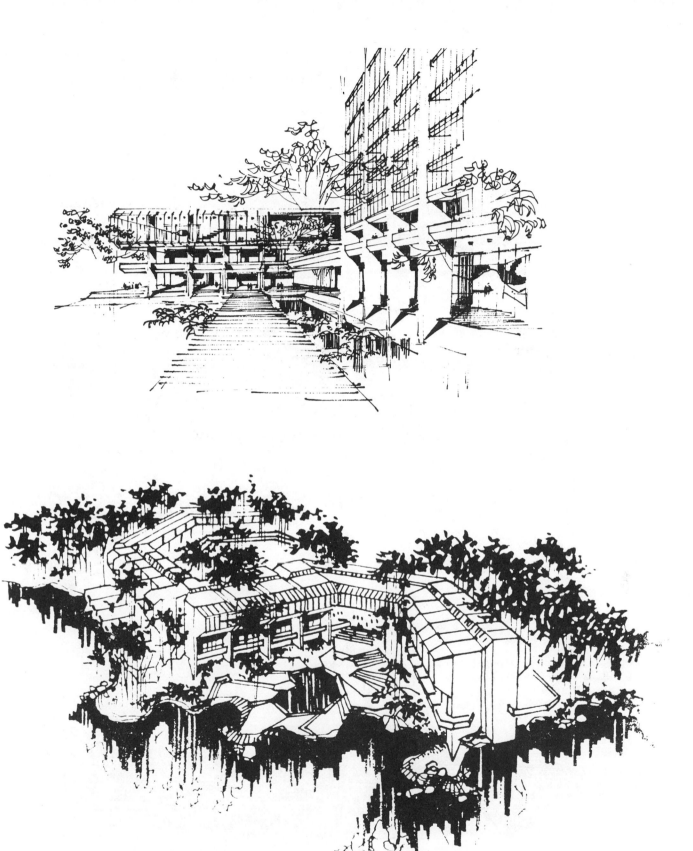

Felt marker design studies by James Langenheim. *This architect achieves a remarkable spontaneity by drawing his concepts directly onto the paper, with no preliminary layout. See next page also.*

Ballpoint pens are handy sketching tools for detailed linework. Results are not as bold as those from free flowing instruments, but intricate effects can be built up by many individual strokes.

India ink, applied by a quill pen or small brush, is less convenient for on-the-spot drawing but, if it is skillfully handled, it gives excellent and permanent results.

Bold patterns and colorful impressions are possible with quick watercolor washes. Outlines and details often are held by linework in soft pencil or ink, applied either before or after the washes.

Freehand pen work is a good technique for more romantic building projects. A preliminary layout was roughly blocked in first for these. See next page also.

MISSION AREA

LEAVITT
DUDLEY

- COSTA SMERALDA

Purity of technique is not a requisite. Several mediums may be combined to save time or to create a desired effect.

These suggestions are helpful hints for sketching:

1. Triangles, T-squares, and other straightedges seldom are used. Your eye can maintain true alignment on the paper, however, with the help of a few drawn-in guidelines.

2. Block out the composition very lightly before attempting any detailing.

3. Do not draw horizon or vanishing points, but assume them; keep a mental picture of their approximate locations in your head as you develop the sketch.

4. When working from an existing subject, comparative proportions can be measured on a pencil or a stick held at arm's length.

5. For clarity of detail, rely on linework with a minimum of cast shadows. For a bolder pictorial effect, go heavier on the shades and shadows and eliminate more detail.

6. Include only enough detail to define the subject or its function. Treat nonessential or repetitive features very suggestively, or leave them out entirely in areas.

Vignettes usually illustrate particular details or effects but also may be a small-scale impression of a larger subject.

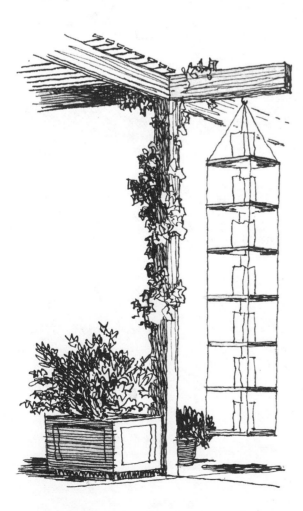

VIGNETTES

Vignettes show only a detail or a portion of a structure rather than an entire subject. Unfinished edges and free forms of composition are distinctive features.

They are used widely in advertising to stress a particular selling point of a building, and in editorial stories to emphasize important features of design or function.

In architectural offices, vignettes illustrate key areas of a structure. During preliminary planning stages, they can indicate a direction of design without the necessity of delineating the entire subject.

Vignettes resemble small architectural renderings rather than freehand sketches. Their layout is quick but careful; the eyeball, the horizon, and vanishing points all come into use. Because fewer elements are needed in the composition, rendering them can be direct and crisp regardless of the mediums employed.

Design Studies

The primary purpose of design studies is to capture and delineate ideas. Attractive drawing is desirable, to be sure, but it is secondary in importance to the visualization of the tentative, nebulous concepts that are the initial steps to any architectural project.

These studies are working drawings. They may become smudged and dirty from erasing and reworking. Lines of former attempts may show through the structure. Tones added over tones may obscure entire sections of detail. If the idea is presented in a tangible form, a neat appearance is less important than a clear explanation of the subject.

By necessity, you must work very closely with the architects, designers, and other planners to translate their thoughts into three-dimensional forms.

Plans are subject to revision at any time. Changes may be only minor alterations, but they also may be so radical as to require a completely new concept.

In an extensive and complex development, this design time can last over a period of a year or more. A proposal may be shelved for months in an incomplete form, to be resurrected for further study at a later date.

An illustrator is not likely to be involved in a continuous process for such work, but he may be on call as more sketches and revisions are needed to move a project toward its final solution.

In the early period of design study your work is the visual formation of tentative thoughts. Later, as the concept jells, sketches help clarify doubtful points of design and indicate areas needing further study and improvement.

When the project is planned firmly enough to need highly finished presentation illustrations, you may plan and detail the layouts to be used (even at this stage, last minute changes are still made).

Final rendering of the presentation art might possibly be assigned to another artist with a reputation for competence in a particular technique, as watercolor, air brush, or other medium.

Through all stages, your work is a valuable means of communication among the design personnel and also between the architect and his client.

Acceptance of the presentation drawings

All studies and illustrations in this chapter were done under the direction of Anthony J. Lumsden, Principal for Design at Daniel, Mann, Johnson, and Mendenhall, Architects and Engineers.

BUMI DAYA BANK

Bumi Daya Bank is a multistory office building in Djakarta, Indonesia, shown in its final design stages in a pencil sketch by Dick Johnson.

Banking facilities, mezzanines, and parking levels illustrated by a section.

Main entry lobby and stairway to the mezzanine.

View from the lobby into the banking section, with a new design for the stairway.

Rear entry to lobby.

Mirror glass model of project.

236

Final airbrush illustration by Uri Hung.

does not necessarily close your part of the study. Design changes may continue right up to the time of construction, requiring sketches incorporating the latest revisions.

Not all projects materialize into completed structures. Some may be proposals only, others bids for a design project. A few sketches illustrating an architect's thinking may be all that are needed.

Design studies may not appeal to all illustrators. Pressures and deadlines can be demanding. Requirements for a sketch are often difficult to specify during initial stages of a project. The appearance of a drawing may suffer from frequent but necessary changes.

However, if you are flexible enough to meet the requirements of this type of work, you will find yourself more involved in the complexities of planning major developments than in any other field of illustration. What you can do with your hands is important, but it's not enough. You will use your head just as often.

Even a very large project is only one of a number of jobs in a big architectural office. The time a busy architect-designer can spare for your briefing is limited. In initial stages, information sometimes is nebulous or suggestive at best.

You must be able to perceive a general concept quickly, and take it from there without waiting for specific directions. Unless you are given definite instructions, your most important action at this point is to *get something drawn* from whatever information you have. Your first ideas may bear little resemblence to what may come later, but don't worry about that.

An architect can suggest directions and developments more easily from some kind of sketches—even if they are wrong in concept—than from nothing at all.

SEPULVEDA WATER RECLAMATION PROJECT

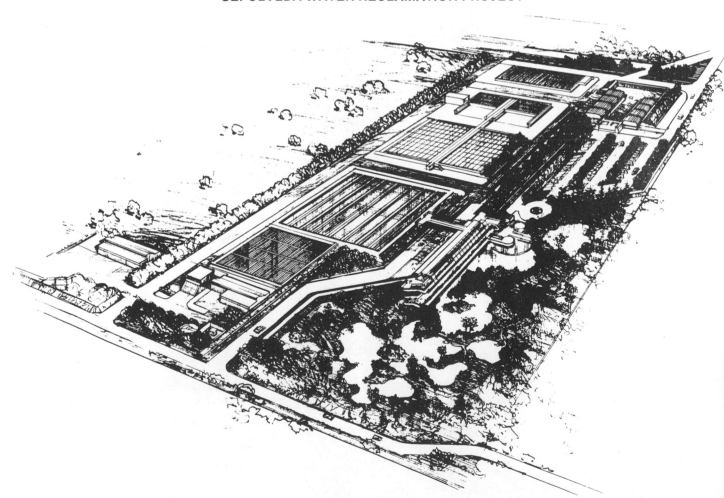

This project successfully combines a water treatment plant with award-winning architecture and an attractive park. Birdseye view shows the complete facility.

After many erasures and design changes, the plant headquarters viewed from the lake. Before rendering with graphite pencil, original layout was done in nonphoto blue pencil.

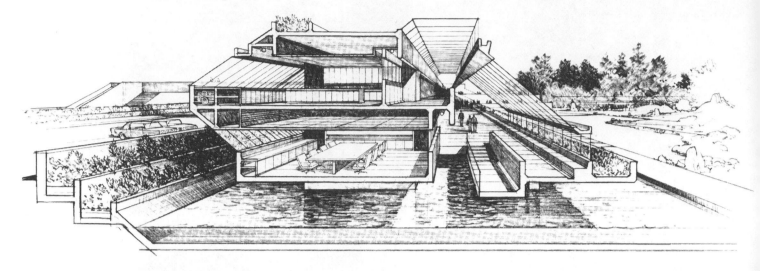

Section through main building.

Interior of main building.

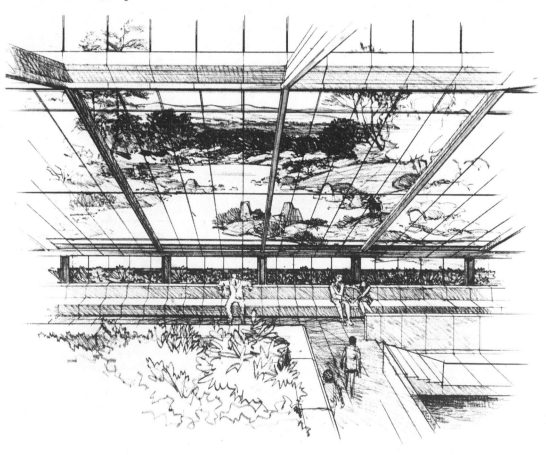

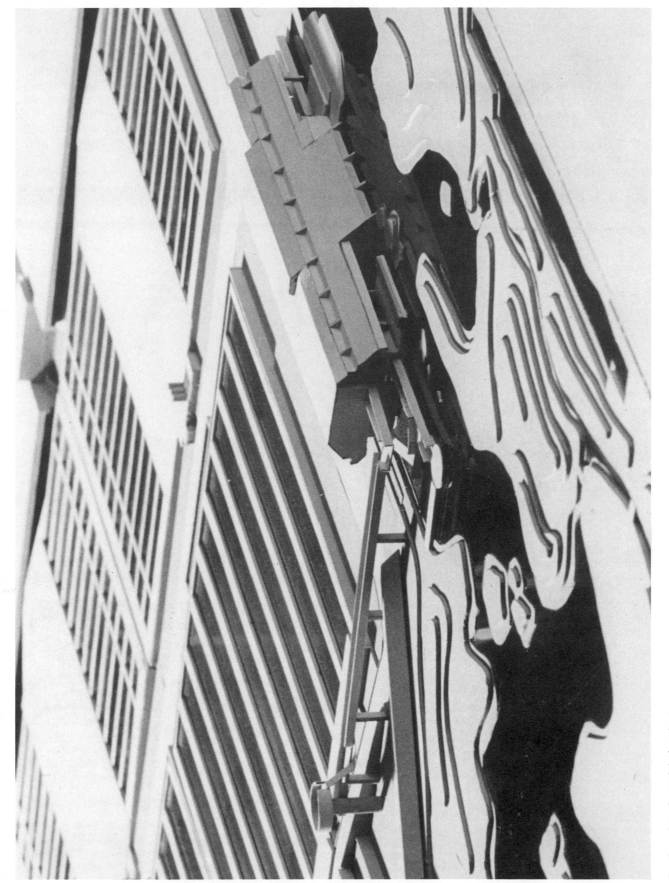

Cardboard study model of project.

A number of small freehand thumbnail sketches, with the architecture treated very suggestively, are better than one careful drawing trying to say too much. For the time being, impressions are more important than specifics. Try several different viewpoints, including aerial perspectives, normal eye-level shots, and close-ups, but don't spend more than a few minutes on each.

From these, the architect may be able to pick out a few compositions or ideas suitable for further study and suggest improvement or revision in the angles of view or the structural massing.

Architectural definition and detail often develop as the sketch progresses, even though proposed solutions have been worked out in elevations. Any of this information is changable at any time up to the completion of the drawing.

You may have to add some of the features from your own conclusions of the project. Although you won't be quite so concerned as the designers about practical workability and mechanics, your ideas must be compatible with practical building methods.

Each artist must work out his own way of coping with the variables of this type of illustration, but the following method is one satisfac-

MARINA DEL REY

Marina del Rey is a large residential development at a busy small-boat harbor. These are early thumbnail studies, each drawn in a few minutes.

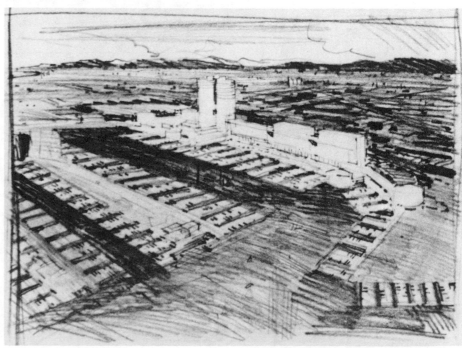

Design possibilities of the initial concept were further explored through quick pencil sketches.

When the final solution evolved, with the help of quick sketches and study models, it was carefully delineated by pencil.

tory solution to the necessary working and re-working of the paper surface:

On 1000H technical paper, from a thumbnail layout, establish the horizon and vanishing points, and work out an eyeballed perspective.

Use a nonphoto sky blue pencil. Its color is recessive but strong enough to be readable, does not smear, and erases easily. Include all the detail necessary for approval of the layout.

The illustration is rendered directly over the blue underdrawing with graphite pencils. #2^{5}/$_{10}$, #2, and #1 grades (or similar) cover the range from fine architectural detail to coarse foliage. The blue tones below add a pleasing color variation to the finished sketch, and drop out completely if it is photographically reproduced.

Keep the rendering as quick and loose as possible while still maintaining accuracy of

drawing. Don't get too involved in intricate deline-ation of trivial detail until you are sure it will stay as it is. Remember that drastic changes may be ahead, or a large leafy tree may have to be added to the composition to screen a problem area until time for later consideration.

You will work with light guidelines as your sketch develops. Don't worry if they show through the final drawing. If not dominant, they add to the effect of flexible, thorough study of the subject.

Unlike the crisp delineation of some pencil illustrations, design studies tend toward an over-all smudginess. Some smearing and grayed tones are unavoidable in drawings so subject to revision. This is by no means a drawback, as strength and solidity are built up with the addi-tional penciling.

Erasers are almost as essential as pencils

Mariners Bay is another waterfront development, and its early design studies show how drastically a concept can change in its formative periods. Circular shapes featured in the first ideas gave way later to a stepped design (see next page also).

BALTIMORE COLLEGE

This large college was confined to a small building site because of its downtown location and existing adjacent buildings. The 3-D plan shows its structures fitted into less than two city blocks. Building at upper left is not a part of the project.

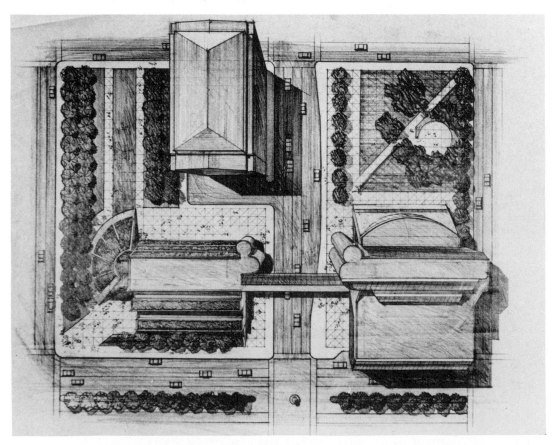

The college as seen from the street. Its basic design was fairly well established when these drawings were made.

An interior view of the library, with adjacent buildings seen through the window.

for this work. If an area to be changed is heavily coated with soft graphite, remove its top layer first with pliable kneaded rubber to reduce smearing. Remove the balance with a firmer type, as a pink pearl or one on the end of a pencil. An electric eraser effectively takes out stubborn lines. Use an erasing shield for clean edges, or for lifting highlights from dark areas.

Cardboard bridges at the sides of a drawing help reduce smearing by preventing excessive drag of a T-square or straightedge across the surface. Workable fixative helps to hold the graphite during the rendering and after the completion of the job. Don't spray too much fixative: every application lessens the ability of the surface to take additional pencil lines or tones.

LUGANO

The project is a proposed hotel on the shore of a lake in Switzerland. Its scenic environment was an important consideration for both exterior and interior views and was a part of nearly all of the design studies used in its planning.

PART **III**

Special Processes

A completed architectural illustration is not always the finished product. Some are modified or altered for better presentation or to serve additional uses. Others receive widespread distribution when reproduced for advertising or publicity.

Your value as an artist improves when you can increase the flexibility of existing artwork or understand the particular requirements of special-purpose artwork.

17

Presentation Tips

It is healthy to view your finished artwork with a critical eye. Only the most complacent craftsmen see no room for improvement.

However, an architectural illustrator lives in a world of deadlines and realistic financial returns for his work. Unless he feels the delineation is completely unsatisfactory, he cannot take the time to render it again. Also, another observer is more likely to overlook minor faults than the artist who produces them.

However, even basically good drawings can stand modification or improvement sometimes. Shortcuts can save drawing time. Major corrections or changes can be made on existing art. Through simple processes, the composition and character of renderings can be changed, or can adapt themselves to serve other purposes.

CROPPING

An illustrator has a natural tendency to include too much in a composition. When this fact is realized, he has an equally natural reluctance to eliminate portions of a rendering over which he has worked so diligently.

Drawings are often improved greatly by some judicious "cropping"—removing areas that detract from the center of interest or reduce the effectiveness of the composition. (If it is difficult to steel yourself for the amputation, turn the job over to someone whose artistic judgment is not hampered by a creator's sensitivity.)

A pair of L-shaped cardboard strips simplifies cropping. Adjust them to form a flexible rectangle, and move them about till you are satisfied with the composition.

Indicate their selected positions with "crop marks," or reference lines, marked on the margins of the illustration.

None of the rendering actually need be cut away or destroyed. It may be cropped differently for another use, so preserve the entire drawing. If the original is for presentation, the eliminated area can be screened with a mat. For reproduction, the crop marks are a framing guide for the photographer or engraver responsible for the copies.

MATS

These cardboard frames set off illustrations for more attractive presentations. They square up the ragged edges of paintings, or crop too generous compositions. Their usual material is mat board, fairly rigid but not of the same weight or quality as illustration board.

The center of the mat is cut out to fit the size indicated by the crop marks on the drawing, with a mat knife or single-edged razor blade. Use only a metal straightedge as a cutting guide; never use one made of wood or a T-square. The knife will nick their edges. Place a layer of heavy cardboard under the cut to protect the table top and the point of the knife.

A white mat is most suitable for a colored or halftone rendering. Artwork which is basically light in value, as a pen and ink drawing, is complimented by a contrasting frame of gray, a light earth tone, or a muted color.

The width of the border varies with the size of the drawing and the preference of the artist, but 4"-5" is sufficient for setting off the average 20" x 30" drawing. Reduce or enlarge it proportionately for other sizes.

Keep the same margin on all four sides, unless titles or other copy require increased space at the bottom.

If lettering is used, ready-made type, which transfers with pressure from a sheet of paper to the mat, is quickly applied and professional looking.

PRINT TOUCHUPS

Sepia, blue, or black line copies from a whiteprinter are quick, convenient, and inexpensive reproductions of pencil sketches.

The process often diminishes the contrast, however, weakening the lines and toning the

Though the drawing in the original was strong, some of its line and tone quality was lost in this sepia copy. The second illustration shows how an hour's work with white, sepia, and black Prismacolor pencils can deepen the tones, heighten the contrasts, and improve the lighting effects of a weak print.

white areas. These copies are suitable for office circulation or filing, but are improved for presentation if some of the values are strengthened.

Touch-up of key areas with black or colored Prismacolor pencils sharpens the contrast. Black for lines and darker areas combines well with all the whiteprinter tints. White pencils are used to pick out highlights or lighten the values of other areas.

Mount the finished print on cardboard and frame it with a mat to further improve its presentation.

SPLICING AND PATCHING

CORRECTIONS

On a lightweight drawing paper, cutting and splicing a portion of a pencil drawing is sometimes a neater, quicker method of alteration or correction than extensive erasing.

Cut the part to be saved along a dark tone or strong line, as the edge of the building, so the splice is less noticeable and will not interfere with additional rendering.

See that the new surface completely backs up the old section. Fasten the two layers together with rubber cement.

A similar process can be followed with a whiteprinter copy, if a sky or other area is desired in clear paper rather than toned by the reproduction. Touch-up rendering is possible on the addition with Prismacolor pencils matching the print tone.

A different cut and splice method is used for unobtrusive patches on watercolor or ink techniques, rendered on heavyweight illustration board:

1. Tape a tracing paper overlay over the area to be changed. With a sharp pencil, carefully outline the area to be removed. Use strong regular lines or dark tones as edges.

2. Peel the thin top ply from the cardboard backing of another piece of illustration board. Cover the area to be patched and tape firmly in place.

3. Replace the tracing paper overlay. Make sure the patch outline is still in the same position over the original drawing.

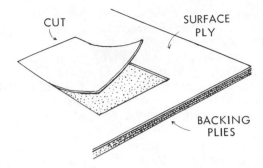

The surface ply of illustration board can be cut through with a frisket knife, peeled away, and a new section cemented into its place for correcting or revising a drawing.

4. With a sharp frisket knife, cut cleanly and firmly along the outline through both the new surface and the top ply of the old. Use a metal straight-edge as a cutting guide, and to help hold the paper securely.

5. Remove the overlays and peel away the top ply of the old surface between the cut lines.

6. Rubber cement the new patch to the old surface. If the job has been carefully and neatly done, it will fit exactly with its surface on the same level as the original.

7. Render to match original drawing.

VARIATIONS

Several different studies of a project, each visualized in the same environmental setting, may be necessary before its final design is accepted.

Drawing a complete new background for each proposal is time consuming. Instead, draw only the architectural variations. By reproduction processes, each may be spliced into the same background in the following method:

1. Render the entire background carefully, omitting the proposed architecture. (The space occupied by the smallest size proposal can be left blank.)

2. Draw the variations to the same scale and perspective.

3. Set each in place on the background, touch up to match, and reproduce. If the process is photographic, leave the architecture in place on the background. If the whiteprinter is used, print the background and architecture separately and cement the variations in position.

4. Extensive revision on sepia prints is possible with the use of liquid print eradicator. Applied with a small brush, the eradicator removes any unwanted lines or tones from the print. Corrections or revisions may be made directly on the print with either a sepia or a graphite pencil.

Changes can be made either before or after use of the eradicator, as the liquid affects only the printed linework. Blot up the liquid immediately after application, and be sure that the surface is thoroughly dry before attempting any further drawing.

The whiteprinter can copy illustrations only on translucent paper, of course. Photo reproduction must be used for those on board.

SALVAGE JOBS

Not all illustrations proceed smoothly. Accidents can happen, mistakes are made, or rendering can reach a discouraging stage.

Cut and splice methods are suitable for some salvage operations. Others may be too minor to warrant their time, or too extensive for them to be practical.

If a tracing paper drawing is torn or badly wrinkled, cement or dry-mount it to a backing of mat or poster board. Apply it smoothly to a non-textured surface if the drawing needs further rendering. Transparent tape on the back of the drawing mends minor rips.

Corrections are made on pen and ink illustrations with white tempera and a fine brush. Add revisions before the correction, as ink does not take well over tempera. If it is necessary to add lines over the paint, use lampblack watercolor and a small brush. If the correction is planned and executed carefully, a drawing can survive even such a tragedy as a spilled bottle of ink.

Changes can be made on a tempera rendering by overpainting, or by masking an area with tape and sponging lightly to remove paint.

The more delicate surface of a transparent watercolor is a different matter. Additional tone buildup in areas may help, and tempera washes can alter values to some extent.

If the overall rendering is muddy, too dark in tone, and generally unsatisfactory, a part of the drawing can be saved at least. With a large soft sponge, and plenty of clean water, wash off the paint. The pencil drawing will remain, together with a light residue of the color absorbed by the surface. Give the back a thorough wetting as well, so the board will not warp as it dries.

Start the rendering over when the surface is dry. Salvaging by this method can often produce effective and interesting results, using the color residue for some tonal values.

Sepia prints can be altered with Prismacolor pencils, using two or three shades of color intensity. A white pencil can reduce the values of lines and tones substantially, but not remove them entirely. Major alterations are possible

A

B

A *A sepia print of a background for several variations of a proposed building. When* **B** *is rubber-cemented in place, the whole is touched up with sepia and white pencils.*

A

Three grades of photocopies. **A** *A high contrast negative emphasizes blacks and whites and is suitable for linecut reproduction.* **B** *A halftone negative is softer and holds gray tones better.* **C** *A continuous tone negative prints a gray background over the entire picture.*

when they are drawn in the darker values and blended into the rest of the print with additonal rendering.

PHOTOGRAPHIC PRESENTATIONS

Pencil, or pen and ink sketches, are drawn more conveniently at the smaller dimensions, but their finished sizes may be insufficient for easy visibility as presentation pieces.

Photo processing can enlarge an original to any size up to a legible 30″ x 40″, or an even larger photo mural. The blowup emphasizes the character of the linework, bringing it to a bold and massive scale.

Dry-mounted on heavy weight illustration board, with its edge "bleeding" (running off the sheet), a little sketch can be transformed into a striking presentation.

Ink drawings are consistent in their black and white values and are usually reproduced in high contrast.

The character of pencil sketches, with their tonal variations, changes with differences in the photo process. A high contrast negative cuts out middle values, resulting in a composition of strong black and white patterns. Halftone prints are less dramatic but retain better the values of the original art. The gray cast of the continuous tone negative gives the softest effect.

When ordering these photos, specify the size of the mounting board, the type of negative, the print surface (matte or glossy finish), and whether or not the edges bleed. Size the drawing with crop lines, with the print dimensions indicated between them.

For large display panels, as might be used on sales office walls, a drawing is sometimes printed on a translucent photographic surface. Areas on its reverse side may be tinted with color. In front of low intensity lights, these are effective attention-getters.

COLOR ADDITION

Versatile pen or pencil drawings are unequaled for many purposes, but sometimes are faulted for their lack of color.

After the drawings serve their black and white uses, however, it is not difficult to add color to the original artwork or reproduction.

To originals on 1000H technical paper or other lightweight translucent material, colors may be applied with Prismacolor pencils or felt markers in the more subdued tones. Color is bolder when it is added to the front of the drawing. On the back, it shows through as a suggestive tint. Prismacolor also works well on whiteprinter copies.

To a pen drawing on illustration board, add

B

C

tints of transparent watercolor. Keep the values flat, simple, and not too intense, as the ink lines and tones already carry the delineation.

Get a good photographic negative of an original before applying color, to ensure line copies for further black and white usage if necessary.

If the original is to be kept as is, or if larger color presentations are desired, several possible ways of tinting a high contrast photoprint are possible. Specify a mattefinish working surface, mounted on heavyweight board to prevent buckling.

The surface takes Prismacolor or felt markers well. Watercolor tinting is more difficult because of adhesion problems, and needs the addition of soap to the brush for even coverage.

An oil paint process is one of the smoothest, most sophisticated methods of adding color to a black and white print. A good medium is Marshall's Photo Tinting Oil, used by photographers to color portraits and other camera studies. The transparent material is available in tubes, in a wide range of colors.

The drawing to be tinted should be printed on a matte finish photo mural paper, the surface best suited for the process.

To apply color, squeeze a dab on a piece of marble, porcelain, or other broad palette. Rub with a swab of cotton to pick it up, then apply

A pen and ink line drawing, by Ben Althen *for Gruen Associates, after coloring with oil tints.*

it smoothly, to the desired intensity, onto the print. The cotton should be of the finest possible texture. A small swab can be used for windows or other restricted areas.

Color can be confined to a given section with masks of tape or paper. If it covers too much area, a vinyl eraser and a shield removes the surplus cleanly. Be sure to remove all eraser crumbs with a soft brush to prevent their marring a treated area.

Tinting oil is slow to dry completely, requiring a day or more. However, additional coatings may be overlaid immediately if the layers are applied thinly.

When thoroughly dry, windowframes, highlights, or other white areas can be masked and picked out with an eraser, or can be painted in tempera.

The color is a permanent addition to the print, but can be erased with vinyl up to a period of several months if changes are required.

Colored oil pencils also can be used for the same purpose, alone or in conjunction with the paint.

Airbrushing with colored inks produces equally smooth results. Masking is necessary, as in any airbrush job. The surface is more susceptible to damage, however, and is not removable.

Acetate color films, transparent and adhesive backed, are perfect for adding areas of brilliant flat color to smaller pen and ink drawings or prints. Available in many bright tones, shades of gray, and black, they are pressed to the artwork. The excess is trimmed with a frisket knife and peeled away.

Different applications of color tints can completely change the character of a drawing although the original line artwork is the same. Barry Zauss *did these for* Gruen Associates.

Pen and ink artwork can be reproduced photographically on transparent acetate sheets. Color is brushed on the back with acrylic paint, and the sheet is mounted on colored mat board.

In another method, the main shapes of the architecture and landscaping, to match the print, are drawn on illustration or mat board. Major areas and planes are painted broadly in tempera or watercolor. The acetate print as an overlay defines the detail.

A

B

Ross Barr *added color to a line drawing printed on a clear acetate sheet, for architect Marvin Johnson.* **B** *shows the application of acrylic paint to the back side of the transparent film.*

18

Reproduction Techniques

Sooner or later, a large percentage of contemporary architectural illustrations are reproduced in some form. Examples of all rendering styles are seen in the advertising and editorial columns of newspapers and magazines, brochures, and other types of promotion and publicity.

Any competently executed drawing is usable, although its quality and legibility can suffer unless it is printed in a publication compatible with its technique or prepared particularly for reproduction.

The most common printing methods are letterpress and offset lithography. The former uses a photographically engraved plate; the latter reproduces from a photographic image on a metal sheet.

Most artwork is printed in one color, as a *linecut* or *halftone,* though the original may be in full color.

A linecut is in black and white only, with no gray tones. Pen and ink reproductions are excellent examples. When an apparently gray area is seen, it has been added by the engraver through a *benday* process. A pattern of minute, closely-spaced dots is also printed as a linecut but

appears as a continuous tone because of the density of the dots.

A halftone is totally composed of grays of different intensities, developed by means of a screen covering the entire printed area. Some sections seem near black or near white, but examination will show them to be extremely dark or light shades.

This is the only possible type of reproduction for watercolor, tempera, airbrush, smudged pencil, or other mediums whose techniques are tonal rather than linear. The "dropout halftone" is a variation, where white areas of the drawing remain free of tone through certain engraving methods.

Although the preceding methods are one-color processes, additional hues can be included in the reproduction by means of overlays. Separate sheets, one for each extra color, indicate with flat tones the areas to be tinted.

Expensive, less-used full color reproduction is entirely an engraver's process. Colors are separated and screened into halftone plates of yellow, red, blue, and black. Overprinting combines them into a faithful representation of the original artwork.

A "silk-screen" process is an entirely different printing method. Bold patterns, strong hues, poster-like effects, or delicate detail all are possible through the use of silk-screen. Different colors are forced through a series of fine mesh screens onto the printing surface.

Preparation of an overlay-type drawing for each separate color is the artist's responsibility. Screens are processed photographically.

The methods and the quality of the printing of different types of publications also concern the art preparation.

Printing stock and reproduction screens used by newspapers tend to be coarse. A full halftone of an average wash drawing may be dim or muddy when reproduced, especially in extreme reductions. Advertisements, using drop-out halftones and more space for the art, are usually more sparkly. Pencil linecuts may or may not turn out well, according to the caliber of the drawing and the care of the engraver. A strong pen and ink linecut is always the safest technique for any purpose or publication.

Rotogravure, often used for newspaper supplements or special sections, also employs a coarse stock, but reproduction processes are kinder to halftones. Pen and wash drawings, handled with flat definite tones, are usually successful.

Magazines and brochures, printed on smooth, high-grade stocks with finer reproduction screens, can reproduce well-prepared drawings in any technique capably.

LINECUTS

Pen and ink or pencil illustrations are usually drawn larger than they will appear as reproductions. Reduction refines the quality of good linework, but can close up the spaces between too delicate strokes and result in blotchy loss of detail.

Too much shrinkage has the same effect on a competently detailed drawing. One of average quality can reduce to half size without problems. Coarser linework is recommended below that amount of reduction.

A safe and convenient working range for an original is from 1¼ to twice its reproduction size. If you are not sure of its ultimate dimensions, keep the drawing on the bold side. If you want to retain the same line character, draw to the same size as the reproduction.

To emphasize the lines for bold display, work at smaller than final scale. A quick, well-executed thumbnail-sized sketch can be enlarged with striking effects. Be careful with your

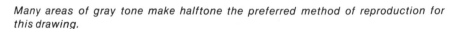

Many areas of gray tone make halftone the preferred method of reproduction for this drawing.

A pencil drawing reproduced as a linecut.

draftsmanship though, as errors or sloppiness are also magnified.

An illustration may have additional usage as a very small reduction, as on a letterhead or in a two-column ad. Don't take a chance on the original. Redraw it at a smaller scale, strengthening the light and dark pattern and eliminating the delicate linework.

Even for minute detail, pen or pencil strokes for all linecuts must be firm and definite. Don't let lightweight lines taper off in weak, vague endings that will be lost in reproduction.

If you are in doubt about line quality, examine the drawing through a reducing glass, which diminishes the artwork to a scale closer to its reproduction size.

Linecut art is simple to change or correct. Cut a piece of paper off the top ply of an illustration board and cement it over the area to be redrawn. Seams and joints will be dropped out during reproduction procedures.

HALFTONES

Illustrative techniques for halftone reproduction depends on variations of tonal values rather than lines for their definition.

To remain separated through the screening process, planes must change definitely and distinctly in the original artwork. Shadows and highlights must be very contrasting, particularly if the halftone will be the overall rather than the drop-

out type. Emphasizing the value separation helps prevent reproductions in drab monotones.

Because an illustration is more difficult to detail with a brush than with a fine quill pen, halftone originals are drawn to a larger scale than linecut art. (Their larger sizes are often due to initial preparation for presentation or display; reproduction in this case is a secondary usage.)

If reproduction is a primary purpose, keep the original as close as possible to the enlargement recommendations for linecuts while maintaining clear definition of detail.

Wash and ink renderings, with finishing touches added by a pen, are easier to draw to smaller sizes.

Illustrations for full-color reproduction are prepared to the same value standards as other halftones. The separation process often tends to distort or dull the original hues, and so drawings for this purpose should be colored with above-average intensity and brilliance.

Black and white reproductions are also made from full-color art.

PENCIL DRAWINGS

Sketches for halftone processing may be drawn on any kind of paper, and smudged or toned for any desired effect. The reproduction subdues the strength of the lines but holds the shading and middle values better than a linecut.

As in a wash drawing, tones should be

strong and distinct enough to contrast and separate from one another.

A pencil linecut reproduces in black and white only. Gray areas are apparent by the white spaces and flecks interspersed with the black. Strong lines become darker and bolder; weak ones tend to drop out. Rendering must be crisp, clean, and free of smudges or smears.

Paper used for the drawing must be textured enough to permit the intermixing of black and white, but not too rough to make fine detailing difficult or impossible.

One-ply Strathmore meets these qualifications and is thin enough for tracing over a light table. Medium to soft grades of pencils are recommended for the rendering. Because of its coarser texture, a slightly harder grade is used than for a similar operation on smoother paper.

A careful outline layout, including major details, is first drawn on lightweight tracing paper and taped to a light table. The finish surface is taped over it, and the drawing is traced. Minor details, toning, and other features not included in the initial layout are added.

To help protect the surface, use cardboard bridges under the T-squares and triangles; spray finished areas with fixative and cover them with tracing paper before proceeding to the next section. Avoid erasures as much as possible, but if they become necessary, protect the rest of the surface with an erasing shield.

Highlights can be added—or smears cleaned up—with white tempera.

OVERLAYS FOR BENDAY AND COLOR

With overlays, benday tones may be included in reproductions of linecut artwork for additional depth, variety, and unity. They also are used when more than one color is specified in the printing process.

A rough pencil layout for a catalog cover.

Finished artwork and overlay for the illustration.

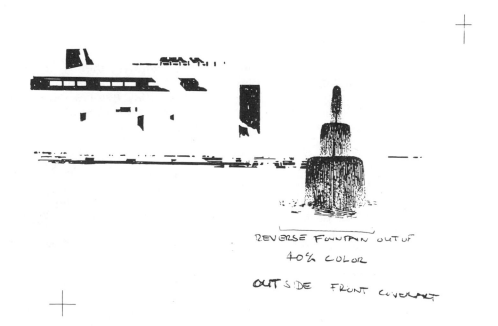

REVERSE FOUNTAIN OUT OF

40% COLOR

OUTSIDE FRONT COVER ART

The printed cover.

These features are primarily additions to pen and ink artwork, but they also are adaptable to pencil linecuts. Color overlays are made as well for halftones.

The overlay is simply an indication of the portion of the illustration to be bendayed or colored, and it is photographed during reproduction as an additional piece of artwork.

Appearance and preparation of the overlay for either purpose is identical—a flat tone of any desired size or shape at the same scale as the master drawing.

A sheet of clear acetate is placed over the drawing, and a transparent, adhesive-backed film called "mylar" is applied as the tone. With a frisket knife, the mylar is carefully cut to fit the area to be toned, and the surplus film is peeled away from the acetate.

Mylar, which is red, photographs black, but the master drawing is clearly visible, because of its transparency, for easy trimming to shape.

An overlay may involve more drawing and detail than simple, easy-to-cut flat shapes. If so, a piece of translucent acetate with a slightly roughened surface may be used. The drawing may be in pen and ink, brush and ink, grease pencil, graphite pencil, or any medium that will stick to the acetate.

If adherence of the medium is a problem, dust the surface with talcum powder and brush it off with a cotton swab to remove the oiliness.

All overlays must coincide perfectly with the base drawing for the additional tone or color to be in proper "register," or alignment, during reproduction. Register marks are drawn on each overlay in the identical positions as those on the master drawing. Ready-made marks are also available as commercial products.

An overlay for pen and ink artwork, its accompanying drawing, and with its accompanying drawing.

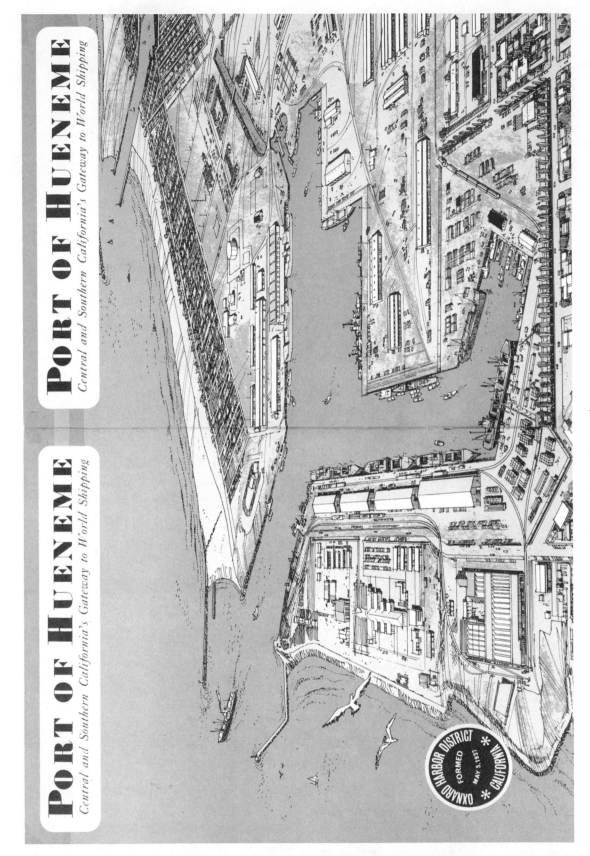

PORT OF HUENEME

Central and Southern California's Gateway to World Shipping

PORT OF HUENEME

Central and Southern California's Gateway to World Shipping

OXNARD HARBOR DISTRICT
FORMED
MAY 5, 1937
★ CALIFORNIA ★

Three overlays were required to print the different tones and colors (black, blue, and red) of this artwork.

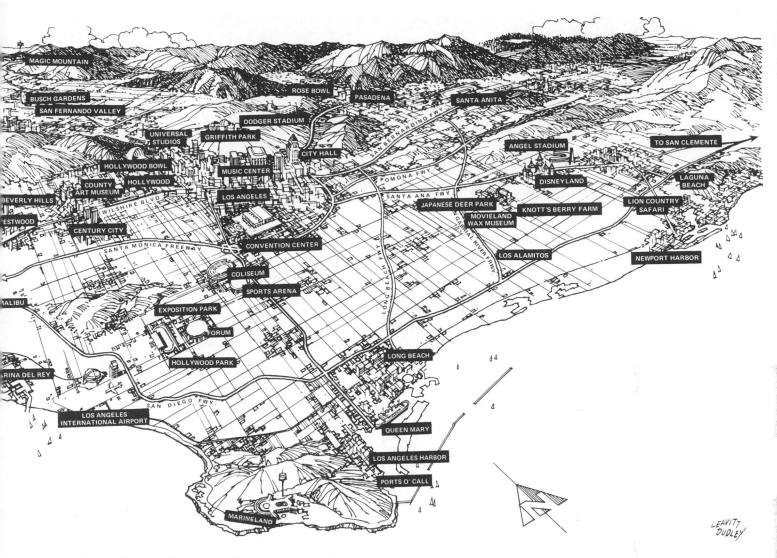

Typography for this artwork was pasted to an acetate overlay.

Benday may be specified in several shades, from a light ten percent to a dark seventy percent, as an average working range. Dot patterns of the screens also vary from fine to coarse, and other textures are available.

As long as it is limited to one color, more than one shade of benday can be indicated on a single overlay. Definite divisions must show where values are to change.

Each different color, however, requires a separate overlay. Variations in a single color are possible by "screening" areas with benday. By overlapping the designs on overlays, additional colors are obtained as the initial ones overprint.

A typography overlay is the best and simplest method of labeling streets, points of interest, or other features in an illustration. The origi-nal artwork is not disturbed by the process, and can be adapted to other purposes by additional overlays.

On a tracing paper layout, the artist or art director specifies the positions and sizes of the information to be included. The copy is typeset and mounted on an acetate sheet. If white letters are desired, the copy may be photographically reversed.

The overlay is superimposed over the art for reproduction, and results in clean, legible labels.

Silk-screen reproduction also depends on overlays for each different color, prepared as linecut artwork. Because each layer may be an important element to the definition of the finished product, its drawing is often intricate and detailed.

This silkscreen print was reproduced from four separate drawings.

REPRODUCTION AIDS AND SHORTCUTS

Commercial products help eliminate much of the drudgery of incorporating routine patterns or shapes into reproduction drawings or other artwork. Adhesive backings and press-on methods simplify their transfer to the drawing surface. They save time and labor, apply neatly and accurately, and are professional in appearance.

Many are also useful for the addition of tones, textures, and entourage to rendered elevations, plans, and perspectives. After their application to colored illustrations, figures and foliage may be brightened by painting them with tempera.

Typography, production tapes, arrows, and other symbols are versatile aids to the preparation of charts, titles, and other presentation material.

Shading Film: Similar to benday when reproduced, flat tone patterns can be cut from sheet and applied directly to the drawing. Artwork shows through the transparent backing. Graduated tones are also available.

Pattern Film: Application is similar to benday, but a variety of different textures are produced.

Press-on Type: Titles and other lettering are quick and professional and come in a wide range of type faces and sizes. Rub characters with a burnisher to transfer.

Symbol Sheets: Vehicles, figures, shrubs and trees, arrows, and geometric shapes are available. Though mainly for draftsmens' elevations and plans, they are also useful for some types of illustrations.

Production Tapes: Solid and broken lines, tone patterns, register marks, and other aids are useful for decoration or reproduction procedures.

A line drawing animated with press-on figures, available commercially in different sizes.

A drawing that can be produced quickly and easily by any careful craftsman using available reproduction aids. Pen lines of the architecture are nearly all drawn with a straightedge, trees and shrubs are press-on types, and three grades of shading film are used for the toned effects.

A few of the many styles of press-on trees. A plan view is useful for 3-D plans. Foliage may be cut up for shrubbery.

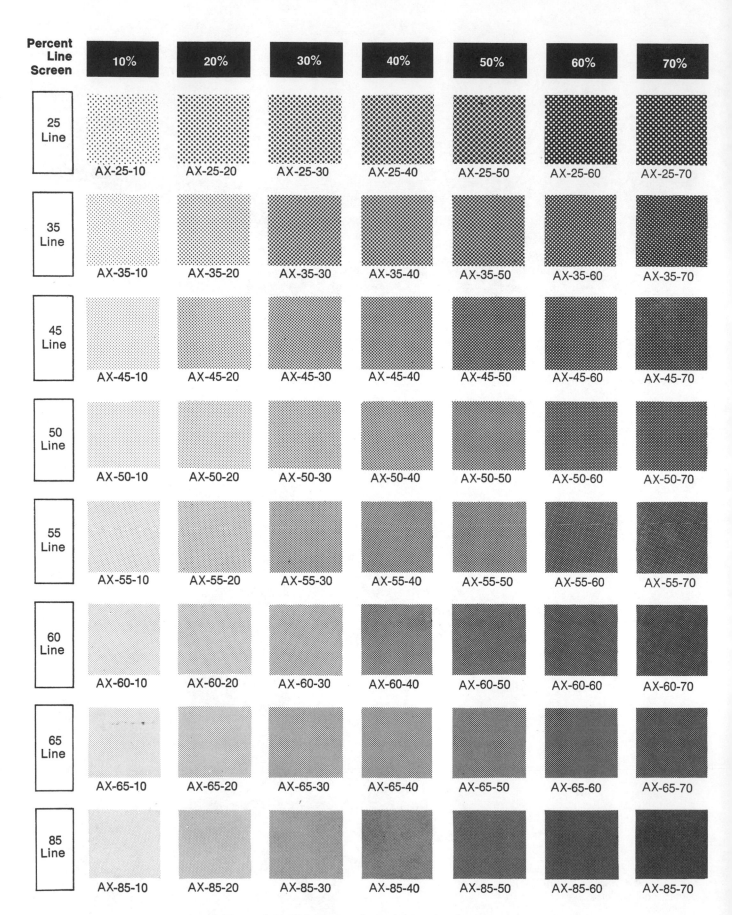

Percent Line Screen	10%	20%	30%	40%	50%	60%	70%
25 Line	AX-25-10	AX-25-20	AX-25-30	AX-25-40	AX-25-50	AX-25-60	AX-25-70
35 Line	AX-35-10	AX-35-20	AX-35-30	AX-35-40	AX-35-50	AX-35-60	AX-35-70
45 Line	AX-45-10	AX-45-20	AX-45-30	AX-45-40	AX-45-50	AX-45-60	AX-45-70
50 Line	AX-50-10	AX-50-20	AX-50-30	AX-50-40	AX-50-50	AX-50-60	AX-50-70
55 Line	AX-55-10	AX-55-20	AX-55-30	AX-55-40	AX-55-50	AX-55-60	AX-55-70
60 Line	AX-60-10	AX-60-20	AX-60-30	AX-60-40	AX-60-50	AX-60-60	AX-60-70
65 Line	AX-65-10	AX-65-20	AX-65-30	AX-65-40	AX-65-50	AX-65-60	AX-65-70
85 Line	AX-85-10	AX-85-20	AX-85-30	AX-85-40	AX-85-50	AX-85-60	AX-85-70

Shading film tones are indicated by percent, the degree of coarseness by the number of lines.

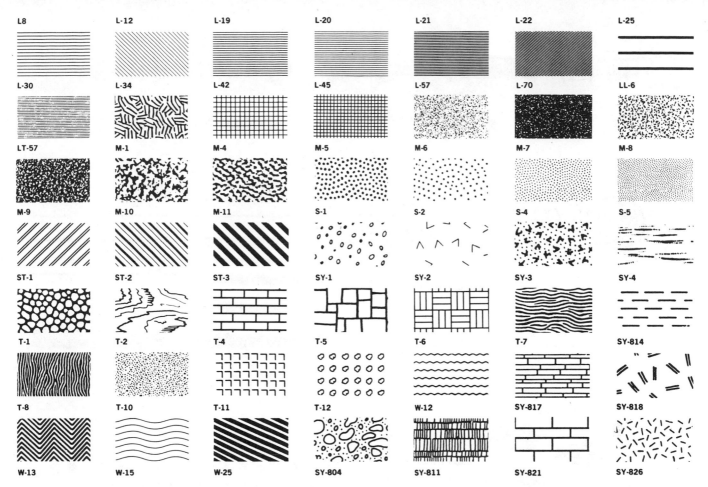

Examples of pattern films, many usable for textural effects in illustrations.

Letter sizes in typography are identified by the number of points (24 pt., 12 pt., etc.). Press-on type is available by the sheet, including a complete alphabet of a particular style and size. Characters most used are more plentifully provided. Numbers and letters are also available in circles or other symbols.

No. 118   24 pt.

ABCDEFGHabcdef

No. 193   18 pt.

ABCDEFGHbcdefg4567890

No. 192   14 pt.

ABCDEFGHIJKmnopqrstuvwx567890

No. 191   12 pt.

ABCDEFGHIJKLMNOnopqrstu234567890

No. 190   10 pt.

ABCDEFGHIJKLMNOfghijklmnopqrst234567890

AAAAAAAAA;
BBBBB CCCC DD
DDD EEEEEEEEE
EEE FFFF GGGG
HHHHH IIIIIIIIII
JJJJ KKKK LLLL
L MMMM NNN:
NN OOOOOOO
O PPPP QQ RR
RRRR SSSSSS T
TTTTT UUUU V:
VVV WWW X;
X YYY ZZ & ?¡

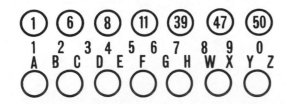

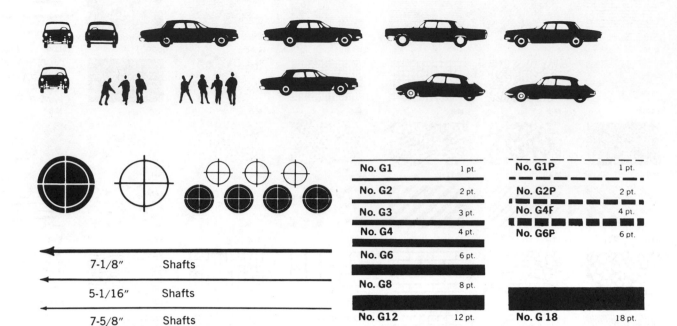

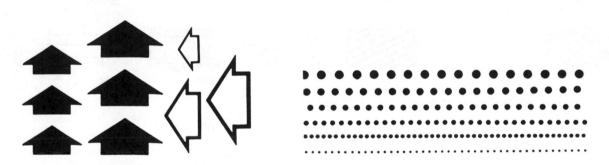

No. G1	1 pt.
No. G2	2 pt.
No. G3	3 pt.
No. G4	4 pt.
No. G6	6 pt.
No. G8	8 pt.
No. G12	12 pt.

No. G1P	1 pt.
No. G2P	2 pt.
No. G4F	4 pt.
No. G6P	6 pt.
No. G 18	18 pt.

7-1/8"	Shafts
5-1/16"	Shafts
7-5/8"	Shafts

Small-scale vehicles and figures, register marks, arrows, tape strips, and a variety of other symbols are commercial products that are convenient and time-saving reproduction aids.

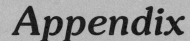

Appendix

Perspective layout is the primary procedure for any architectural illustration. The almost competent rendering will not disguise an ignorance of its principles.

Many drawings must compromise between strict adherence to its rules and variations for better pictorial composition or emphasis of particular elements of a subject, but adjustments must be made within the framework of the basic regulations presented in this section.

PERSPECTIVE PROJECTION

Perspective by approximation, or "eyeballing," is easier when you are familiar with the mechanical methods of translating flat planes and elevations into three-dimensional perspectives. Even the most experienced illustrators rely on mechanical procedures for the accuracy of their drawings, except for the loosest type of freehand sketching.

ORTHOGRAPHIC PROJECTION

Orthographic, or right angle, is the simplest type of projection. Given measurements of a plan are projected at the same size to the views of elevations of the structure. Vertical dimensions are measured off at the same scale and projected directly from one elevation to another. Figure A-1 shows the procedure.

Although orthographic projection is used more by draftsmen than by illustrators, it is often useful for setting up preliminary steps of perspective drawing.

TWO-POINT ANGULAR PERSPECTIVE, "OFFICE" OR "COMMON" METHOD

This is a basic and accurate type of perspective. Information is projected directly from scaled drawings of plans and elevations. If it is carefully executed, any student can produce a mechanically correct three-dimensional view of a structure.

The subject used as an example is the building shown in Figure A-1. Dimensions are given in feet, and the roof overhang is two feet on all sides.

Procedure:

1. Draw the picture plane (PP) line, then the plan (to any desired scale). Align the walls at 30° and 60° to the picture plane, with one corner touching the PP line. (The 30°/60° orientation is most commonly used but can change to any desired angle. The 45°/45° emphasizes both sides of the structure equally.)

2. Draw groundline (GL) at any convenient location below the PP.

3. Add horizon above GL, measured at same scale as plan. The example sets it at 6 feet, a normal eye level, but it may be any desired height.

4. The center of vision is midway in the cone of vision, which locates the station point (SP) from which the subject is viewed. The width of the cone, for this type of structure, ranges from the 30° shown here to about 45°. The wider angle moves the SP closer to the subject and makes the perspective more angular.

5. Locate vanishing points (VP) by running lines, parallel to the walls of the plan, from SP to the PP line. From their intersections with the PP, drop verticals to the horizon for the left and right VPs.

6. Draw end elevation as shown, at the same scale as the plan.

7. Where plan touches PP, drop vertical true height line (THL) to GL. Where plan and PP touch, all points projected horizontally from the elevation will be at their true height in the perspective. (Figure A-2 includes all the above procedures.)

8. From the plan, project reference points which will be visible in the drawing to the SP, but stop the lines at their intersection with the PP. Drop vertical lines to locate the lateral positions of these points in the perspective. (To simplify the drawing of this example, many projection lines are omitted or not completed.)

9. Heights of points are projected from the elevation to the THL. Projection from their intersections with the THL to the proper VPs continues the same height in perspective around the structure.

10. Heights for points not directly related to the THL can be established in two ways:

    A. Project the height line from the elevation to the THL. From the intersection, project to the VP for the point to be located. The intersection of this projection and the reference line, dropped from the plan, determines the height in perspective. (This method is used for the chimney in the example.)

    B. Extend reference points to the PP. Lines dropped from their intersections establish auxiliary THLs. Project true height from elevation to desired auxiliary THL, then to proper VP from the intersection for correct perspective height. (This method is used for the long ridge in the example).

11. Gables are constructed by connecting measured reference points. Extend their slope lines to establish auxiliary VPs to simplify drawing additional structure at the same slant. (Figure A-3 includes the above procedures.)

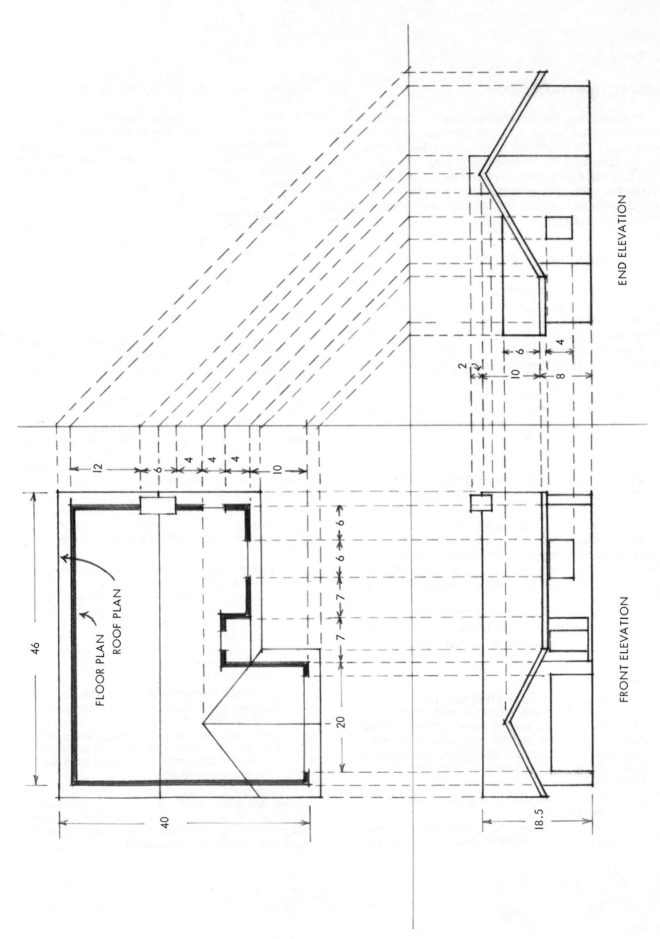

FLOOR PLAN

ROOF PLAN

46

40

12

6

4

4

4

10

6

6

6

7

7

7

20

END ELEVATION

2

10

6

8

4

FRONT ELEVATION

18.5

Figure A–1

278

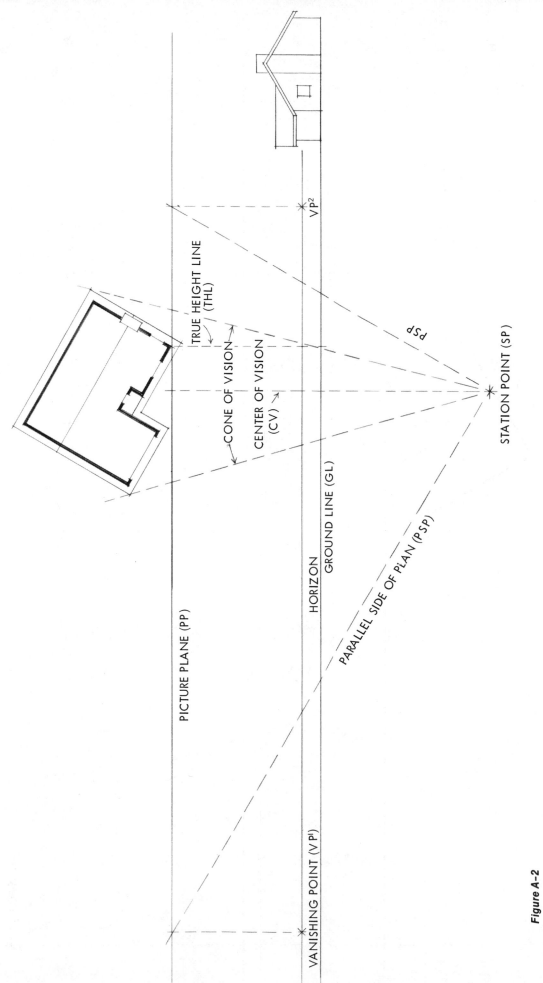

Figure A-2

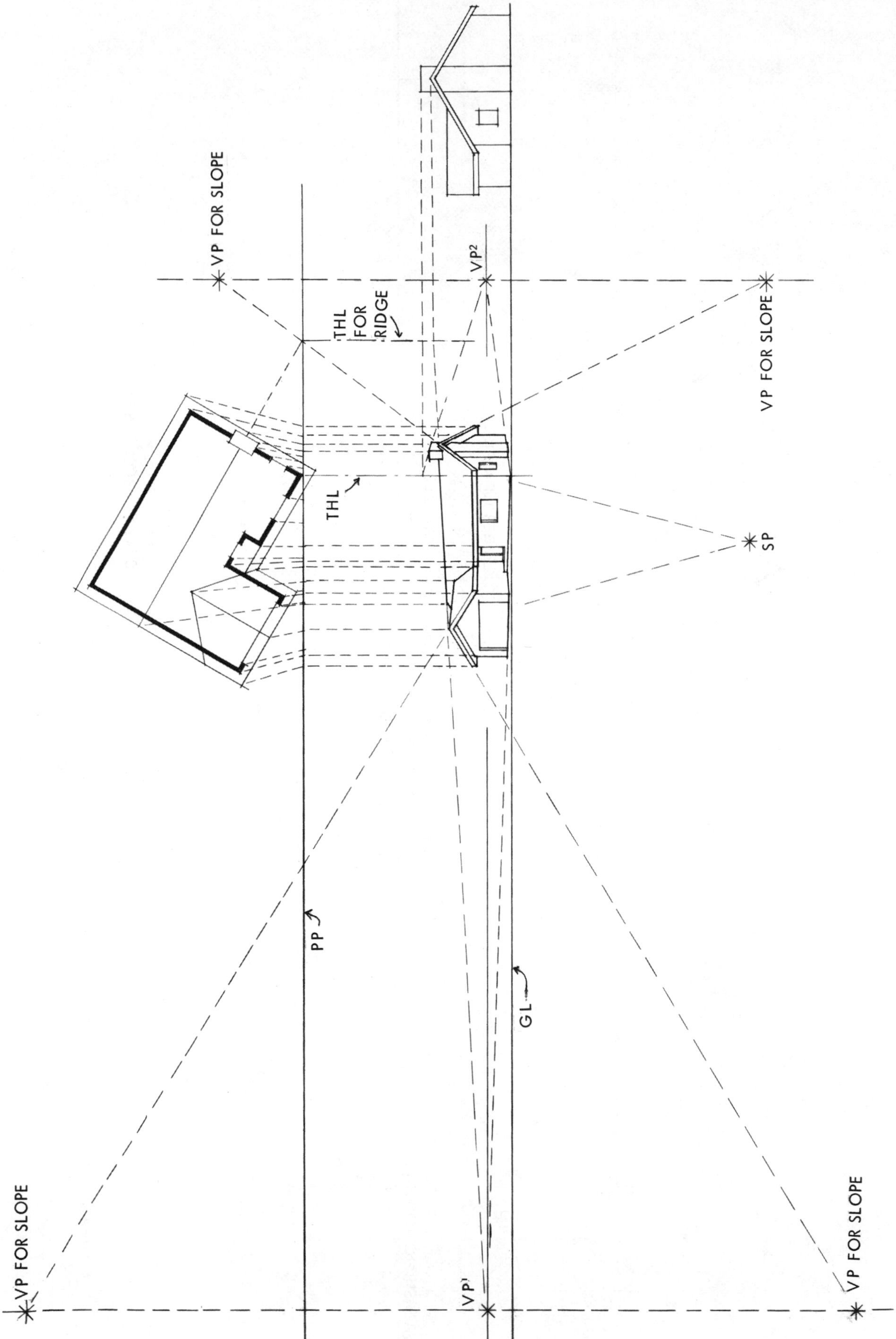

VP FOR SLOPE

VP FOR SLOPE

THL FOR RIDGE

THL

VP²

VP FOR SLOPE

SP

PP

GL

VP¹

VP FOR SLOPE

VP FOR SLOPE

Figure A-3

PERSPECTIVE-PLAN METHOD

Quick and direct, this method is favored by artists for the layout of more complicated types of buildings. The preliminary procedures differ, but the principles of perspective projection are the same as in the office method.

For comparison, the same subject is used for both.

Procedure:

1. Lay out the horizon, PP, GL, SP, VP¹ and VP² as shown in Figure A-4. Horizon height is six feet here, but can be any desired height. Combination of angles at the VPs can also vary, but must add up to 90°.

The plan is not drawn in practice at the PP, but it is included here to relate it to the projection process.

2. Locate measuring points MP¹ and MP². Add measuring line at a convenient distance below GL, but far enough away to project the plan from a high-angle view.

3. From plan, transfer its dimensions to the measuring line as shown in Figure A-5. Note that dimensions for both sides of the plan read in a continuous sequence around the corner of the building.

4. From the corner touching the measuring line, project base lines to the VPs.

5. Project the dimensions to the MPs to establish their measurements along the base lines. Project from the base line intersections to the VPs to form the plan in perspective. (To simplify the diagram, some projection lines are omitted or not completed.)

6. Structure extending beyond the base lines, as the ell of the garage and the roof overhang, are constructed as shown in Figure A-6. The distances of the projections of the garage ell, ten feet, and its roof overhang, two feet, are marked off on the measuring line *to the left of the corner*. The base line from VP² is extended; lines from MP¹ are projected to it where the dimensions of the ell intersect the measuring line. From their intersections at points *D* and *E*, the proper size of the ell in perspective is projected to VP¹. The overhang of the roof corner at *A* and *B*, in

Figure A-4

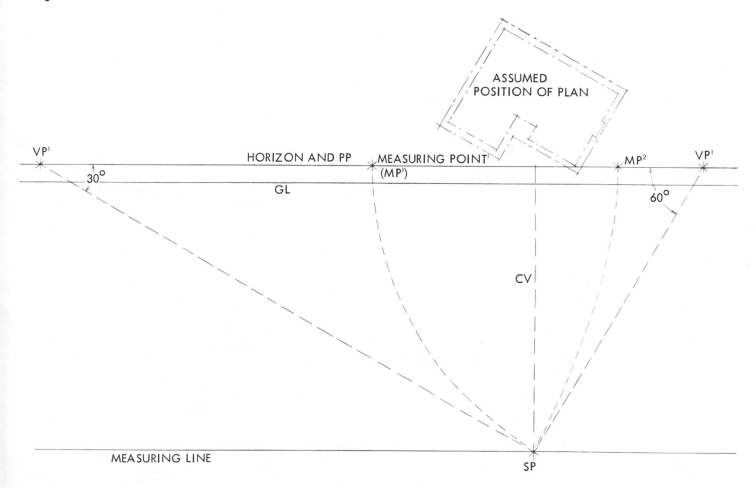

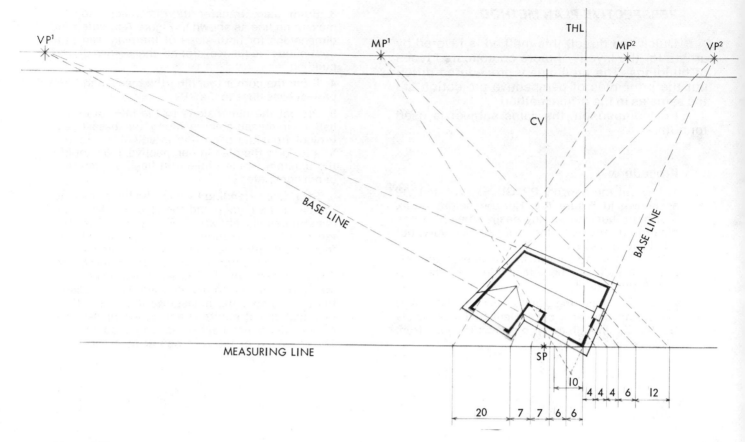

Figure A-5

Figure A-6

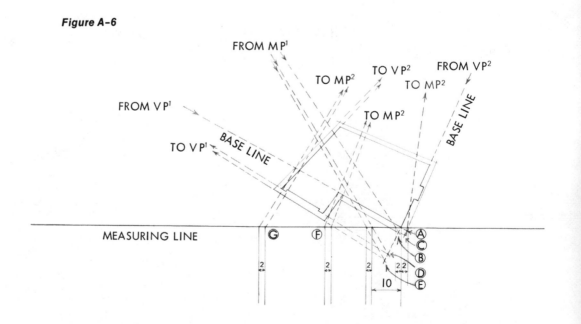

front of the measuring line, is measured in a similar manner, and projected from intersection C to the VPs. Roof overhangs at F and G are measured and projected as any other points along the baseline.

7. Project a THL from the corner of the building to the horizon.

8. Project the reference points from the perspective plan to the drawing (Figure A-7). Measure vertical distances on the THL and construct the perspective by projections to proper vanishing points as in the office method.

ONE-POINT OR PARALLEL PERSPECTIVE

This is the simplest and quickest method of perspective projection, as all surfaces parallel to the center of vision (CV) are drawn to a single VP. Surfaces perpendicular to the CV are all drawn parallel to the horizon.

Buildings, walls, or furniture not aligned in positions parallel or at right angles to the CV, however, must be projected in two-point perspective.

As three elevations of a subject can be shown in a single drawing, one-point perspective is useful for street scenes, interiors, or U-shaped buildings.

Procedure:

1. Lay out plan, elevations, picture plane, and groundline as shown in Figure A-8. Height of horizon above GL is arbitrary, according to the desired type of view. The center of vision may be centered on the plan or offcenter if one parallel elevation is to be favored over the other. (If too far offcenter in a very wide cone of vision, however, some apparent distortion of heights in the far elevation may be noticed. This can be corrected by a slight eyeballed adjustment to an assumed distant VP.)

The VP is located at the intersection of the horizon and center of vision.

2. Perpendicular elevations of subjects located on the PP are drawn to the same size and in the same position in the perspective. Others are located and measured by projections to the PP and VP (Figure A-9). THLs can be added wherever necessary.

3. An interior view is drawn in the same manner as an exterior (Figure A-10). VPs for differently-aligned subjects are located by lines drawn parallel to their planes from the SP to the horizon.

Figure A-7

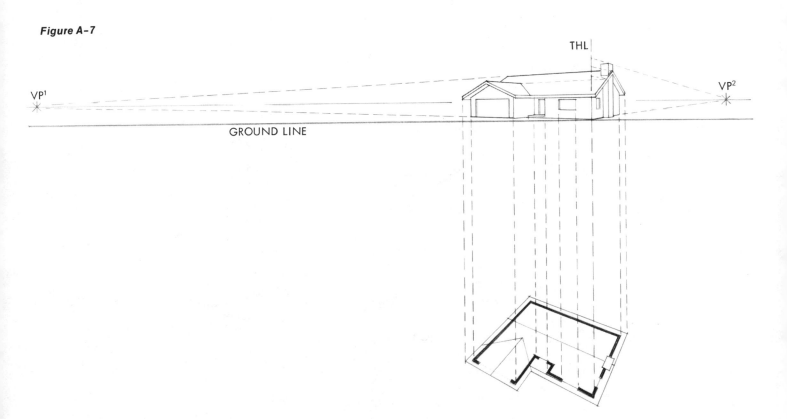

APPENDIX   283

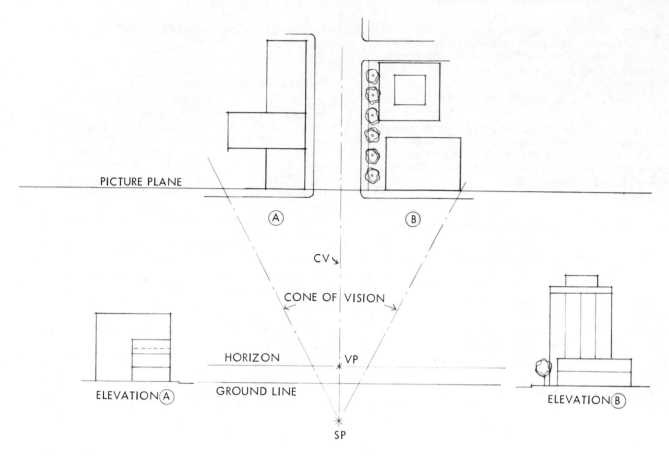

PICTURE PLANE

Ⓐ   Ⓑ

CV↘

CONE OF VISION

HORIZON   VP

GROUND LINE

ELEVATION Ⓐ

ELEVATION Ⓑ

SP

Figure A-8

Figure A-9

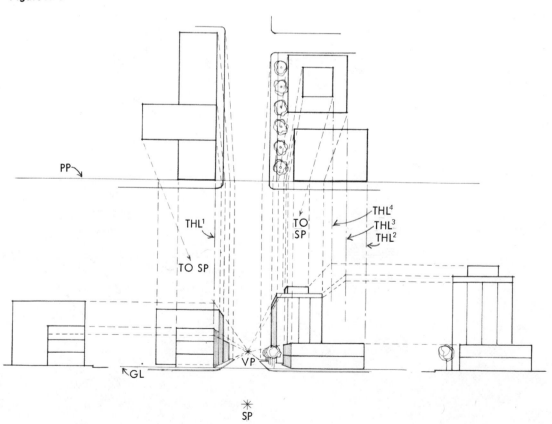

PP↘

THL¹   TO SP   THL⁴
                              THL³
TO SP   THL²

GL   VP

SP

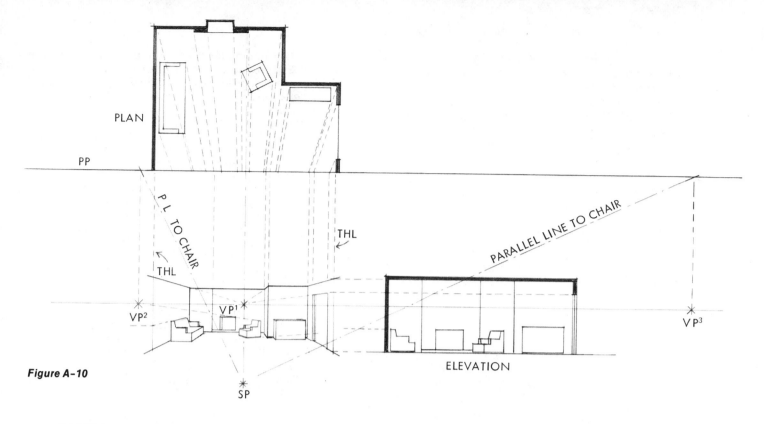

PLAN

PP

P. L. TO CHAIR

THL

THL

PARALLEL LINE TO CHAIR

VP²

VP¹

VP³

ELEVATION

Figure A-10

SP

CAMERA ANGLE PERSPECTIVE

Perspectives drawn for motion picture or television usage must be drawn quickly, but they must show the exact field covered by the lens of the camera. As the stage sets are only partial structures, an incorrect illustration is misleading. The lens in the same position as the station point might pick up an unfinished edge of a wall or ceiling in its cones of vision.

Artists lay out their sketches with the help of *camera angles.* These aids, of clear plastic or

acetate, are marked with both horizontal and vertical cones of vision. (See Figure A-11.)

An angle is calibrated in feet, at ¼″ to the foot, the same scale used for the working drawings. A floor line, 4½′ below the center line/horizon, indicates the most commonly used eye level.

Placed over a plan or elevation, the angle enables the artist to locate the station point for the perspective quickly and accurately.

Camera angles of 35, 28, and 50mm are used most. The frames of drawings made from them

Figure A-11 *Camera angle courtesy Universal Studios.*

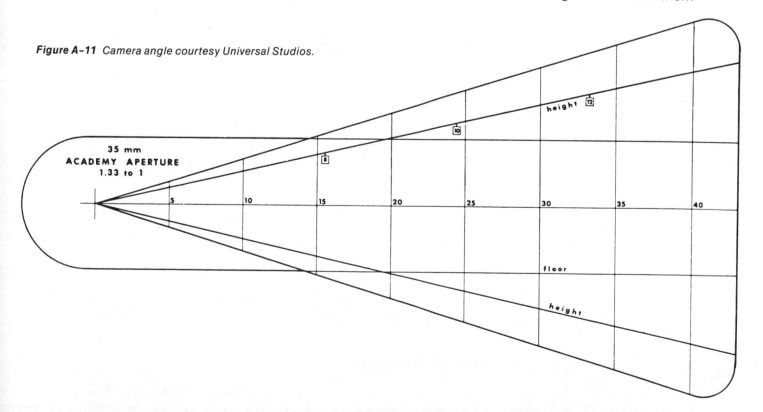

35 mm
ACADEMY APERTURE
1.33 to 1

height

height

floor

5   10   15   20   25   30   35   40

are three by four in proportion. Wide motion picture screens use other angles calculated for their proportions.

Basic procedure for camera angle use is the same, and similar to conventional perspective projection, but professionals in the business usually work out their own methods of speeding up the process.

Angles are used for drawings of both interior and exterior views.

Procedure (using 35 mm angle):

1. Lay angle over plan, select SP and PP (Figure A-12). Draw horizontal cone of vision on plan, divide as shown (1, 2, 3, 4). Draw lines parallel to walls from SP, extend PP to locate VPs.

2. Lay angle over elevation, with center of vision same distance from the same point on plan, and floor line aligned with ground line (Figure A-13). Draw vertical cone of vision on elevation and divide as shown. (Horizon height can be changed by moving floor line position and adjusting camera angle accordingly.)

3. Draw frame for drawing to any convenient size in 3:4 proportion, locate horizon at center, and divide to correspond with divisions on plan and elevation (Figure A-14). Locate VPs on horizon, using same proportions for distances as extensions of PP on plan to parallel wall lines. Choose a convenient reference point, from the plan, on a wall or at a corner to establish a vertical scale. In the rectangle on the perspective (CDEF), corresponding to the same points on the plan and elevation, locate the point for the floor line by proportionate division (proportional dividers are helpful here).

Divide the distance from the floor point to the horizon to correspond to the height of the horizon (4½ ' in the example), extend to the desired height. This gives the scale in feet at this point, which can be projected to establish heights at other points.

4. Locate other reference points by proportional positions in rectangles, and project in two-point perspective to construct the drawing.

Establish the auxiliary VPs as necessary for furniture.

Camera angle projection also is used for one-point perspectives.

Figure A-12

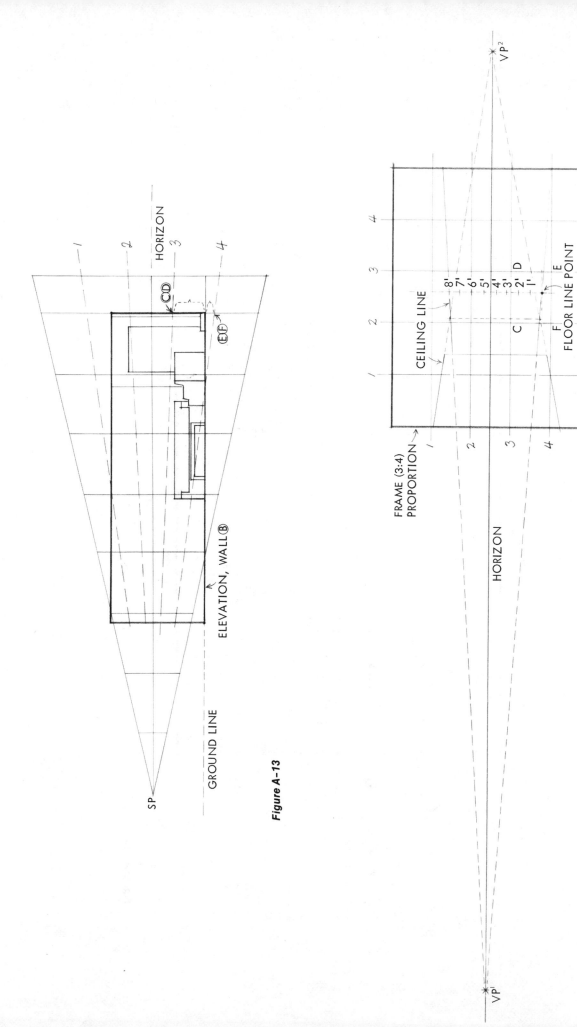

Figure A-13

Figure A-14

287

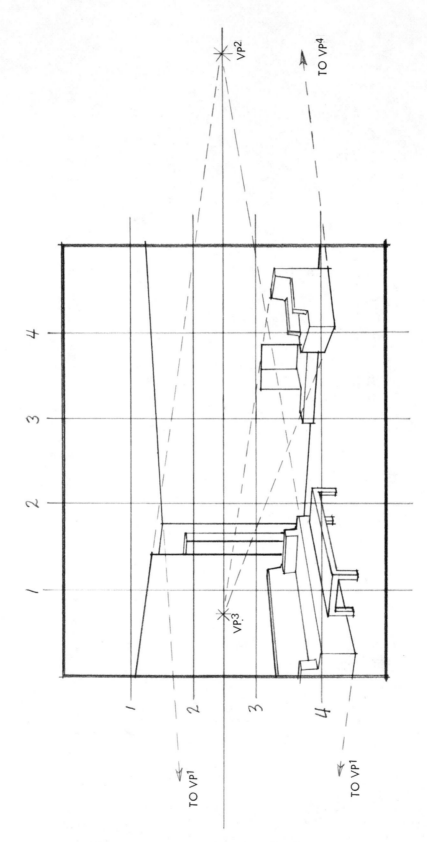

Figure A-15

288

Bibliography

Some of the publications listed are directly related to architecture. Others are not involved with the subject per se, but include information concerning methods and techniques applicable to architectural illustration.

BARBOUR, ARTHUR J.
Painting Buildings in Watercolor
Watson-Guptill, 1973

BURDEN, ERNEST E.
*Architectural Delineation: A Photographic
    Approach to Presentation*
McGraw-Hill, 1971

CAPELLE, FRIEDRICH
*Professional Perspective Drawing for
    Architects and Engineers*
McGraw-Hill, 1969

CARDAMONE, TOM
*Advertising Agency and Studio Skills:
    A Guide to the Preparation of Art
    and Mechanicals for Reproduction*
Watson-Guptill, 1970

COULIN, CLAUDIUS
*Step-By-Step Perspective Drawing for Architects,
    Draftsmen, and Engineers*
Van Nostrand Reinhold, 1971

COVINO, FRANK
*Discover Acrylics With Frank Covino:
    An Academic Approach*
Watson-Guptill, 1974

GUPTILL, ARTHUR L., AND MEYER, SUSAN E.
Watercolor Painting Step-By-Step
Watson-Guptill, 1967

HALSE, ALBERT O.
*Architectural Rendering: The Technique of
    Contemporary Presentation*
McGraw-Hill, 1972

HOBBS, CHARLES I.
Pencil Drawing for the Architect
Transatlantic, 1954

HOGARTH, PAUL
Creative Ink Drawing
Watson-Guptill, 1968
Drawing Architecture: A Creative Approach
Watson-Guptill, 1973

JACOBY, HELMUTH
New Techniques of Architectural Rendering
Praeger, 1971

KAUTZKY, TED
Painting Trees and Landscapes in Watercolor
Van Nostrand Reinhold, 1952
Pencil Broadsides
Van Nostrand Reinhold, 1960

KAUTZKY, TED
Ways with Watercolor
Van Nostrand Reinhold, 1963

KEMPER, ALFRED M.
Drawings by American Architects
Wiley, 1973

LALIBERTE, NORMAN, AND MOGELON, ALEX
Pastel, Charcoal, and Chalk Drawing
Van Nostrand Reinhold, 1973

LAWSON, PHILLIP J.
Perspective Charts
Van Nostrand Reinhold, 1940

MORELLO, S. RALPH
Complete Airbrush Book
Tudor, 1954

MULLER, EDWARD J.
Architectural Drawing and Light Construction
Prentice-Hall, Inc., 1976 (2nd edition)

PILE, JOHN (ED.)
Drawings of Architectural Interiors
Watson Guptill, 1967

PITZ, HENRY C.
How To Draw Trees
Watson-Guptill 1972
Ink Drawing Techniques
Watson-Guptill, 1957

RAMSEY, CHARLES G., AND SLEEPER, HAROLD R.
Architectural Graphic Standards
Wiley, 1970 (6th edition)

TAUBES, FREDERIC
Acrylic Painting for the Beginner
Watson-Guptill 1971
Pen and Ink Drawing
Pitman, 1972

WATERS, NIGEL V., AND BRONHAM, JOHN
Principles of Perspective
Watson-Guptill, 1974

WELLING, RICHARD
Drawing With Markers
Watson-Guptill, 1974
Techniques of Drawing Buildings
Watson-Guptill, 1971

WOOD, ROBERT E., AND NELSON, MARY CARROLL
Watercolor Workshop
Watson-Guptill, 1974

Index